SIX
REELS
UNDER

SIX
REELS
UNDER

by David Del Valle

BearManor Media

2012

Six Reels Under

© 2012 David Del Valle

For information, address:

BearManor Media
P. O. Box 71426
Albany, GA 31708

bearmanormedia.com

Typesetting and layout by John Teehan

Published in the USA by BearManor Media

ISBN— 1-59393-696-6
978-1-59393-696-9

"Come up to the lab,
and see what's on the slab."

– The Rocky Horror Picture Show

Table of Contents

MEMORIALS

Acknowledgements

SIX REELS UNDER WOULD NOT EXIST if not for the advice and support of the following people. As with my first book, *Lost Horizons: Beneath the Hollywood* sign, A. Ashley Hoff has given hours of his time to help research this book. I am so lucky to have him in my corner. Alan White contributed so much in designing the cover art for both my books. Next my dear friends Charles and Peggy Sherwood, who believed in me from day one and offered their support in seeing this project through until the end. I love them very much. Also special kudos to Derek Botelho for his much-needed advice and my old friend Russ Lanier for a lifetime of support. Every writer should have such encouragement. Many of the articles here were created for different venues over the years. My colleague Eric Kuersten, whose remarkable website, The Acidemic Journal of Film and Media, is a must read with his amazing insight into film. I only wish I could write as well as he does every week. My pals over at The Night Crew podcast, Sean Smithson and Thom Curnell, gave me an outlet to try new material with my very own column, "Tales I never tell twice." Roy Frumkes, my long-suffering editor at *Films In Review,* has remained loyal to the cause of film history longer than most. Victoria Price with whom I shared a stage in 2011 honoring her father Vincent. Her generosity in praising my continued efforts to keep her father's memory alive led to me adding the chapters on his films in this edition. The staff of *Diabolique Magazine: Horror Unlimited* became fans of my work and then allowed me into their inner circle. I remain in their debt for supporting this book. And lastly, my mother Jeanne Del Valle, who has spent 62 of her

97 years watching her son remain loyal to his dreams while encouraging me to always be true to myself. This was indeed a labor of love with every film and personality in it...a piece of the fabric of my movie going existence. I can only hope to always be six reels under the influence of the films that still shape our imaginations.

DD

Introduction
by David Del Valle

Six Reels Under

WELCOME TO SIX REELS UNDER, a personal homage of sorts to the much honored HBO cable show *Six Feet Under*. Since I have always been drawn to macabre material in the arts, it is no surprise that I would enjoy this series, which seemed to be six reels presented, literally, by Death each and every episode. For those that may not know the series, each episode began with someone's death, and that death would then in some way be fashioned into the plot of each show. The era it represented spoke to me as well, having lived so much of my life in the Los Angeles area, then discovering my cousin, Robert Del Valle, was one of the show's producers just made the whole experience all the more personal. The manner in which I came to enjoy many of the films in this volume was at the neighborhood drive-in; a now forever lost pastime that, back in the late 1960s, allowed me to see nearly every film produced by American International Pictures as well as countless triple features that were the staple of such venues back in the day. Another reason the title seemed so right from the beginning was my discovery that while the drive-in might be a thing of the past, watching films under the stars was not all thanks to an enterprising cemetery in Hollywood. One of the most star-studded graveyards this side of Forest Lawn is the Hollywood Forever Cemetery which has been screening films out of doors much like the old days with the drive-in, only this time you are not sitting in the comfort of your car but resting on blankets with picnic baskets near the very stars (now deceased) that you are now watching projected in the very graveyard in which they now remain six feet under.

1

I have attempted to follow the cemetery theme into the chapters, as well as dividing up the essays as either tributes or memorials for the films and the people that were a part of them in one way or another. The films in this collection are all favorites of mine from a childhood spent either at the drive-in or seated under the glowing reflection of a TV screen watching the late late show revival of films like *Dracula's Daughter* or more recently *The Magician*, perhaps the first "mad lab" film ever made. In each case I had a personal encounter with someone connected with the film and I hope this will add to your understanding of the film or perhaps give a sense of Déjà vu to why we both love these particular films so much. One of the guilty pleasures in this collection is *The Dunwich Horror* which I saw at a drive-in on several nights since I was such an admirer of the writings of H.P. Lovecraft that to see his name finally on the screen was enough to keep me coming back, even if Sandra Dee was not what anyone had in mind as the proper leading lady for the abyss.

As with my first book, *Lost Horizons Beneath the Hollywood Sign*, the real pleasure in sharing these memories is having the chance to preserve what might have fallen through the cracks of film history, not to mention my memory banks, which always seem to be six reels under, thanks to Netflix. I was indeed fortunate to have encountered such reclusive personalities like Alice Terry, living her golden years in the loving shadow of her departed soul mate, the director Rex Ingram, or the bittersweet last days of Gloria Holden, forever remembered as Dracula's daughter, who suffered the most devastating loss a mother can have; to outlive a child. The films and personalities in these pages are all very dear to me and it is with that sense of dedication that you should not forget any of them that I put into this volume. As I used to say on my cable show, *The Sinister Image*, may all your nightmares be in 70 mm. May I now add: try and stay six reels under your favorite films. Perhaps we will catch sight of each other one night over at the Hollywood Forever cemetery watching those films out there in the dark...

Resurrections

Director Daniel Haller supervises the dream sequence in
The Dunwich Horror with Sandra Dee.

1

Wilber Whateley Has a Girlfriend

The Dunwich Horror

IT IS EARLY FEBRUARY OF 1970; former teen princess Sandra Dee is in between takes reclining as best she can on a faux druidic altar, surrounded by lighting experts, focus pullers, hair and make-up stylists. Completing the picture is a continuity girl running lines as Ms. Dee puffs on an endless string of cigarettes to quiet her nerves. Her own mother, Mary, comes to her speaking words of wisdom: "Keep your clothes on, Sandy, wait for the body double." In other words, "Let her be," to a lurking assistant director eager to get on with it.

This was to be a radical change of image for Sandra Dee, whose last two films, in 1967, were *Rosie* (a Roz Russell comedy) and the ironic (under the circumstances) *Doctor, You've Got To Be Kidding* with George Hamilton. One can only assume the "doctor" in the title would have said something along those lines if he had been informed that Sandra Dee's next role would be that of a willing sacrifice to an inhuman deity known only as "Yog Sothoth," with the end result of her being impregnated with his unholy seed.

The difficult transition from debutante to mature actress was simply not happening fast enough to suit Sandra Dee and her then-management, which included, of course, her mother. When this project was offered it must have seemed like a golden opportunity for Sandra Dee to mature practically overnight; that is, if the film achieved any of the same success *Rosemary's Baby* did with Mia Farrow. Ironically, both actresses would be divorced during the time of each of their respective films—Mia from Frank Sinatra, and Sandra from Bobby Darin. Sandra would miscarry during *The Dunwich*

Horror post production, compounding the depression that was about to envelop her for the rest of her life. *The Dunwich Horror* sadly did not energize the career of Sandra Dee; in fact, this would be her final motion picture. The 1970s would yield only occasional work in television as she retreated more and more into the shadows of depression and substance abuse. Iconic status as a pop-culture figure would finally come for her, but not until nearly the end of her life.

The film in question is, of course, Daniel Haller's production of *The Dunwich Horror*, based somewhat on H.P. Lovecraft's 17,500-word "short" story of the same name, first published in "Weird Tales" magazine in 1929. Lovecraft was at the time unknown to the general movie-going public, making his name above-the-title an impossibility in Hollywood terms. However, with this, his third adaptation for the screen, all-produced by American International Pictures, after eight successful collaborations with his only rival in the horror genre, Edgar Allan Poe, all that was about to change.

The first attempt to bring Lovecraft to the screen was fumbled by the suits at AIP who had no confidence in Lovecraft as a box-office draw; so *The Haunted Village* became Edgar Allan Poe's *The Haunted Palace*, grafting Poe's poem onto the conclusion of *The Case of Charles Dexter Ward*, making it the sixth Poe film directed by Roger Corman. The second attempt retained the Lovecraft name…in small caps. But at least the master did not have to masquerade as Poe. Another novella was chosen this time, The Color Out of Space, re-titled from the stylish *The House At The End of The World* to the oddly Germanic *Die Monster Die*, a rather unfortunate name for a Boris Karloff vehicle since it was well-known how many years the then 78 year-old Karloff had to act under the shadow of the Frankenstein monster.

If all had gone as planned, Karloff would have been one of the stars of *The Dunwich Horror* alongside Christopher Lee, with Italian horror master Mario Bava directing. But this was not to be, and after languishing on production schedules since 1964, the project finally got green lit as *The Dunwich Horror* with a decent cast headed by Peter Fonda, Diana Varsi and Ralph Bellamy as Professor Armitage. However, by the time the script went from Ray Russell to a very youthful Curtis Hanson, the cast changed again with Dean Stockwell, having just done *Pysch-Out* the year before, replacing Fonda. Sandra Dee assumed the role of "Nancy," known amongst the crew as the "Mia Farrow" part since *Rosemary's Baby* became a worldwide box-office success, paving the way for this film to get produced. More than likely this was the reason for casting Ralph Bellamy as the academic, since he was the infamous "Dr. Saperstein" in the Polanski film. (Bellamy's character name so intrigued Polanski that he named his dog after him). Bellamy would bow out soon after, leaving a mad scramble for a replacement in the guise of another equally respected character actor, Sam Jaffe (*Gunga Din; The Asphalt Jungle*).

With the cast now in place, Daniel Haller would finally have the long-awaited opportunity to utilize all the set decorations and symbols that he had designed around Joseph Curwen's dungeon altar beneath *The Haunted Palace,* and then continued on in the UK with the decor of the Whateley mansion of *Die Monster Die.* As the art director and set designer for all of Corman's Poe films, Haller brought great style and beauty to the floor during the making of *The Dunwich Horror.*

Daniel Haller always regarded Roger Corman as his mentor and well he should, considering working with Roger was a crash-course in filmmaking like no other at the time. With Corman producing *The Dunwich Horror,* he was given a free hand as long as things flowed smoothly on the set, and more importantly, that the film be brought in on time and under budget.

The first order of business was to modernize Lovecraft's tale, originally set in the backwoods of New England, circa 1928, into the counter-culture phenomenon that existed in Mendocino County throughout the late 1960s, playing out in early 1970. Haller had done the very same thing with his previous film, *Die Monster Die,* changing the locale to rural England, and in both cases, setting the scene in gothic mansions rather than the farmhouses favored by Lovecraft.

I know that this change in time and location separated *The Dunwich Horror* in terms of Corman's Poe cycle. While it is true that everything AIP did in the horror genre since then was based almost entirely on the initial success of *House of Usher,* with each film that followed using the same basic formula as it were, *The Dunwich Horror* remains unique because of the pop-culture references. It reflects both the success of Polanski's film and the devastating aftermath of his wife's murder at the hands of the Manson family, forever changing the landscape of Hollywood from that day forward. It is no coincidence then that Dean Stockwell would adopt a "Manson vibe" or, depending on your point of view, a "Timothy Leary" vibe as well, since the hippie movement of the day was all about getting high or following a cult — at least this is how Hollywood chose to interpret the lurid headlines.

None of this material was lost on Dean Stockwell (an avid Lovecraft fan) who realized early on that to play Wilber Whateley as written in Curtis Hanson's screenplay was to abandon Lovecraft's concept enough to make his "goatish features" sexy rather then repellent. In Lovecraft's tale, Wilber dies attempting to steal the Necronomicon from the library wherein the reader is given the payoff of discovering just how otherworldly and deformed he really was under all those bulky clothes. All this was abandoned to give Wilber the plot points involving Sandra Dee's character, to make the film more like *Rosemary's Baby* instead of the monster on the loose tale Lovecraft originally created.

Ever since the film's debut in 1970 much has been made over how far it has strayed from Lovecraft's original short story: by including a love interest for Wilber Whateley, also allowing him to live beyond the attack at the Miskatonic Library to perish on Sentinel Hill while performing the ritual, and allowing his cosmic sibling to have his way with Sandra Dee, thereby satisfying the fans of *Rosemary's Baby* as well as producer Corman.

In spite of all this, *The Dunwich Horror* is as faithful an adaptation as one can expect for a low-budget film with few resources at its disposal. During my interview with Daniel Haller he remarked that the only way to keep his film from becoming "another Poe film in the Corman cycle" was to update the storyline and take full advantage of the psychedelic flower children motif which, by 1970, was about to fade from view.

The mythos as created by Lovecraft was long-considered un-filmable since his prose is clear about this unimaginable race of beings that exist outside of our known reality. Cthulhu and his followers worship Yog Sothoth, who is described as being composed of giant spheres of light. Yog is the keeper of the way, as Robert Bloch once described it. He has the power to open the gates, allowing the old ones to re-enter and take back the earth they once inhabited long ago. The Whateleys used the Necronomicon to summon Yog Sothoth long enough to interbreed with their women. The blood of Yog Sothoth now flows through Wilber's veins and, because of the ritual at the film's end, Nancy is now creating what Lavinia had created in the films opening credits: another offspring of Yog Sothoth.

In reexamining the film, Nancy's drug-induced nightmare (in which she awakens only to find herself surrounded by demonic-looking flower children in body paint) makes more sense if you understand that this is her reality of what she is experiencing in her dream state. When we glimpse the "old ones" walking side by side, looking for all intent like witches in long flowing robes, could one interpret this to be the only way such deities can reveal themselves to human kind without them losing their mind completely? In the 1997 film *Contact* with Jodie Foster a similar device is used when she finally confronts the alien life forms. They choose to reveal themselves to her in the form of her dead father. Everything Nancy experiences is on her level of reality, which for American International would certainly be the Haight-Ashbury/counterculture of the late sixties (not to mention easy to present budget-wise). The psychedelic effects work for the film in the sequence in which Nancy's friend Elizabeth confronts Wilber's twin. The sound effects, coupled with the shock visuals, filmed with a distorted lens, allows the only bit of real nudity in the film when the inter-dimensional twin made up of tentacles ravages her, pulling away her bra revealing her breasts before devouring her completely. The camera-work as the Horror moves across the Dunwich landscape towards the Devil's Hop Yard is beautifully realized and very much in keeping with Lovecraft.

The other remaining bit of Lovecraftian lore comes with the death of the elder Whateley (Sam Jaffe). As he lies dying on the floor of the Whateley mansion we hear the sound of birds; whippoorwills to be exact, and as the breath leaves his body the sound subsides. This was a myth used by Lovecraft to indicate the soul leaving the body, but having to fend off the whippoorwills, who wish to take the soul to the underworld. The psychopomps, as they are known, is a concept found in Egyptian lore as well as Nordic mythology with the Valkyries, regarding the guiding of one's spirit into the afterlife.

All in all, if AIP and Haller had set out to make a travesty of Lovecraft's work (the film's detractors seem to think they did), then why bother to put such details into the project in the first place? In view of the recent remake of *The Dunwich Horror* by Leigh Scott, I believe the original film needs to be reexamined as the first real attempt to put Lovecraft's work on the screen and as such, despite the liberties taken, it still remains an entertaining film with much to recommend it if you keep in mind the time and place in which it was made.

I for one believe that to film the works of H.P. Lovecraft successfully you must remain true to the period in which he set them, which is always in the past. Dan O'Bannon's film of Lovecraft's *The Case of Charles Dexter Ward*, known as *The Resurrected*, is perhaps one of the best Lovecraft films done so far, but it suffers from updating the material to the present day as well as going for a film noir flavor that does not work. In the case of Haller's film, part of its charm is the time capsule it gives us of that moment in time when hippie communes flourished along the California coastline from Laguna to Big Sur, with topless chicks in full body paint passing joints to the cowled figures of the "old ones" as seen in the aforementioned drug-induced nightmare. She goes to sleep in a giant four poster bed which is then transported to a Vaseline-framed meadow filled with stony freaks in body paint humping each other madly in a manner which Aleister Crowley would have approved.

Two of the things most admired about *The Dunwich Horror* have always been Les Baxter's unique score and Sandy Dvore's imaginative animated opening titles. What I never realized until later on when I began collecting stills from the film was the discovery of a sequence that Haller filmed and then deleted which might have enhanced the proceedings. It appears he filmed the birth of the Whateley twins as seen in the credits. Sam Jaffe and Joanna Moore Jordan make their way to the Devil's Hop Yard where the same figures draped in black hold ritual goblets while Jaffe performs a ritual as his daughter gives birth. I have nine stills of this sequence, which proves it was done and then discarded. If Haller had retained this footage then his film would have had an Alpha and Omega, since it climaxes, so to speak, with Sandra Dee being impregnated by Wilber's other-dimensional brother.

Dvore was very popular at AIP at this time, having provided the titles for such films as *De Sade*, one of AIP's most expensive bombs, with the credits being singled out as the best thing about the film. He did *Blacula*, the first blaxploitation take on the Dracula myth, and *Three in the Attic*, a sex romp with Christopher Jones. Dvore also did the credits for Otto Preminger's *Skidoo*, a film from which he never recovered even though it now has a large fan base as a cult film.

I made an attempt back in 1979 to interview Daniel Haller regarding not just this film, but an overview of his whole career. We met at his favorite restaurant/watering hole on Santa Monica Boulevard known as the Studio Grill. The interview began over a wonderful lunch with the white wine flowing. Dan did his best to fill me in, which is to say he was a hired gun at AIP looking toward Roger Corman for guidance in every way, so when it came his time to step up and finally assume the director's chair he knew his way around the crew better than most, and with Corman as a mentor he also knew how to bring in whatever the project was, on schedule and under-budget.

Haller seemed to enjoy recalling his two attempts at bringing Lovecraft to the screen, even though until he started working with Roger he had never read any of the Lovecraft canons, nor really knew his background at all. His memories of *The Haunted Palace* were clouded by time as he remembered the whole thing as being hard work, involving sleeping on the set, being ready 24/7 to get the thing done on time and, of course, what a great guy "Vinnie" was to be around since he was always prepared and more than willing to meet his fans when they chose to drop by the set.

When we finally got around to talking around *The Dunwich Horror* he was getting a bit high from all the wine and our conversation loosened up enough for him to reflect on the hazards of shooting too fast and in some cases wishing the effects could have been better. He had nothing but praise for Sandra Dee whom he found to be charming and professional at all times, even though she was going through a rather rough time after her divorce from Bobby Darin. He laughed at the notion that Sandra was ever nude in the film saying to me, "Sandy's mother made very sure her daughter was never in any situation that would paint her in a negative light. Unfortunately she was never allowed to really make up her own mind." He felt Dean Stockwell knew his character and managed to bring as much of the Lovecraft flavor as the script would allow him to bring. Since he had actually read Lovecraft as a boy he knew the background inside and out. "At first Dean was a bit put out that we were moving too far away from Lovecraft's original concept with the girl, but as soon as we began to block scenes he was totally committed to doing his job. Dean was a pro, as he had been in the business all his life."

As our lunch was coming to an end I reached in my case for a photo of him directing Karloff in *Die Monster Die*. He looked at it for a moment and then wrote, "For David, Lovecraft be dammed." Haller obviously enjoyed working with Boris Karloff, telling me, "When we did our picture together in London, Karloff was in the process of moving into a new flat, so he would call me to ask if there was anything he could be doing when we weren't using him as he did not want to be home until all the moving was out of the way. He was such a pro to direct and the crew loved him."

My experience with Dean Stockwell was not as much fun, since we met at one of those autograph shows in Burbank in the mid-90's and he was not in the best of moods. I was there working a table myself with Martine Beswicke, so I had an opportunity to catch him in between signings. When I first brought the film up he laughed a bit saying, "Hey man that was a very long time ago. I really don't remember it all that well. Shit, I can't even remember what I did last week. What exactly is it you need to know? The film was done very quickly since it was a Corman production, and it made a lot of money for AIP while I did not." When I asked about Sandra Dee he softened a bit, recalling her with some affection, "Sandy was a better actress than she was given credit for in that film." I asked him to sign a couple of stills, one as Wilber Whateley and then one as Ben from *Blue Velvet*. When he asked me what to say on that one I replied, "Well, how about your famous line?" Dean looked at me for a moment and said "Listen kid, I have made over 300 motion pictures. How the fuck am I supposed to remember a line of dialogue from any of them?" I was a bit surprised, since among even 300 films it would be hard to forget the one that restarted one's career as *Blue Velvet* did his. So I reminded him by asking for him to write "For David, Here's to your Fuck, Dean Stockwell." After he wrote it he said, "Well, I dare you to hang this one in your office." I replied, "Well, Mr. Stockwell, that is just where it's going."

In the time since its original release *The Dunwich Horror* has ceased somewhat to look as cheesy as it did compared (as it was) to *Rosemary's Baby* which, like *The Exorcist* a few years later, would completely redefine the genre and all that would follow in its wake.

What I find so ironic in 2010 is that with all the technological advantages that have taken place since Haller made his version, when someone finally got around to remaking the film, they not only employed Dean Stockwell to play the Ed Begley role of Dr. Armitage, but they made the same mistakes that dogged the original 40 years ago by making a film with a zero budget for special effects and a climax that makes you appreciate the original, which of course took its cues from the old Universal horror films of the early 1930s, with the venerable Edward Van Sloan essaying the essential prototype of the crusading monster-demolisher.

The new version was directed by a young man named Leigh Scott, who did his best under the circumstances, referencing Lovecraft in much the same way as the crew over at AIP had to do in 1970, updating the material and adding what they could from the master without actually doing him any favors. Aside from casting Dean Stockwell from the original film, they also hired Jeffery Combs, who has made a career out of playing Lovecraftian parts

Sam Jaffe as "old Man Whateley" in the prologue for *The Dunwich Horror*.
This sequence was turned into the animated titles at the beginning of the movie.

like Herbert West in Stuart Gordon's *The Re-Animator*. Gordon is another director who has made his share of Lovecraft films, all updated to the present as well.

The best moment in the new version lasts about a mega-second and it is worth seeking out for a true Lovecraft moment: our reluctant hero, who is also a professor and friend of Dr. Armitage, wanders with the girl (yes, they made that mistake as well) into an old house wherein lies a secret room. He begins to peel at the wallpaper until a small peephole is made where, for a moment, they observe an alien landscape that captures the pulp covers of the old *Weird Tales* that first published *The Dunwich Horror* back in 1929. Otherwise, this remake must defer to the 1970 version as superior in every way. So much for waiting 40 years to take full advantage of all that time had given us in the way of special effects and CGI perfection. I think it is safe to say that the best Lovecraft adaptations to come will be animated without the problems of always having to cast women in parts that never existed in Lovecraft's stories to begin with, and keeping the narratives in the 1920's where they work best.

It is my contention that time has been more than kind to Haller's version. After 40 years, one can better appreciate the exceptional cast, all of whom have died except for Stockwell and Talia Shire. The passing of Sandra

Dee made this film all the more bittersweet in that it was her swansong from films and she remains in the film a beautiful young actress who could have made the transition to more mature parts if Fate had been more forgiving and taken her in a different direction.

Lovecraft is now an icon in weird fiction second only to Poe, which is something Lovecraft himself would have applauded, since he regarded Poe as a god in his personal worldview of fiction and letters. I think we can all safely assume, based on Lovecraft's own observations of the horror films he *did* live to see in the early 1920s and 1930s, that he would have loathed each and every adaptation that has been made from his works…that is, if he could have even made it through one of them. He famously walked out after watching 20 minutes of Lugosi's *Dracula*.

However some of us that have read his fiction and then seen the films made from them might be a bit more forgiving. I remember when I first watched *The Haunted Palace*: it was a thrill just to hear the familiar names from the Lovecraft canon being spoken in a film for the first time. When Frank Maxwell uttered the names Yog Sothoth while referring to the old ones, well, it was great just to realize Lovecraft was no longer such a well-kept secret among his followers. By the time Dean Stockwell was yelling his name on top of Sentinel Hill, I felt like all we needed was Doris Day singing "Once I Had a Secret Love," which definitely was not a secret anymore.

The final moments in the original are still enjoyable while being faithful in execution to the source; the bursting out of the Whateley house of Wilber's other dimensional brother who then rampages through the countryside until he arrives at the Devil's Hop Yard to fulfill his date with destiny, not to mention Sandra Dee.

May I close with my personal favorite moment: when Dean Stockwell finally gets hold of the Necronomicon in the library at the beginning of the film, he delves right into the text that is relevant to the ritual he is ready to perform to bring the old ones across. For reasons nobody needs to know, Dean reads the following to himself while Les Baxter's score provides the proper mood:

"Yog Sothoth is the gate whereby the spheres meet. Only them from beyond can make it multiply and work. Yog Sothoth is the key. And with the gate open, The Old Ones shall be past, present, future…All are one… The Old Ones walk serene and primal, un-dimensional and unseen…The Old Ones broke through of old and they shall break through…

Well, you know the rest…One day even Death may die…

Bette Davis ponders her fate while sister Joan Crawford lies dying on the beach.

2

Whatever Happened To Peter Lawford Happened To Baby Jane

What Ever Happened To Baby Jane?

ONE OF THE MOST WIDELY DISCUSSED yet underappreciated films of the 1960s has to be Robert Aldrich's *What Ever Happened to Baby Jane?*

In spite of the fact *What Ever Happened to Baby Jane?* made millions for Warner Bros., not to mention restarting the careers of both Joan Crawford and Bette Davis, the film itself is trapped in camp adoration by gay men who have placed a reality check at the theater door when it comes to just how much Davis and Crawford really did hate each other, and just how impossible it was to get them to appear together on camera without bloodshed. I mean, how many times have you heard the one about Davis actually kicking the shit out of Crawford during the scene downstairs when Crawford tries to use the phone? In reality, a stand-in was used and if you watch the film, it is clear Crawford is not really being kicked at all. These two highly professional talents worked together seamlessly and made a classic in the process. Then we have the director; Robert Aldrich, who has more than proven himself in every genre he ever chose to make a film in, and still *What Ever Happened to Baby Jane?* is regarded as a guilty pleasure that can only come out at horror festivals on Halloween or drag balls at New Year's Eve.

What Ever Happened to Baby Jane? was the beginning of what genre buffs now refer to as the era of the "Horror Hag." Hopeless as that phrase has become, it does cover the territory well enough when we are discussing films like *Lady in a Cage, Dear Dead Delilah, The Anniversary, Dead Ringer, Berserk* and *Strait-Jacket.* The real beginning came a bit earlier with *Sunset Boulevard* with the unforgettable moment when Gloria Swanson descends her staircase in search of "those wonderful people out there in the dark." The role was supposedly based on silent screen star Mae Murray. Miss Murray was in the audience when the film was finally previewed in Hollywood. Her take on the subject was priceless: "None of us floozies was that nuts."

As the 21st century is well upon us, it is time to place *What Ever Happened to Baby Jane?* back in the realm of serious filmmaking and reassess it as we have done time and again with Hitchcock's *Psycho*. The comparison is certainly there, if you wish to see it as both Norman Bates and Baby Jane Hudson have been reduced to monstrous creations at the hands of family dysfunction. When Anthony Perkins was forced to make sequels to the Hitchcock film because, as he told those close to him at the time, "I want to make as much money as I can so my children will be looked after," his character of Norman Bates (the role that forever became his doppelganger) was to become in these films a sympathetic pawn in the hands of others, especially his mother, the real monster of *Psycho*. Now if *What Ever Happened to Baby Jane?* had been allowed sequels, we might well have seen the character of Blanche become the real bitch of *Baby Jane II*, which would probably pick up at the beach after Jane goes for those damn ice cream cones—the ones she would not let Blanche have in the 1915 flashback.

Robert Aldrich must have realized just how much his work in this and its unofficial sequel *Hush, Hush Sweet Charlotte* was a part of his legacy, as he requested that the songs from both films be played at his memorial. Aldrich had already worked with Crawford in the mid-1950s in *Autumn Leaves*, which bears a number of similarities to *What Ever Happened to Baby Jane?* in the dysfunction of Cliff Robertson's character who is traumatized by his father (an oversexed bully who ridicules his son from childhood and as an adult steals his young and willing wife away from him), leaving the scars for Joan Crawford (as the older woman starved for love as well) to heal. It was this relationship with Aldrich that probably did lead to insecurity on the part of Bette Davis, who as legend would have us believe, actually had a conversation with the director before filming as to whether or not he could work with Joan without favoring a former lover over Davis. Robert Aldrich apparently reassured Bette that there were no worries in that department.

In reexamining the film, we must refrain from the diva-like behavior of its stars long enough to focus on just how well this film addresses the aging process, along with the trauma of family dysfunction in the lives of two women living out their lives in the worst place on earth to cope with the inevitability of losing one's looks, which is Hollywood and the motion picture business itself. All of the scenes where Jane goes forth on her own are cruel and spiteful; it is only because she is so wrapped up in her own reality that she can ignore the outside world for so long. The moment she can no longer do this is the "pièce de résistance" of the film. When Baby Jane sings "I've written a letter to daddy" into her own reflection, that fantasy and reality come crashing together allowing the greatest primal scream in the history of movies as Jane Hudson finally gets her comeuppance many fold, to quote a similar moment in *The Magnificent Ambersons*.

If one can move past the rats and parakeets for din-din and see beyond the clown-at-midnight facade of Davis, we move into the stuff operas are made of in the intense longing of acceptance both the sisters craved as Hollywood players, allowing only Blanche a spotlight from which to move up into the stars above Hollywood Boulevard. In a series of brilliant set pieces, we see the Hollywood back lots of the early talkies where studio execs sit in screening rooms yelling, "Kill it!" to screen tests that might as well put another place-card up at Forest Lawn for the actors left hanging on the screening room wall. Jane Hudson made her share of early talkies and they use the two of Davis's early films, *Parachute Jumper* (1932) and *Ex-Lady* (1933); it's a shame they didn't include *The Cabin in the Cotton, in which* she utters one of her early howlers, "I'd love to kiss you but I just washed maw hair." We are never allowed to see the women at this stage except in film clips. Crawford shines in her private moments sitting in front of her television staring at her own image in a scene with Edward Arnold during it she mutters to herself, "I told Lloyd to hold that shot a bit longer. Oh, why didn't he listen?" It is during these moments that the audience is allowed into the private world of these two sisters, both lonely and desperately in need of the outside world. Blanche remains indoors as her vanity prevents too many fans from seeing her in a wheelchair. However, it is with the accident that put her there that the dysfunction began to erode within the mind of both Jane and her sister and it is not until the final reel that we learn fully the degree of guilt between the two women. Perhaps only the casting of Joan Fontaine with her real-life sister (and bitter rival) Olivia De Havilland would have drawn the same amount of blood between the real life sisters and the make-believe world of Blanche and Jane.

Hollywood itself becomes a character as well; in one of the blacker moments in the early part of the film, Jane goes into the LA Times to place an ad, reminding the puzzled staff writer that he might just remember who is standing in front of him by declaring, "I am Baby Jane Hudson. You may have heard of me," to which he replies with a sincere lack of conviction, "Oh yeah." As Jane exits, he then says after her, "Who the hell is Baby Jane Hudson?" and so say all of us. In Hollywood, the only thing worse than being dead is being forgotten. It is with the revival of Blanche Hudson's films at a local TV station that the drama begins to boil to overflowing as Jane reads and then tears up or writes profanity over the bags of fan letters coming to her rediscovered sister making the past even more unbearable. The neighboring house has two more Blanche Hudson fans in a mother and daughter, played by Anna Lee and Davis's real life daughter B.D. The character Anna Lee plays is called Mrs. Bates (considering this was made less than two years after *Psycho*, one can guess what Robert Aldrich was paying homage to here—or was it just an uncanny coincidence? Bette Davis would live to disown her daughter for writing a warts-and-all memoir of life with Mom not that long after Crawford's adopted daughter did her own poison-pen letter to Mommie. These two are also glued to the television during the Blanche Hudson festival. Overwhelmed, Mrs. Bates brings flowers over to Blanche, only to be told off by Jane and the flowers dumped into the trash, all this behavior brought about from decades of resentment going back to their childhood in 1915 when Baby Jane was the breadwinner and spoiled beyond redemption by her father. If *Psycho* had such a flashback, we might have been allowed to see just what the other Mrs. Bates was up to with her gentleman callers at the motel while little Norman watched through keyholes and openings in the wall; this would have made him a victim as much as those he killed while assuming his mother's role as avenger.

Hollywood history tells us that not only did Joan Crawford discover the novel for *What Ever Happened to Baby Jane?* but brought it to the attention of Bette Davis in the first place, dispelling any notion of feuds to begin with. It seems Crawford had long been looking for a property to bring the two of them in one film and at last, this was it. The project could not have come at a better time, since Davis was in debt to the tune of $30,000, with no nest egg except her guarantee of playing in Tennessee Williams' *The Night of the Iguana*, which was a living nightmare from day one, since the play's leading man, Patrick O'Neal, hated Davis to the point of trying to strangle her before a run-through. These ladies needed each other at the time the film was made and it was only afterwards when the film was a hit and Davis was nominated for the Academy Award that things went toxic for the two divas; so much so that the second attempt to bring them together went so far south it would place Joan Crawford in the hospital, shutting down the whole production for weeks before a replacement could be found in, of all people, the woman with a sister-feud for real, Olivia De Havilland.

It is time to begin to give credit to these two stars for creating, together with Robert Aldrich, a masterpiece of suspense in the Hitchcock tradition with such detail to the breakdown of the family as presented by Hollywood to the world of what is supposed to be "normal" family values within the American dream after World War II. David Lynch has made a career out of the same territory while openly admiring this film for its artistry.

The process of aging is difficult at the best of times within a family, as loved ones become a burden that leads to premature burial in a nursing home and this was not lost on Jane Hudson either, when she discovers Blanche's plan to sell the house they shared for years simply because Jane was a handful, to put it mildly, so it was time to "take care of me" as Jane puts it to her sister.

The scene that always stays with me is one of the scenes between Blanche and her maid Elvira. At this moment Jane has been caught writing profanity on the letters marked for Blanche from the station when Elvira forces the issue of a rest home for Jane as "she is getting worse by the day." Crawford plays this scene to perfection in close-up. "You didn't know Jane as a child. It wasn't that she was just pretty. She had something about her. She was special. I can't just tell her, she will know. After all, Elvira, we're sisters. We know each other very well." Davis certainly had the plum role, but it takes a great star like Joan Crawford to pull scenes like the aforementioned one to life, and Crawford more than held her own with her old rival from Warner Bros.

This essay was originally prepared for a book project on women with issues for Fab Press a few years ago and read quite differently at that time. I became interested in it all over again when I discovered a casting choice early in the filming of *What Ever Happened to Baby Jane?* that has gone unnoticed for decades: it is the fact that the role of Edwin Flagg (played so brilliantly by the late Victor Buono) began filming with Peter Lawford and was terminated by Lawford when he simply left the set and never returned. It is rumored that he could not reconcile the character's flaws (i.e. mother-dominated, possibly coded homosexual/loser living in Hollywood on welfare and his mother). It is interesting to notice that after the success of *What Ever Happened to Baby Jane?* with its effect on the careers of both Crawford and Davis allowing them to continue on in films quite similar in tone to *What Ever Happened to Baby Jane?*, that Davis made sure Peter Lawford had a substantial role in *Dead Ringer*. Lawford plays a golf pro with a sideline as a gigolo, and a very butch one at that.

Peter Lawford's career, as everyone that follows the Kennedy family knows, was dealt two death blows: one from Joe Kennedy himself (in making Lawford the messenger in a tactless response to Frank Sinatra) and the other from Old Blue Eyes himself, who blacklisted Lawford in Hollywood for the rest of his life. Lawford's last days were tragic in ways that redefine the term: he was reduced to game shows and episodic television. His social life was ruined as only Hollywood can ruin it by making you a last minute replacement at posh dinners making you the z at an A list event. My personal experience with Lawford came around 1979 when I was working for Paul Tiberio in Beverly Hills. Paul resembled Lawford and was frequently mistaken for him in public. One night, Paul and I were in a landmark West Hollywood gay bar on Santa Monica known as "The Four Star", which also booked entertainment from time to time on weekends. On this particular evening, Peter Lawford came in only to be told at the door that there was a guy that everyone thought was him, so Lawford came over to where we were sitting and

Victor Buono embraces a "Baby Jane" doll. Buono replaced Peter Lawford in the film.

introduced himself. I will always remember how polite and well-mannered he was in complementing Paul on how much they did favor each other and so on. Paul introduced me as a film buff who loved movies and when Peter Lawford asked me what my favorite film of his might be I blurted out, "Well I just saw you in *Sherlock Holmes Faces Death*. Peter was taken with that because it was almost his first screen appearance (Lawford has one line as a sailor at the bar). I spent the rest of our time together trying to make up for it by naming films in which he had a more substantial part. We discovered that he lived in West Hollywood and was there at the request of the woman who was booking a singer he wanted to hear.

After the initial shock of my discussing his cameo in the Holmes film, of which he remembered "what dear men Rathbone and Bruce where and how much they were a team in films like Laurel and Hardy, not to mention that black bird that could not be tamed during the brief scene in the pub and how many takes were ruined by it's missing its marks and running amok." I mentioned what a favorite of mine *The Picture of Dorian Gray* was and how good I thought he and everyone else was in it. Lawford smiled at the mention of this film and responded with, "You're much too kind about me. I was a green kid who was in great company like George Sanders, who really hated acting even though he was made to be one. I never understood why Hurd Hatfield was chosen; when I first heard about the film being made at M-G-M, I remember Robert Taylor was being considered, since there was no man in Hollywood at that time as handsome as Taylor. Albert Lewin, our director, was a real intellectual and gave the film class, no question. The sets were stunning, especially the house they created for Dorian. That staircase; I still remember walking down it with Donna Reed for nearly ten takes before we got it to Lewin's satisfaction. Hatfield was very professional and aloof during the film, staying in character, I believe. Still, I will always wonder what Bob Taylor would have been like as Dorian; not that he would have understood the perversity of it one bit. I still see Angela. What a great actress she became after that film."

I always remembered him fondly after that. A few years later, his death was announced on ten o'clock news with a clip of him from what was his very last appearance on some sitcom playing himself alone sitting at the end of a bar nursing a drink; the image was unforgettable in it's sadness.

Whether or not Peter Lawford would have worked in the role for which Victor Buono received an Oscar nomination we will never know. Buono became a sought-after performer on television himself. Davis tried to get him fired as she thought him too young and inexperienced, however, halfway through filming, she confessed, "I tried to get Bob to fire you but I am glad you stayed. You are absolutely marvelous in the part." Could this have also been partly because of Peter Lawford's attempt to play the same role, only to flee the set when the mama's boy references proved too close to home?

Victor Buono's own take on acting alongside Davis and Crawford was classic: "I felt like an altar boy being asked to the Ecumenical Council in Rome in an advisory capacity."

Candace Hilligoss is Mary in *Carnival of Souls*.

3

There's Something About Mary

Carnival of Souls

WHILE THE DRIVE-IN WAS A RITE OF PASSAGE for the baby boomers of my generation, I must give television its due as an influence as well. Outside of the Shock Theater packages of Universal horrors televised in the early 1960s, the one film that really made a lasting impression on me was *Carnival of Souls*. This low-budget mood piece is best served if you are by yourself late at night watching it unfold between station breaks advertising used cars.

While not a great film by any means, the lack of star power, (in fact the whole film was done by unknowns in front of and behind the camera), allows the viewer to drift into a dream state within the film itself. The scenes that really make you jump involve the film's director, the late Herk Harvey. His phantom-like performance while in white face—a walking dead man the likes of which we would see again in the films of George Romero—is a tour-de-force.

Now this is a film which those of us that saw it at an impressionable age, best remember it as being much better than it really was and much more frightening when trying to convince one of your friends to sit through it as well. I held a place of honor for *Carnival of Souls* in my memory for decades until 1997.

In 1997, I was sitting in my kitchen on the corner of Beverly and Oakhurst when I noticed a tall, blond woman walking across the courtyard; even from a distance I seemed to recognize this woman as someone very familiar to me from my distant past. She continued down the path until she reached the manager's apartment and then went in. The manager was a woman who

23

had worked in Hollywood for years and was now doing script-doctoring to make extra money, since she had been long retired from any professional endeavors. The woman in question turned out to be none other than Candace Hilligoss, the lead in *Carnival of Souls*.

Candace had the kind of face with shape features and large expressive eyes that made you notice her, especially when she appeared to be frightened. Candace had, in fact, written a script entitled *Dakota Ashes*, a western of sorts in the manner of *Lonesome Dove*. Helen, the apartment manager, told me later that she thought Candace had written a very commercial script and should find an agent to help her place it for a potential mini-series.

The entire afternoon was so surreal. I mean, to see someone you had watched as a child on the late late show all of the sudden materialize at your front door, really needed to be fully taken in. Candace came over to my apartment after she finished her business with Helen as she wanted to meet me, having heard I had been an agent in the business as well.

A plan had begun to take shape in my mind as she sat in my living room sipping a cup of tea; here was a bona-fide cult figure from a highly regarded horror film who has never done the convention circuit that was so much a part of my life that year, having just come back from Kevin Clement's Chiller Theater in New Jersey. I had taken both Martine Beswicke and Barbara Steele to that venue as well as Mary Woronov.

At that time, Candace was doing temp work as a secretary and was not the least bit averse to making some money signing autographs. I explained the situation to her as best I could, knowing that, at least for the first few shows, she would more than likely do very well since none of the fans had ever seen her outside of midnight screenings of the now legendary film that forever sealed her image with that of Mary Henry, a young woman trapped between the veil of life and death.

Now, I need to explain that, in spite of the passing of time from 1962 until 1997, Candace Hilligoss looked exactly like she did in the film. This, coupled with the fact that she seemed to be Mary Henry in almost every other way as well. I remember joking with her about it at the time, and she quickly explained that she had studied the method with Lee Strasberg in New York as well as having done a great deal of stage work back east before marrying Nicolas Coster, another New York actor who was quite successful in his own right working non stop in soaps on television as well as commercials. They divorced in 1981 and not on good terms at the moment. In fact, it was her dream to sell her script to television, where it would then become the next *Lonesome Dove*. Then it would be her great pleasure to rub all this in his face when the series went on to glory at the Emmys.

After our initial meeting Candace Hilligoss and I began working together in earnest to launch her first appearance as a cult star at the Ray Court's

Autograph Show at the Beverly Garland hotel. The first order of business was to secure photographs from *Carnival* for her to sign. The real problem with a film like this is the advertising was almost non-existent. The posters were amateurish, with only half a set of lobby cards, with only two featuring her. The video poster was the best artwork, so we looked around for as many of those as we could to sell at a higher price. It would be the 8" x 10" stills that would provide the foundation for a table at the show. There were no National Screen Service stills from this to be found, so in a moment of inspiration, Candace decided to call her late director's wife Pauline, who was now very old and nearly blind. The next day Candace came by my apartment with the news that she had indeed spoken with Pauline Harvey and she was sending us all she could find on the film to help with Candace's plight. Candace was somewhat concerned about whether or not a nearly blind woman could locate, much less choose, what would be useable for fans to purchase at our table. After a few days the package arrived and she was horrified to discover all that Pauline Harvey could come up with were 35mm frames from the film itself. As soon as I saw what they were, I calmed her fears by explaining these were pure gold as they were all the great moments from the film, many of which were fantastic shots of Herk Harvey himself as the leader of the undead in that amazing pavilion at Saltair.

It took us nearly two and a half months to get the material ready for the show. One of the more time consuming aspects of this were the tee-shirts that Candace insisted upon producing at her own expense, which were costly and, in my opinion, not the wisest of investments for a show like Ray Courts. Barbara Steele and I made the same mistake with *Black Sunday* tee-shirts in New Jersey and we were still trying to sell them months later at the Dark Shadows Con in LA. However, Candace would hear none of my arguments against them, so *Carnival of Souls* tee-shirts we would sell with Candace's ironic signature across them saying, "Hauntingly yours."

During this time I tried to discover just what did happen with her career that she only had two feature films to her credit, *Carnival of Souls* and the Del Tenny film *Curse of the Living Corpse*, whose only real claim to fame was introducing Roy Scheider to films (which of course led to a very successful career including an Oscar). Candace could barely remember making the film such as it was, but did tell me that Roy Scheider was okay on that particular film and they did socialize a bit after it was done; but in her own words, "Roy was never really interested in helping other actors and really never tried to help me secure parts after he became a star."

Carnival of Souls is still highly regarded by genre fans and certain critics that observe that, while the film itself is cheaply made with amateurs, except for perhaps Candace and Sidney Berger (who by the way was selling his autograph at conventions as well) who play well in their scenes together,

Candace Hilligoss looks on in horror as the undead waltz at the *Carnival of Souls.*

the real power of this movie resides in what we imagine long after we have watched what has become a collective nightmare for all that have fallen under its spell.

Whatever John Clifford or Herk Harvey had in mind when they began this project, while far removed from their educational films as Centron Studio employees, the film somewhat looks like an educational film about the dangers of reckless driving as well as the pitfalls of straying too far from God's grace, as Mary Henry surely does to find herself in the hellish limbo of non-existence. Perhaps *Carnival of Souls* is best served as an influence on more prolific directors like David Lynch, George Romero and especially Francis Ford Coppola, who's *Apocalypse Now* has Martin Sheen emerge from the water in much the way Herk Harvey does in *Carnival's* best moments of ghostly splendor.

Meanwhile, the day of the Ray Courts show is finally at hand. Three days of sitting at a table with Candace Hilligoss meeting her public and hopefully selling much of what we spent the last two and a half months preparing for this celebration of all things ghostly. At this point, all of our conversations had been about the show or her plans for her script, but now another bitter demon was coming out of the closet: the dreaded remake of *Carnival of Souls* produced by Wes Craven and without any input from Candace, which was all the more galling for her because of a long-cherished treatment of her own design that she showed me. In it, she was back from the dead with a ghostly assistant to bridge the portal from one dimension to another. I was rather impressed with her concept of filming all the sequences in the land of the dead in black and white, while the living remained in color. Candace naturally assumed that any producer intent on remaking the film would have to have its original star in tow or else the legion of its fans would fail to pay to see a remake without her.

Well, we all know what happened with the remake: it went straight into Video Hell, and unfortunately it took Candace's dreams of a comeback with it. The irony of Candace Hilligoss is that her character in the film was a cynical, bitter woman whose lack of faith literally placed her soul in a netherworld of non-existence. Herk Harvey never made any more films like *Carnival of Souls* nor would Candace ever act in anything like a lead role in her career, such as it was. She always told me her ex-husband did not want her to work and as a result she let the momentum go in favor of raising two children, both of whom were now grown up and successful in their own lives.

During the three days of the convention, many people came to our table with glowing things to say about Candace, how well she looked and so forth. It seemed, at least for that weekend, that Candace Hilligoss was a star. On Sunday, a middle-aged woman approached the table and asked for one of the stills of Candace looking quite lovely, I think a headshot of her made right after the film. The woman began to tell Candace about the first time she saw *Carnival of Souls* and how the film haunted her for years afterward, and then she fished around in her purse for a photo of her daughter to show Candace. The woman proudly displayed the picture to Candace, exclaiming, "You know, I named her after you!" For a moment Candace was speechless and it seemed quite touched. Candace smiled and then said, "Oh, so this young lady is named Candace, too." The woman looked at her for a moment and then replied "Oh, no dear, I called her Mary Henry." Candace Hilligoss changed her expression ever so slightly after hearing this, looking even more like Mary Henry than she had all afternoon.

In the Mouth of Madness – Sam Neill.

4

Reality Is Not What It Used To Be

In the Mouth of Madness

AFTER THE ANNOUNCEMENT by the great director Gullermo Del Toro that he would be adapting Lovecraft's *At the Mountains of Madness* (1936) into a motion picture, I began to think back rather fondly to the film John Carpenter made a few years ago as homage to Lovecraft, the decidedly underrated *In the Mouth of Madness*.

At the time of the film's release, the fans and critics both seemed to be impressed with Carpenter's nightmarish visuals, courtesy of Bruce Nicholson, not to mention Michael De Luca's savvy script which managed to balance the celebrity of Stephen King with the legend that still rests at Swan Point Cemetery, the immortal H.P. Lovecraft. The film, however, was not a success, and the end result would affect the career of John Carpenter for years to come.

In the Mouth of Madness is the third in what Carpenter refers to as his "Apocalypse Trilogy", the other two films in the trilogy being *The Thing* and *Prince of Darkness*. If one needed to build a case for Carpenter's infatuation with Lovecraft then you need look no further than these three films. *The Thing* is considered by many to be Carpenter's greatest film and it well may be, since the cast and effects are still amazing to this very day. This film proved that Carpenter could handle a full blown Lovecraft adaptation, as *The Thing* was very close in spirit and atmosphere to Lovecraft's fiction. *Prince of Darkness* also holds the same argument, as Carpenter creates a unique take on the concept of God and the Devil as we watch a large glass canister ooze with an eerie green glow, the essence of evil as the Devil waits for his chance to rule the earth, with a little help from Alice Cooper.

During the 80's and 90's, there was a rash of films brimming with what some critics were referring to as cinematic "elastic reality", fraught with the paranoid undermining of everything we know in pop culture and beyond. This theme was successfully exploited in Wes Craven's masterful take on his own Elm Street films with Wes Craven's *New Nightmare*. Even Woody Allan's *Purple Rose of Cairo* blurred the reality of the film going experience with characters coming right off the screen and living among their fans. The real premise of *In the Mouth of Madness* is revealed when Julie Carmen's character says the line "reality is just what we tell ourselves it is".

The moment we hear the dreaded question "Do you read Sutter cane?" the reality of reading horror fiction, as opposed to living it, is blurred forever. Our protagonist, well played by Sam Neill, is a skeptic who begins to doubt all that he sees and, more importantly, what he reads, as the film takes a turn towards the abyss.

When it comes to adapting Lovecraft for the movies, the real flaw seems to be in misinterpreting what his fiction is all about in the first place. Lovecraft was a specialist in cosmic psychological horror; the indescribable horror filled with eldritch rites invoking timeless Gods. Lovecraft is not about beating about the bush when it comes to his nightmares and demons. They come right out of your dreams and bite you without your ability to see what exactly is sinking its talons into your mortal flesh.

The current popularity of H.P. Lovecraft on screen seems to have started with Stuart Gordon's witty and gory take on Herbert West in 1985's *Reanimator*. The film's that would follow gave audiences buckets of gore and very little else, least of all the atmosphere of a classic Lovecraft short story or novel. Dan O'Bannon's *The Resurrected* was close in mood to the real Lovecraft with a bravura performance from Chris Sarandon portraying both Charles Dexter Ward and his ancestor the warlock Joseph Curwen. (It is interesting to note that Vincent Price also does an admirable job in portraying the same two characters in *The Haunted Palace*. Personally, I feel it is a great mistake to try and update his fiction to the present day.

The Dunwich Horror, made at the height of the "Summer of Love", is more proof that Lovecraft does not update to anyone's satisfaction. Now having said that, I have to admit that I find the film a real guilty pleasure as the "hippy" trappings are so removed from time and space that the film has a unique look and vibe, if you will, and Les Baxter's score is a plus as is the terrific opening credits, which would have made an interesting short all by itself.

If you do any research at all into Lovecraft's world, the first thing you become aware of is his personal misplacement in the 20th Century. Lovecraft wrote and lived as if he belonged in another time and place. He lived almost his entire life with his two aunts in the decidedly gothic house, venturing out only at night. It seems his aunts convinced him that he was ugly and even

In the Mouth of Madness – Jürgen Prochnow.

a brief marriage to Sonia Greene could not shake this belief. His contact with the outside world was done mainly by correspondence. This eccentricity made his fiction remote and otherworldly, which is also part of its allure. If one were to double bill *The Resurrected* with Roger Corman's *The Haunted Palace,* you could see more clearly how, while O'Bannon is more respectful of the story line, setting Lovecraft in the past gives his mythos a mystery that the present day seems to deflate.

In the Mouth of Madness, while most definitely a Lovecraft saturated film, is also by rights a Stephen King tribute as well. The faux author Sutter Cane, played with the right amount of corn ball dedication by Jurgen Prochnow, is at once recognizable as a cipher for King. The films opening sequence is more than enough to let us know that Sutter Kane/Stephen King is selling millions of copies of every book that bears his name. It would not have been as compelling to film a similar sequence over at Sauk City, Wisconsin where the very real publishing company, Arkham House, has been printing Lovecraft's output in limited editions of 2,500 to 5,000 for the last half century.

In reexamining Carpenter's film, I can appreciate the Lovecraftian set pieces all the more than the first time around. I particularly admire everything beginning with the nightmarish car ride to Hobbs End (a tribute to Nigel Kneale's Quatermass film) right up to the confrontation between Trent and Sutter Cane where the very walls and especially the giant wooden door behind the cursed author is literally swelling to burst allowing the slimy monstrosity to gain a foothold into this world. It is also interesting that both the film and Lovecraft's novella At the Mountains of Madness is narrated by men residing in asylums. The film allows one bit of humor as one of the scripts best lines is delivered while Trent is locked away in his cell, the great character actor David Warner, of all people, playing a doctor reminds him that "a man with a pair of swollen testicles says you want out." This was referring to Trent's violent actions to the guards as he was led to his cell.

Carpenter's location scouts scored big-time with the discovery of that superb byzantine church isolated by itself on that hill in the middle of nowhere. The sequence at Pickman's Hotel is a textbook in Lovecratian atmosphere and dread. The surreal painting that keeps changing whenever you look away, and of course, that marvelously wicked old lady with her husband shackled to her leg behind the desk. In many ways this film is really like a short story Lovecraft should have penned in the golden days of Farnsworth Wright's legendary Weird Tales, where Lovecraft first came to the attention of his public.

Time has been more than kind to *In the Mouth of Madness* and its reputation is solid among fans of both Lovecraft and Carpenter. It is now regarded as one of the last good films from Carpenter, whose reputation took a bit of a downward spiral directly after this film. Recently, Carpenter returned to the themes of ITMOM with the series, Masters of Horror. The short film, *Cigarette Burns,* is in many ways a continuation of depicting the corruption of human beings by decadent art in both literature and cinema. In this latest venture, Carpenter uses the very essence of fandom to explore the power of camera to open Pandora's Box, once again in the character of Udo Keir, who plays a wealthy memorabilia collector whose specialty is horror. In an inspired moment, Keir explains to the detective he employs to find this toxic film, that the only reason he was not at the world premier, which caused members of the audience to attack each other, was the chance to meet Vincent Price in person, so he changed his ticket for a screening of *Dr. Phibes*! Instead of trying to locate Sutter Canes latest novel, the object of everyone's obsession is a legendary film called literally "The absolute end of the world." It seems everyone who has seen it destroys themselves directly as a result of being exposed to the film itself. Even a few frames of it can take your soul. The end result is quite satisfying and I consider this to be a successful return to form for Carpenter.

In the years since the original release of *In the Mouth of Madness* the European intelligentsia has taken notice of both the film as a statement on capitalism and schizophrenia and the popularity of Lovecraft's literary output to elevate the author to rather lofty heights. The celebrated cultural critics Deleuge-Guattari consider Lovecraft to be more than a fantasy author. Lovecraft is "an authority or source of formulation." *In the Mouth of Madness* is now regarded as a gothic materialist parable. Lovecraft is referenced several times in Deleuges *A Thousand Plateaus,* as well as his many books on cinema, now translated from the French.

The result of the constant merging of the reality of Lovecraft's fiction from the fantastic to the real world as revealed in Carpenter's film that the possibility that perhaps some of his nightmares are more than just imagination. I have seen so many ads on the internet offering copies of *The Necronomicon* that I dare to ask myself if I ordered the right one, could I?

Peter Wyngarde – *Night of the Eagle, AKA Burn, Witch, Burn!*

5

"I Do Not Believe."

Burn, Witch, Burn!

WRITTEN EMPHATICALLY ON A BLACKBOARD in the presence of his students, Professor Norman Taylor (Peter Wyngarde) dispels belief in witchcraft and all the trappings of the supernatural. However, Taylor's wife, Tansy (Janet Blair), has been liberated from so much scientific logic by a mind-expanding experience in Jamaica, where a witch doctor literally brought the dead back to life, and it is Taylor's discovery of her convictions that serves as the catalyst for *Burn, Witch, Burn!*

Produced in England in 1961 under the title *Night of the Eagle* (at a time when studios on both sides of the Atlantic were making exceptional genre films), American International Pictures chose to distribute the film as *Burn, Witch, Burn!*, adding a deliciously demonic rendering of an incantation voiced by Paul Frees to protect the viewing audience from deadly forces from the pits of Hell. This created yet another similarity to the already renowned Jacques Tourneur film *Night of the Demon* (1958), known as *Curse of the Demon* stateside.

Both films are now staples in most retrospectives of the horror genre anywhere around the world. These two films now have secured the reputation as two of the finest examples of black magic ever put on the screen. Terence Fisher's masterful *The Devil Rides Out* (1967) joins the trio, even having its title changed as well for American consumption to *The Devil's Bride* to cash in on the world wide success of *Rosemary's Baby*.

Night of the Eagle was directed by Sidney Hayers, whose only other excursion into fantastic cinema was 1960s *Circus of Horrors* (featuring the icy

35

villainy of Anton Differing) regarded now as a truly "Sadian" motion picture whose reputation was linked to Arthur Crabtree's lurid potboiler *Horrors of the Black Museum,* as well as the infamous *Peeping Tom* by Michael Powell. I must interject, however, that Powell's film is now regarded as a masterpiece while the other two films pale in comparison. They still form a rather unholy trinity of genre films of the period that created "X certificates" for all three by the British censor. This only made these films more desirable in the future as video nasties, constantly on-demand by collectors and fans alike.

After the success of *Night of the Eagle,* Hayers went on to helm many memorable episodes of *The Avengers* in Britain, continuing to work on both sides of the Atlantic until his death. *Night of the Eagle* still remains his most accomplished work. The fortuitous collaboration of writers Richard Matheson, Charles Beaumont with George Baxt, turned Fritz Leiber, Jr.'s thrice-filmed novel *Conjure Wife* into a taut, gripping screenplay mysteriously overshadowed by the literary ghost of M.R James, whose own excursions into the supernatural *Whistle and I Will Come To You* is referenced in Hayers' film, not to mention Val Lewton's *I Walked with A Zombie.* Peter Wyngarde had just completed a career-defining role in director Jack Clayton's version of the James novella, (his performance was spellbinding as the lustful ghost of Peter Quint without relying on a word of dialogue), when he was cast as Norman Taylor in Hayer's film.

Leiber's work arrived on the screen as part of the Inner Sanctum series Universal Pictures had created to showcase Lon Chaney, Jr. after the success of *The Wolf Man. Weird Woman* featured Evelyn Ankers in a part similar to Margaret Johnston in Hayers' version. This adaptation is certainly not faithful to its source, making *Night of the Eagle* the definitive version of Leiber's novel. In 1980, a third somewhat-pirated version *Witches Brew,* was made without giving Leiber a screen credit. This time it was played for laughs, attempting a "horror comedy" with Richard Benjamin and Teri Garr, and featuring screen legend Lana Turner in one of her final roles. I am sure the producers were hoping for a "Baby Jane" moment here as we watched yet another Hollywood leading lady finally playing a witch.

The witch in Sidney Hayers' version fairs much better in the capable hands of Janet Blair, perhaps the least likely candidate for such a role, and she surprised her director and co-star by rising to the challenge, playing Tansy with great style and conviction. I interviewed Janet Blair for the premiere laser disc presentation of the film. The still-vivacious actress remembers the production with enthusiasm. She recalls her first day of shooting was Tansy's drowning scene off the Northern coast of England. "It was bitterly cold and I had to go over this rocky cliff and continue to walk into the ocean for what seemed to be an eternity. By the time I was retrieved out of the water, I was frozen and soaked to the bone. One of the grips ran up to me and made me drink from a thermos which was filled with brandy. Being a non-drinker, I immediately spat it out; so much for the glamorous work of a movie star."

"Originally I was told Peter Finch was to be my leading man, but he became ill, so Peter (Wyngarde) took over at a moment's notice. I quickly became utterly bewitched by my co-star, Peter Wyngarde, who was so dramatic and sexy that I nearly forgot I was acting. I do believe this was one of Peter's largest film roles at the time, and I remember after a day's shooting, he drove me to my hotel and continued that atmosphere of a happily married couple. I adored working with him."

As Sidney Hayers fondly recalled to me, the shooting was very quick and fun to do. After some initial misgivings about the casting of Wyngarde and Blair, he was quite pleased to find these two professionals had great chemistry together. He remarked that even Ms. Blair said at the time that she gave this role her all and considered it to be some of her finest work in film. Hayers also remembers that the actress playing the true villainess of the piece, Margaret Johnston, had by then become a theatrical agent representing one of the actors in the film. Hayers persuaded her to play the unbalanced Flora, ruthlessly driven to practice the black arts against Tansy's white magic, thereby creating one of the screen's most memorable witches alongside such greats as Kay Walsh, whose turn in Hammer's *The Witches* set such a standard.

The giant stone eagle which terrorizes Wyngarde was in actuality an eight foot styrofoam figure that could do no harm should it fall from great heights. The script called for a full camera as this prop is transformed from its solid state into a living, winged gargoyle. As Hayers put it, "It is Peter Wyngarde's acting and intense focus that really allows the audience to suspend disbelief, that and of course having a cameraman like Reggie Wyeis, a real craftsman with monochrome photography, as well as an editor like Ralph Sheldon."

Peter Wyngarde made a lasting impression in *The Innocents*, leaving audiences wanting to see more of this charismatic performer. As Hayers recalled, "Peter was quite a performer both on and off camera. The crew was very amused by one thing in particular: you see Peter was very aware of his physique at the time, since he took great care to be in perfect shape and remember, in those days it was not so common to see actors going to the gym to work out. We even had him shirtless at one point in the film. However we had to keep tightening his long shots as he wore the tightest trousers in England! I mean, he left little to the imagination as to his endowments if you follow me. I don't think this even came up again as long as I have been directing!"

Night of the Eagle was one of those films I saw for the first time at the drive-in and I carry that memory with great pleasure, since it is difficult to explain to today's film buffs the weekend ritual of going to see a film in your car, at night, out of doors, under the stars. The nocturnal trappings of the horror genre lends itself to such circumstances perfectly. Of course, it helps to be at a certain age as well and the drive-in was a haven for teenagers to escape from the rigors of school and parents. Almost all of the films produced by American International were shown at the drive-in and *Burn, Witch, Burn!* was no exception. I can still see myself sitting in the car windows rolled up, speakers turned to full volume, as Paul Frees begins to speak to us from a pitch black screen. By the time he is through and we are all under the protection of his spell, the titles begin to appear: *Burn, Witch, Burn!* ...

I DO BELIEVE
The Sidney Hayers Interview

I was fortunate at the time *Burn, Witch, Burn!* was being prepped for its first incarnation on Laser Disc by Image Entertainment to be in touch with the films director Sidney Hayers. I phoned him several times until we could finally organize a meeting. He suggested we do the taping at my apartment on Beverly Blvd as I was only a few blocks from Cedars Sinai hospital where Sidney Havers was under treatment so this would prove convenient for both of us.

He arrived at my place on time and ready to chat. He was a charming man who was modest in recalling the two films that would secure his reputation in the genre of horror films even though he really felt both *Circus of Horrors* as well as *Night of the Eagle* were really thrillers disguised as horror films. I would like to thank Bill George and his lady for keeping this interview safe and ultimately transcribing it for publication now:

Q: You started as a film cutter. With that background, did you find yourself a more economical director, making the cuts in your head as you go?

S: I don't actually cut in my head. It's a very difficult thing to do because you make decisions in the cutting room that you may have overlooked on the floor. You find that some of the decisions you make, if you're cutting in your head, don't always work in the cutting room. For proof of that, I was cutting a picture called *Tiger Bay* (1959) for J. Lee Thompson and he started out by giving me instructions on a piece of paper. I found out the sequences wouldn't go together in the best way like that. So I went up to him and told him he had better find someone else to do the cutting because I disagreed with the order in which he wanted the scenes. He wouldn't have gotten the best out of the picture. To my surprise, he tore his notes up in front of me and said "Do it your way".

Q: What steps led up to you directing *Night of the Eagle* (1962), (aka *Burn, Witch, Burn!*)?

S: Well I became an editor and during the course of my career I worked for Julian Wintle and Leslie Parkyn. They were producers at Beckinsdale Studios and I kicked off *Circus of Horrors* (1960), which was the very first picture I made. We went from one picture to another and eventually…

Q: Then, Julian Wintle was probably responsible for you doing *The Avengers*?

S: He and Albert Fennell, yes. That was a bit later, though.

Q: There were three British films made around the same time that seemed somewhat related: Arthur Crabtree's *Horrors of the Black Museum* (1959), Michael Powell's *Peeping Tom* (1960), and your own *Circus of Horrors*. Had you seen either of the other two films?

S: No I had not. *Peeping Tom* was, in fact, made after *Circus of Horrors*. I saw *Peeping Tom*, actually and I thought it was a quite superior picture.

Q: It certainly didn't deserve the criticism it got.

S: No, it was just ahead of its time.

Q: How do you feel about making the audience truly a voyeur when you are creating certain scenes? When watching *Circus of Horrors*, it seems that during certain scenes (ghastly scene on the operating table and in the circus tent, for example) the film takes on a different kind of technique.

S: I think one of the most awful things that can happen to a person is to be spied upon. It takes their privacy away, particularly if the person is unaware of it. It's a thing that always affects me when I see sequences like that, like in *Rear Window* (1954).

Q: How did the casting work out? Anton Diffring enjoyed kind of a side career as a villain, not just as Nazis. Circus of Horrors gave him a definite personality as a mad doctor. There was also a certain element of sexuality in what he does.

S: I was really instrumental in bringing Anton in. There were all sorts of names being bandied around. I felt the character had to have a certain elegance and he had to convey this to the audience—

Q: He had to be attractive—

S: He had to be attractive and elegant and really played against type. He wasn't noticeably nasty unless pushed.

Q: There was one sequence I remember in *Circus of Horrors*: Diffring is very sexually involved with all of the women in the temple of beauty that he recreates. He is so emotionally overcome that he embraces one patient while she is still bandaged and the image of that is very unsettling.

S: That was Yvonne Romaine, who is married to Leslie Bricusse.

Q: I didn't know that. She retired not long after…

S: Oh yes. Stunningly attractive woman.

Q: She did Hammer films. They both did. Had you seen them in Hammer films?

S: No I had not.

Q: Had you ever worked with or known Terrence Fisher?

S: Yes, I knew Terrence Fisher. We weren't close friends or anything like that.

Q: He has enjoyed a certain Renaissance right now because he did all of the Hammer Horrors. Some people think it may have inhibited him from doing greater work, but then one has to re-assess what he did. I think in certain ways, Horror pictures can be very liberating because you can do things you just don't do in regular films.

S: Absolutely.

Q: Your two horror films are quite different in technique and style than the other films you have directed. There are similarities, but I feel these two films made you experiment.

S: Well you do, because you have to create effects on the screen, searching for the reaction you want from the audience. You have to adopt a technique that you hope will achieve that end.

Q: How did you go about finding a circus to use as a backdrop?

S: I remember we went up to Liverpool where Billy Smart's circus was and spoke to Billy Smart about it.

Q: Were there any problems working with the animals?

S: None at all. Only just once on the floor. Donald Pleasence had a scene with a bear.

Q: Oh, the bear that kills him.

S: Yes. They were rehearsing the scene and there was a microphone about a foot long. The boom swinger wasn't concentrating too much. He hit the boom arm and the bear took off chained to the caravan. This is on the set, mark you. The caravan just took off and went straight thru sets and everything else! The bear just dragging it on the end of his long chain and the caravan just wrecked half the sets.

Q: So that is a real bear he is fighting with?

S: No, the one where he is tortured outside the caravan is a real bear, but when he was fighting it, we made him a stuffed bear. I think there was a trainer who doubled for him when there was a bit of action with the real bear.

Q: 'Cause it could have been dangerous.

S: Indeed. A bear that could take a complete gypsy caravan and knock the walls down and smash it through sets…

Q: They're strong. Now Pleasence has, sadly, passed away, but he enjoyed a long and varied career.

S: A very fine actor, I thought. He had great instincts about what was right.

Q: Did he enjoy making *Circus of Horrors*?

S: Very much.

Q: He seemed to be having a lot of fun.

S: He did.

Q: Did you have any censorship problems as far as how you could go with the operation sequences?

S: No we just had a guiding letter at the front that said don't show this or that. We did adhere to that because we it would be stupid to have to ruin sequences with rewrites. In re-editing sometimes the sequences don't go the way they should and the audience doesn't know why, they just feel a sense of loss there.

Q: It holds up well today because it went as far as it could in both violence and sexuality. It is interesting that you were able to convey all of this sexuality without nudity. If that film were made today it would be almost impossible to watch. I'm not much for gore in films because, especially in horror films, you can imply so much.

S: Of course you can. In my opinion, it's many times much more effective.

Q: Well, you have to show some imagination. I think that directors that take the gory path are really taking a shortcut.

S: I always remember when I was an assistant editor working on a David Lean film, he said "You're very foolish if you are too explicit in a love scene. Everybody, no matter who they are, they always fantasize about making love in a different way and if you just show them something that's not their cup of tea, it irritates them."

Q: Same thing, I think, holds true with violence. You can imply so much rather than…

S: Yeah, yeah.

Q: I think that impact of that bear attacking Donald Pleasence and killing him—just the look in the little girl's eyes and the different things you pointed to—you didn't have to show big chunks of flesh being ripped away or lots of blood. Yet that film was considered very sadistic for its time.

S: Was it really?

Q: Yes, when it came over here [the U.S.]. Were you aware there was a record album done?

S: Yes, "Look for a Star". Apparently made it to the top of the Hit Parade!

Q: It was a 45, I think. Did you know that this song was going to... ?

S: No, I didn't. I had a call from someone in the States asking, "Are you aware that this song is at the top of the charts?"

Q: I always think of this as being American International, but they didn't finance it, right?

S: I think they partially financed it. Karen Levy was the distributor in England and I don't know where else.

Q: So that was your first picture.

S: First full length picture.

Q: What had you just cut before that?

S: *Tiger Bay.*

Q: With Haley Mills and Horst Buchholz. When that picture was finished, it was successful; it made money.

S: It was very successful, yes.

Q: What were you offered after that?

S: *Payroll* (1961), which did extremely well. In fact, an American picture called *Ace in the Hole* came out at the same time, on a similar subject—

Q: With Billy Wilder?

S: I can't remember.

Q: It had several titles. *Big Carnival*, I think, was one. Where a man is trapped...or was it a film with Tony Curtis. Now I am confused.

S: Well I'm confused, but I know this: It was a similar type of picture and I know that we did tremendously more business.

Q: Who was in *Payroll*?

S: Michael Craig, Billy Whitelaw, Kenneth Griffith, Tom Bell. It's a very hard robbery picture.

Q: I love Billy Whitelaw.

S: And a French actress called Françoise Prévost. It's a very, very hard-hitting robbery picture.

Q: After *Payroll*, you went to?

S: Well, *Night of the Eagle*...

Q: That was really your fourth picture?

S: Yes, about my fourth or fifth.

Q: AIP also released *Night of the Eagle*; was this something offered to you based on the success of *Circus of Horrors*?

S: It probably was, yes.

Q: So what do you remember about the setting up of that film and the casting, etc?

S: Well the funny thing is the witch, played by Maggie Parker [Margaret Johnston]—who was an agent at the time and wife of Al Parker. She had come to me to discuss another actor for the picture. I got her to audition for the part.

Q: She was so good in that. Wasn't her stage name Margaret Johnston?

S: Yes.

Q: So she was an agent who just changed hats?

S: She had been an actress before and then she was married to Al Parker and she had become a rather super agent. I still remember her address.

Q: Peter Wyngarde… was he already set or did you pick him?

S: He wasn't already set. I think it came out in discussion, I was a little apprehensive about the casting of him and Janet Blair: how they were going to work out, the chemistry between them. I didn't know whether they would really appear like a happily married couple. There was a particular difference in thought about certain subjects.

Q: A lot of people feel that Janet Blair was a mis-cast.

S: I know. That is basically what I'm talking about.

Q: Yet, she doesn't disgrace herself.

S: Not at all.

Q: I think a lot of people were surprised to see her give that performance. She is convincing enough. I mean, if the performances were not convincing, we wouldn't be talking about the picture now. But the fact is she did give the impression that she was so in love with Peter Wyngarde that she would give her life for him. Of course Peter Wyngarde has been the subject of so much controversy because his career took a substantial nose-dive at one point in his life because of his problem with something that—well I guess in England it will always be a problem, unless the laws are changed like they are here to where actors like that are not subject to blackmail. I do feel he was set up and that was terrible. He was a fine actor.

S: He was. I thought he was great the way he opened in the classroom. Very authoritative.

Q: He had a lot of strength.

S: Oh yeah.

Q: There was something very powerful about Wyngarde and I do believe he would have gone on to a really good career in character work. Well, he is still working. This is one of his best films, I think. This was long before he did "The King and I" and all that stuff on the West End. I think it's just a problem when you have a very large female following as an actor. I don't think it would have affected a character actor that much. But to have been a romantic lead and have this come up… But of course, over here, we heard very little about it and the film itself, I don't think anyone has really realized… People have asked me—that don't know his career—"what happened to him? He was so visible for one minute." Janet Blair on the other hand, I don't recall her in another film after *Burn, Witch, Burn!*

S: Nor do I. Isn't that amazing?

Q: Now she lives out here and at one point—may still do it yet—I know someone who knows her, a casting director. Have you not seen her in years and years?

S: No

Q: It might be really interesting to put you two together and video-tape the two of you.

S: That might work.

Q: She apparently remembers this movie very fondly. Do you remember anything that went on during the film that might be an interesting story?

S: It's very difficult to go back and suddenly remember. I could call you later. [Janet Blair] was very effective coming down that corridor with that great knife in front of her. I remember that.

Q: Oh there's a great sequence in there too because she's limping.

S: Like Maggie Johnston.

Q: Which is a marvelous way of transferring … and of course you have a cat that starts the fire. It's a very effective film. I always thought you must have really been torn about how to convey this eagle coming to life.

S: I was really. I spent some hours thinking about this. I thought "This could really be the Achilles heel of the film, if this doesn't work; people are going to think 'What does all this mean? What is it about?'" This stone bird suddenly comes to life and it's chasing him around...

Q: Were you familiar with the films of Val Lewton?

S: No I was not.

Q: You know his movies dealt with a lot of themes like people changing into animals. He believed that you just kept everything in shadow and let the audience come up with far worse scenarios than he actually could have put on film. I do feel there is a great sense of tension when he's running through the building and he goes back into the room where he has written "I do not believe". And using a very modern apparatus to convey supernatural control, like a telephone or tape recorder ... and the use of music—I don't think we can underestimate that. The music in that film makes it work. Was that Lori Johnson?

S: No, it was Hans...??

Q: I'll look him up in the press book here. The music is really effective. The press book doesn't say; isn't that bizarre? Did you choose the composer?

S: No, I think it was a committee sort of decision.

Q: Do you remember when it opened in London?

S: It did very well. My then-wife went to the toilet after and told me "You can't believe the conversation I just overheard. Two women were discussing how "This sort of thing does happen!" [in regards to the witchcraft].

Q: Witchcraft in England is something that's kind of taken for granted. There are people who will go out at midnight in Highgate Cemetery and prance around in the nude because it is an old religion. How did you come upon that sequence where it's all subjective and you see the graveyard through Janet Blair's eyes, while she's being carried? It was kind of innovative for the time. I can't think of any films that you see from the point of a person who is unconscious or dead.

S: I can't remember too much about the actual graveyard part of the scene but I can remember thinking "How am I going to get a real effect of her coming to and she's in a trance?" And what I did, which was an awful thing to Peter Wyngarde, really, I got a nine millimeter lens, which if you hold it to your chest you can see your feet and you can see the roof of the building at the same time. I stuck (Wyngarde's) face almost in the mat box so his nose had a big hook like an eagle and his ears sort of stuck out. I Vaselined the edge of the lens, too. His face was very intense. When she came to, Peter looked a bit like an eagle, actually.

Q: Yeah, I had thought about that. It's very effective. It takes that far into the film for him to start practicing witchcraft. These different sequences one remembers very well. The music is very effective.

S: I think it was Hans Reisenstein who did the music.

Q: Now, that's interesting. Of the two films, the score from *Night of the Eagle* would have been the superior one, but it didn't have a hit song in it so it didn't get on vinyl like *Circus of Horrors*. What University did you use for the—

S: We didn't. We used a very old house in.....? On the gates it had eagles. We mounted this enormous eagle, which was about 8 feet high, over the door.

Q: You know in America that they tapped on a sequence at the beginning of the film before it starts where a spell is read that protects the audience. Have you ever seen that?

S: Well, I've heard it.

Q: 'Cause they read it here at the Newark Theatre. The audience really loved that. It was a bit campy now but it's rather effective to go into a darkened theatre and have that spell read.

S: How did the picture go down with an audience today?

Q: You would be very pleased. I think it would be very satisfying that a contemporary 1990s audience gets into a state of disbelief. They don't yell back at the screen. There's not camp in this film whatsoever and what's amazing is you had some rather campy people.

S: I know.

Q: I mean Kathleen Byron—-one forgets that this is the woman that goes berserk in Michael Powell's *Black Narcissus* (1947). And you've got Margaret Johnston that could chew scenery and Peter Wyngarde who could be over the top if he wished. And several other people that are in smaller parts.

S: In fact the boy got a bit upset because he thought Wyngarde was having an affair with Judith Stott—he used to come a little bit near the edge and I was always pulling him back.

Q: He was a bit hysterical.

S: He was supposed to be, but I was always pulling him back.

Q: But he seems unstable at the beginning of the film. With regard to wardrobe—did you decide to show that just ordinary, academic people could secretly be witches? Were you tempted to dress anyone in black?

S: No not at all.

Q: You kept it to where the sense of the normal world—

S: I thought it very necessary that Margaret Johnston was, if anything, more than correct.

Q: Was her husband unaware that she practiced witchcraft? Because that is the implication.

S: Yes, he was unaware. Until the end.

Q: And of course, she's killed by the very thing that she tried to use on him. I think this is why the film isn't laughed at today, because this film is so deadly serious about its subject matter and the dramatic intensity of the music, plus you've got very competent performers. It all works. I'm very surprised you haven't seen any Val Lewton—you'd be amazed, there are three major set pieces you have that were used in Val Lewton's films, in a completely different context. The scene where she's walking on the beach is not unlike the scene where a girl is walking into the sea in *I Walked with a Zombie* (1943) that Mark Robeson directed. The sequence in the graveyard is similar to some things in *Isle of the Dead* (1945). In Lewton's movies, he always does one shock sequence that you remember like a woman that is buried because she has catalepsy and the camera, after everyone has left, zooms in on this empty coffin. As it pans away, you hear a scream. It is so much more effective than showing any explicit scenes. How is the scene done with the bus and the car going side by side? Is that a stunt? Did Wyngarde use a stunt driver at all?

S: Yes, we had to do a tiny bit of stunt work.

Q: Did you ever meet Richard Matheson?

S: I did on one occasion, when he visited England.

Q: He was very pleased with the results.

S: Yes, he was.

Q: That was your final horror film, I believe.

S: Yeah. Absolutely.

Q: Yet it was so successful; did you ever want to make another one? Was anything offered to you?

S: I would've. If I could have found the right material, I think I would like to have done. They're very fascinating to work on. I mean, *Burn, Witch, Burn!* I wouldn't call it a true horror film.

Q: It's more of a thriller.

S: Yes. It's fascinating because of its subject matter. Even *Circus of Horror*, in my opinion, is not really a horror film.

Q: That also could be construed as a kind of psychological love story.

S: I like the lull of the music of the circus.

Q: One doesn't think of circuses as being sinister.

S: No.

Q: But yet, a long time ago, Lon Chaney Sr. said that if you take a clown out of the circus and put him at your front door at midnight, the clown takes on a whole… it just depends on your environment. The circus is kind of a magical place and yet you're dealing with a lot of danger because of the animals. You show the different tragedies that can befall people—-trying to stay on the high wire or people that place themselves in danger without a net.

S: The girl on the horse. The girl on the revolving—

Q: Well, that is a famous sequence. It was considered very nasty for its time.

S: Oh was it?

Q: But you look at it now and its tame. I'm sorry to say it's tame be-cause I remember as a little boy, I may have even looked away. I'd pay good money to watch a horror film from between my fingers. In that movie, for that period of time, I'd never seen anything so violent. But then, I hadn't seen *Peeping Tom* yet, which then again, isn't as violent but it—

S: The image is awful of these girls—

Q: In a death throe, yes. See, but that's what made it nasty. Yet there's really nothing explicit.

S: Some of the shots going up the stairs—

Q: It's scary. I think Michael tapped into everyone's fear of a Jack the Ripper character. Seeing women propped against lampposts and going up stairs—-it really all goes back to Pandora's Box. You almost think that there are no tricks new in cinema. You can always think of a movie in some obscure decade before where these things were possible.

S: I regret today that somehow the majority of film people are not really interested, fascinating filmmakers. Today, in my opinion, there is very little technique, very little true interest in the subject matter. All they think about is—

Q: Sex and violence.

S: Sex and violence and making money. We never approached films like that in the old days.

Q: That's very interesting. Why do you think that was?

S: All you thought about was making the best possible thing you could and you'd spend days of your own time working on this. I know, working among these people today there's not the interest at all—-this dedicated interest.

Q: And the actors cared too. Do you recall with *Night of the Eagle*, did you show it to the cast? Was there a screening before it opened?

S: That, I don't think happened.

Q: Did Peter Wyngarde ever compliment you on the way that –

S: Oh yeah, he thought it was a very good film. He liked it very much indeed.

Q: And Janet Blair too, I suppose, was pleased with her work?

S: Yes. She wrote me a letter because she had come back to the States by that time.

Q: It's amazing you didn't end up with a contract to do three or four more [films]. You never really strayed from what we would call Cinefantastique. In your television work, your Avenger episodes went right back to this material and what I love about *The Avengers* is that you never see any blood. No matter how many bodies pile up at the end, they are all beautifully done. The men are all in Pierre Cardin suits, whether they've got umbrellas impaled in their backs... and it's not dwelt on. I'm sure this is intentional because this was television.

S: Yeah.

Q: But those shows are as entertaining today as they were—-I mean the ones you directed especially—-I can remember some of the titles even, like *The Joker*.

S: That's one of my favorites.

Q: Isn't that where she keeps hearing "*Mein Lieben, mein lieben*"

S: Then she comes out from the curve of the road…

Q: That's a very creepy episode. She was so divine to work with.

S: Yeah, I really enjoyed her.

Q: Now, her part was written for a man. Ian Bannon, originally.

S: Really?

Q: I don't think they really altered much.

S: Oh that's right. The very, very beginning. Was that even pre-Honor Blackman?

Q: Yes, originally it was a police sergeant.

S: Who was the other actor? There was a pair of them.

Q: Ian Hendry and Pat McKnee. McKnee is just so—-I did a long interview with him and he is just so… he thought your work—-He said that "You know, we were very lucky in the show, in that we had directors like Sidney Hayers. We had the best. Going to work every day, I never knew who was going to be on the floor working for a day or so." Actors that were really fine..

S: I remember in *The Superlative Seven*. I had Charlotte Rampling, Donald Sutherland…

Q: What a group! Had Charlotte done many movies? Had she done *Georgie Girl* already?

S: I can't remember the actual order but she was well known.

Q: That was one where you got to take Steed off to a—

S: An island. Dressed up like the Duke of Wellington.

Q: When A&E brought them out here in the morning, it opens with champagne and their always drinking, I thought, my God, they shouldn't put this on at ten in the morning—-its following is mainly alcoholics! [laughs] That's the thing with this new show *Absolutely Fabulous* with Joanna Lumley, that's so popular. They do things there that in America is just frowned upon like driving while intoxicated and taking drugs and being promiscuous. All the things that really were the swinging 60's which alas, what's going on now prevents all that. Which is what makes these fantasies so enduring. I guess we're all becoming voyeurs now.

S: It seems to be that way, doesn't it?

Q: Sex is gone as we knew it, movies have changed, but I still think great things can be done with TV. It gets to so many people. It's just finding a happy medium for talented people to work. I just think that everyone is following the leader here, don't you?

S: They always did. There seems to be no original thought, that's one of the problems.

Q: Did you retire? What brought you back to California?

S: No. I came here in '78. Made a mini-series and lots of TV—things like *Remington Steele* and *Magnum P.I.*

Q: But you haven't made any more features in a while?

S: No I haven't. I did mini-series and stuff like that.

Q: Well, that's like making a feature, really.

S: It's much worse—you're doing 8 hours of stuff

Q: Do you miss the kind of camaraderie and way things were done in Britain?

S: Very much so, yes.

Q: Doing all this television work out here, you can really tell the difference... is it because everyone is rushing to get everything made?

S: Yeah, well everything is done—time and money are the things that matter here.

Q: Yet, you were on tight schedules not only with these films but *The Avengers* had to be put together quickly.

S: That's true.

Q: So what would you say was the difference between trying to meet deadlines in Britain and trying to meet them here?

S: Well it's a much more mechanical approach, here.

Q: And you don't have men like Julian Wintle.

S: No you don't.

Q: That caliber of people to produce.

S: You're right. You don't.

Q: Have you been aware of *The Avengers* being shown on A&E? They started showing literally all of them.

S: Yes, I have been aware. 8 months of the last year I was in England making a series called *Space Precinct.*

Q: *Space Precinct?* Is this science fiction?

S: Yes, it's about another planet.

Q: Who is in that?

S: Two American leads. There is a man called Ted Shackleford. Actually he's quite a good actor.

Q: He was in *Knot's Landing.*

S: And a man called Rob Youngblood and they've got a Danish lead girl and that's about it. It's really fascinating.

Q: How many episodes have you done?

S: Six of those out of twenty-four.

Q: Now, is that going to be released here?

S: It will be, yes.

Q: So, you're very active! I guess I was under the assumption you had retired. How have [your films] turned up in your life since you made them? Obviously, they are being written about by people like me. But they are also being shown different places. Have you ever been invited to any film festivals?

S: Not really. No, I haven't.

Q: I think *Night of the Eagle* has been shown in France at the different festivals devoted to films like this.

S: I think half the time, they don't know how to get a hold of you.

Q: Talking about television; have you ever noticed how fast the credits roll by? If you're not alert, it's very hard to watch the credit crawl. Mostof the time they will just cut it off.

S: Also, I think it's almost indecent what they do here when it comes to the credits.

Q: It's not fair.

S: It's not fair to the people. They just slam straight through to a commercial. That's what I mean, you see. There is no feeling.

Q: There's no ceremony anymore.

S: It's just a raw, calculated way to earn money. It's disgusting. It makes me laugh when they ask if I am "network approved" as a director. I say "Well, in whose eyes?'

Q: It really is something to have someone ask you for your credits. I feel in this town there is no sense of history. It's rare that anyone in ICM or William Morris would know about your films. Or that you had done *The Avengers*. They are just blissfully unaware of who you are. I've interviewed a lot of directors and all of them say just about

Janet Blair as Tansy in *Burn, Witch, Burn!*

what you do, that are not even in your age group. I've known several tremendous actresses that have come over here from the BBC that cannot get work here because they aren't blonde with big bosoms. There is no respect for their stage work. Did you ever direct any stage plays?

S: Not really, no.

Q: So, you're really more that breed of British director that started out in the cutting room like David Lean, Terry Fisher, Fred Zimmerman. Where are you going to learn your craft if you're not continually working on something?

S: You always see what a good director does. You see why he does it. You can analyze it.

Q: What did you work on with David Lean?

S: I was his assistant. Jack Harris was the editor. *Great Expectations*.

Q: With Martita Hunt.

S: Yes. My first day in the industry, this very attractive woman came up to me and said "Do you know if Larry has wrapped, yet?" I said I didn't know. It was Vivian Leigh.

Q: Oh my god…. I wonder what he was working on…

S: Probably *Henry V.*

Q: She was beautiful. Those were movies. The television things you did—you must have done something besides *The Avengers*.

S: *The Professionals*.

Q: And…

S: I did several things.

Q: What was the thing that made you move over here? Was it the lack of work over there?

S: No. They asked me to do a mini-series. I came over and did that and they asked me to do another and another.

Q: Next thing you know you're here.

S: Right.

Q: Well, there's not much going on in England to keep anyone there. It's kind of dreary now. It's sad.

S: It is, yes.

Q: So, Michael Powell saw *Burn, Witch, Burn!* and *Circus of Horrors*

S: Yeah, he came out here and he was at the studio with Francis Coppola. What they were doing, I don't know. They were there and I met Michael, we knew each other very well and he came to my home in Westwood. He told me he had seen both of those pictures and thought they were interesting.

Q: What a nice comment. I wasn't love on you that *Circus of Horrors* was kind of a trilogy with *Horrors of the Black Museum* and *Peeping Tom*. Have you ever seen *Black Museum*?

S: Yes, many years ago

Q: It wasn't as sophisticated as your film. I don't know anything about Arthur Crabtree—that's the only time I've seen his name. The film was rather nasty.

S: It wasn't well received.

Q: It made a lot of money.

S: Yes but not critically well received.

Q: No it was just a bit. They were pretty harsh on Michael too, but *Black Museum* was truly a nasty piece of work. Awful. Ghastly. The only scene in *Circus of Horrors* I would even compare to that is when the girl takes the bandages off too quickly. That is comparable, shock value wise, but not nasty. All three films have shocking beginnings. That circus motif allows you to bring the shocks in. At every circus there is the potential for disaster.

S: Absolutely.

Q: I guess that's what you imply, that people's voyeuristic appetites have really not changed that much from the time of the Romans.

Don't you believe that it's possible someone could make a show about people being fed to the lions and people would watch?

S: Absolutely. In *Circus of Horrors*, I also went for the music because it gives a false sense of security.

Q: And you cut away to children eating popcorn.

S: And very gay music, a girl twirling, very gay stuff.

Q: It's amazing from a male point of view—every woman (in *Circus of Horrors*) has an incredible body. You must have had a lot of fun casting.

S: I would say so.

Q: But your current wife is Erika Remberg.

S: She played Elissa.

Q: I liked the actress who had the line, "It was a marriage made in Hell."

S: Jane Hylton.

Q: She's an interesting actress.

S: She's an English actress.

Q: She was kind of the Maggie Johnston role.

S: That's right. Kenneth Griffin was Diffring's little nasty.

Q: Is that Diffring's only starring vehicle? Or one of two times he was the lead.

S: I can't recall any other.

Q: At the end of his life, he was playing Nazis and later played a mad plastic surgeon.

6

Give Me My Skin

Blood On Satan's Claw

THE DEFINITION OF A "CULT FILM", I am told, is one that stands the test of time while maintaining a growing fan base of admirers that see possibilities not altogether apparent when the film was released. In the case of Piers Haggards *Blood on Satan's Claw,* it was love at first sight and time has only heightened the enjoyment of this remarkable film, at least in my eyes.

I was in London at the time of the films release and, as luck would have, in direct communication with the head of Tigon films, Tony Tenser. I had come to know him by writing letters to his Wardour Street offices, introducing himself as a journalist and film buff who was determined to find out all I could about a certain film known as *Curse of the Crimson Altar* with a dream cast and H.P. Lovecraft as the source of its screenplay.

What Mr. Tenser did not know was that he was corresponding with a high school student who was mad about horror films, and one that placed Boris Karloff and Christopher Lee with Barbara Steele was mind boggling, to put it mildly. Tony Tenser proved himself to be a man of his word and upon my arrival in the UK, his was the first stop as soon as I got over my jet lag from California. The year was 1969. Since that time, he and I developed a rapport and when I returned to London in 1970 he invited me over to see him and while I was in his office he asked if I would like to check out his latest double bill of horror films that was about to open the following day at the Victoria. The double bill was *The Beast in the Cellar* with two legendary actresses of the British stage, Dame Flora Robson and Berl Reid, the star of *The Killing of Sister George.* The second film was *Blood on Satan's Claw.* The

Linda Hayden is Angel Blake, seen here with Satan.

stills Tony had given me the day before had the original title on them; *Satan's Skin*. Tony was concerned about these films, as he had been editing them and reworking one aspect or another for months and still was unsure just what to do with them, as one was too talky and the other too violent with sex and rape among teenagers in a rural 17th century village beset with witchcraft.

Having seen much of Tigon's cinematic output, I was prepared for anything and everything. His first feature was disappointing, considering the two actresses who were perfectly tuned to each other but at odds with the script, which was rubbish and beneath them both. I think Tony knew this from the first edit he sat through. The second film was an unforgettable experience for me, from the first note of Marc Wilkinson's beautifully realized score, which remains to this day one of my all time favorites along side *Dance of the Vampires* and *Blood and Roses*. Having seen *Witchfinder General* I was accustomed to the rural mythology presented here; the difference being in *Witchfinder General* there was nothing occult or supernatural in the offering because, aside from the imposition of Edgar Allan Poe's poem, the film was a historical thriller that just happened to star Vincent Price. *Blood on Satan's Claw* is a bona fide horror film in the tradition of *Curse of the Demon* and *The Devil Rides Out*, both made in England as well.

The focal point of my seeing *Satan's Skin* during it's then current run was Tony's concern over one particular sequence which was troubling him, as he felt perhaps it went too far. The sequence was the removal of the Devil's skin from the leg of Michele Dotrice. In his view, the whole bit was too graphic, the irony of this being by today's standards this would probably be left in on any network broadcast of the film. I was prepared for a gross out, but when the offending sequence arrived, I knew that it had remained as it was important to the plot and was in no way too vivid for audiences to handle. I wish my memory was more specific when it came to the scenes involving Angel and the Devil in the guise of the hooded goat like figure. I do remember seeing the sequence where Angel appears to be pleasuring the Devil; however this takes place a bit off to the side and I am sure it was meant to be vague from its conception. The next morning, I arrived at Tenser's Wardour Street office filled with praise for the film, and I am confident that it helped keep not only the skin removal scene in tact but also gave Tony an idea just how the horror fans might react as well. All my memories of this man are good ones. Tony Tenser was unique in that he really loved making films and in a sense was at one with his audience; a real fan that just happened to run a film company. The best moment of all came when he invited me to his local. To celebrate my liking his film so much, we toasted with Guinness complete, with an egg dropped in, which was a first for me. Tony explained that this was the way to do it if I wanted "lead in my pencil." I was on the plane headed for California when I realized what he meant… A real lad, our Tony.

Looking back nearly four decades, I can see just why the time was so right for such a film to come into being in the first place. Tigon had been trying since 1967 to topple the stronghold Hammer films had in the UK as the main producers of horror films and Tony had managed to lure the likes of Boris Karloff, Vincent Price and Christopher Lee into his films, so why couldn't his company become the new Hammer? The other reason, of course, was the era all this was taking place in. In 1969, the world was stunned by the Manson killings and that, coupled with the innuendo by the world press that the director of *Rosemary's Baby* may have brought the whole thing on himself by making a film about Satanic forces, only made the matters more sensational.

In 1970 alone, there was *Witchcraft 1970, Sex Rituals of the Occult* and *Sinthia the Devil Dol*. All three of these films depicted hippies as agents of demonic influences; when the Devil commands, hippies obey. We then had to witness *Werewolves on Wheels; I Drink Your Blood* and last and definitely least, *The Deathmaster* produced by Count Yorga himself, actor Robert Quarry.

Piers Haggard was only 31 years old when he agreed to helm the production of what was at first known as *The Devils Touch*. Originally the film was to have been a portmanteau of three tales of a judge who dealt with dark forces and this was then revamped into a feature length film in which the judge investigates the infestation of evil of the young in a farming community where witchcraft had long been thought dead. The screenwriter, Robert Wynne Simmons, remained on set doing rewrites throughout the production and much of the confusion was lessened by his input. I still wonder what happened to the mistress of the manor whose face is mauled by what can only be described as "Satan's claw." At one point we see her bedridden and the next she simply disappears into the woods, supposedly to give that part of herself to the Devil like the rest of the marked ones.

Satan manifests himself in an animalistic sense throughout the film as bits of fur and claw are lodged in the flesh of his helpless followers, only to be asked to give them back by cutting literally them out of the skins of the afflicted as their unholy master becomes whole again after each sacrifice.

All this being the result of a deformed anatomy being unearthed by a farmer played by Barry Andrews (the atheist from *Dracula Has Risen From The Grave*). This is then brought to the attention of the judge played with great aplomb by Patrick Wymark, who had also appeared briefly in *Witchfinder General* as Oliver Cromwell. Wymark was a favorite of Tenser's and had given Polanski's *Repulsion* a delightfully sordid cameo as the randy landlord who picks the wrong moment to ask Catherine Deneuve for the rent. The part was written for Peter Cushing, who declined in order to take care of his mortally ill wife. Wymark is in full flood as the judge giving expert line readings to all his dialogue. He is most effective in his early scenes with Simon Williams and his aunt, the toast he offers "to his most Catholic majesty King James the third may he remain in exile" is spot on for his character who, along with his old paramour, gloats over their domination of the young as they themselves know the perils of youth and now are too old to do anything about it. The Judge takes the mystery of the disappearing aunt with an air of regret, but still abandons the village to the Devil for the moment. His exit line is beautifully realized: "you must let it build. Only then will all be revealed. I will return when the time is right." He takes with him a book of occult knowledge that just happens to be at his disposal and with that he departs.

While Patrick Wymark gives the film it's Van Helsing. The young ingénue, Linda Hayden, gives the film its center. Her performance as Angel

Patrick Wymank as the judge, seen here putting Satan to the sword.

Blake is the equal of Barbara Steele's performance in *Mask of the Demon* aka *Black Sunday*. In that film, Steele's character is described as "a high priestess to Satan." Unfortunately we never really have an opportunity to witness any of her satanic behavior until the last reel. In this film, Linda is on screen giving a tour de force as the young girl transformed before us into a disturbing erotic devil-woman who literally goes down on the Devil. This sequence was filmed and then darkened as it was just too much for the censor to bear. Piers Haggard goes on record in the DVD commentary for this film describing Linda Hayden "as a very good actress who had no problem with nudity whatsoever." Barbara would have approved.

The signature scene in the film takes place in the rectory of the church where the young come for Sunday lessons. After the Devil takes his foothold in the village, Linda literally becomes an angel for Satan, which ironically is the title of Barbara Steele's last Italian horror film. The Reverend is played by actor Antony Ainley who became well known for his role as The Master on *Dr. Who*. I had the opportunity to correspond with him about this film and here is what he had to say. "I remember this film well and with true fondness, as we were like a family except all the other actors were from famous acting families…Tamara Ustinov was Peter's daughter and Michele Doltice was Roy's daughter and so on.…Piers was a great organizer and possessed a visual sense that his cameraman, Dick Bush, was totally in sync with. They were team in that sense. When it came to doing the nude scene, where Angel comes into the rectory at night and disrobes, this was done at least three times and Linda was spot on with every take. She was a total professional with a refined sense of the erotic unusual for her age…I believe she was only 17 at the time."

In spite of all the nudity and violence, *Blood on Satan Claw* is decidedly a pious and conservative film, where adults are in charge and religion and goodness always prevails. This was an attitude which was changing as they filmed, and the atmosphere was charged with this duality of purpose with the Devil taking the young and infirm from the countryside to build his coven, only to have it destroyed by the same figures of authority we saw in Hammer masterful *The Devil Rides Out* when Christopher Lee drives his motorcar right into the altar of the Goat of Mendes, tossing a cross into the Devils lap. Wymark does much the same thing with a giant sword blessed, no doubt, and held by Milton Reid of all people, from many Hammer productions including *Night Creatures*.

As with the Hammer film the budget, or rather the lack of one, contributed to the finale being what it was. Done in slow motion, it is the concentration of the actors like Wymark and Hayden that bring this film out of its origins as an exploitation programmer into the realm of cult appreciation and ultimately its growing reputation as one of the classic horror films on a level with *The Wicker Man* and *The Devil Rides Out*.

I cannot say enough about the score for this film. The use of the ondes martenot and the cimbalom which gives the music that lower range the composer wickedly refers to as "the Devils Interval", invests the film with a timeless quality that adds immeasurably to the visuals and, for once, the repetition of the title theme never wears out its welcome, as say Les Baxter's theme for *The Dunwich Horror* over at AIP.

Witchcraft in films has always seemed to be about female sexuality and how damaging its power, whether it is suppressed or denied by the reigning authority of the 17th or 20th century in which these films take place. The sexual hysteria of films like Ken Russell's masterpiece *The Devils* or Michael Reeves *Witchfinder General*, even Mike Armstrong's ultra violent *Mark of the Devil* is energized by the denial of the sexuality not only of the accused but the witch finders themselves. In Mike's original script, the witch finder Herbert Lom, is traumatized by discovering he is really homosexual and therefore conceals his desire for Udo Keir by torturing women.

As for the growing cult around *Blood on Satan's Claw,* in time, I think more and more fans will come to appreciate the music and performances of this beautifully crafted film. While not without its flaws, it's still the only film on the subject of witchcraft and the Devil where the evil one gets a blowjob on camera by the most provocative devil-child since Lolita took up the hula hoop… give me my skin…

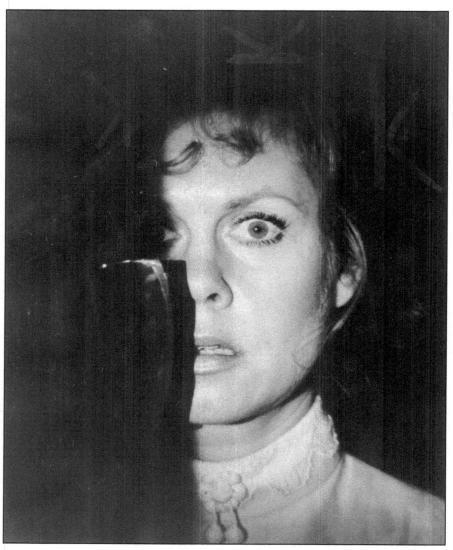

Elizabeth Montgomery as Lizzie Borden.

7

Gettin' Lizzie With It

The Legend of Lizzie Borden

DURING A LAZY SUMMER MORNING in August in the year of our Lord 1892, while the township of Fall River, Massachusetts, went about their simple daily pleasures, a crime was taking place that would rock not only that sleepy little New England hamlet to its very core, but would create a legend in both criminology and pop culture a century later. A middle-aged spinster known far and wide to the townsfolk of Fall River as a church-going, God-fearing woman was about to be accused of murdering her father and step-mother with an axe. The spinster in question was Lizzie Borden, and the circumstances behind the gruesome slayings have long since taken their place among those unsolved homicides of Jack the Ripper and the Zodiac Killer as a mystery that only gets more compelling with time.

Now, one would think that a story as colorful and gothic as Lizzie Borden's would have made the transition to the silver screen dozens of times by now, given the public's fascination with serial killers and unsolved murders. However, there has been to this day not one single major motion picture regarding Lizzie Borden or her trial, which captured the entire nation for the fourteen days it took to find her not guilty. What could it be about this material that refuses to fire up the imagination of the vast array of writers and directors that have been working in the genre since the turn of the last century?

The one and only adaptation of the Lizzie Borden saga thus far was produced in 1975 by Paramount as a made-for-TV movie-of-the-week. The actress chosen to play Lizzie was Elizabeth Montgomery, who discovered after the fact that Lizzie Borden was her cousin, sixth removed, which means the first actress to play Lizzie in a film was also a blood relative. After the first run on television was over, the show was repackaged for theatrical release in the European market, which included nude footage of Montgomery doing the killings in flashback. One of the surprise elements in this adaptation was the theory that Lizzie performed her dark deeds in the nude, followed by a "Victorian shower" to remove any chance of bloodstains appearing on any of her garments, since she was being questioned within 45 minutes after the second murder by a doctor who happened to be nearby.

Elizabeth Montgomery is remarkable in her dedication to the role; for example, she used eye drops during filming to give her a drugged look, since Borden was on morphine during the entire time she was a prisoner, right up through the trial itself. Anyone expecting a glimmer of her *Bewitched* persona will be impressed with how quickly she shed her sitcom image for this project.

The critical response to the production was positive, including Emmy nominations, of which it won three, which makes the fact that no other versions were ever mounted on the subject even more surprising. Montgomery was surrounded by a top-flight group of actors, with standout performances from Fritz Weaver as her father Andrew Borden, Katherine Helmond as her older sister Emma, and Fionnula Flanagan as Bridget Sullivan the maid. Even the smaller roles were filled with people like Ed Flanders, Don Porter and Gloria Stuart (in a clever cameo as one of Fall River's residents who witnesses Lizzie shoplift a hatchet).

However, before I speculate even more as to why this–one of the best TV movies ever made–has all but disappeared from view with no DVD release on the horizon, I must explain my personal interest in its background. A few years ago, I was having dinner with Curtis Harrington who was a very good friend of mine, when the subject of lost opportunities in his career came up, and he lamented being passed over to direct *The Omen*, which as we all know was a box-office juggernaut and would have undoubtedly changed his life for the better had he been its director. After a moment Curtis said, "Well, there was another project that would have done much the same thing for my career, and I was already on board to direct, not to mention having researched the entire project, and that was the Lizzie Borden film over at Paramount in which Elizabeth Montgomery was set to play Borden. Now, Montgomery was a client of The William Morris Agency and as such, they had the upper hand in calling the shots when it came to who was going to direct their stars. Paul Wendkos was a client of theirs, and at the 11th hour I was replaced without any provocation whatsoever. It was highly illegal, so I took it into arbitration with the Director's Guild and won. Paramount had to pay me my full salary. It was a bittersweet victory at best, since I had spent a year of my life researching the Borden murders, even so far as going to Fall River and examining all the records of the trial. The worst thing about it was the damage it did to my friendship with Bill Bast, who wrote the screenplay, since he simply folded up when it came to standing up for what was right. They had no right to replace me and he knew it."

"Afterwards, I ran into Elizabeth at a party and she made a point of telling me it was not her call as to whether or not I stayed, yet we all know she had tremendous cache at that time, coming off eight seasons of a hit show. Yet they all benefited from my research. It was my idea to present Andrew Borden as this debauched father figure who may have sexually abused Lizzie as a child. When I discovered he was a mortician, it wasn't hard to imagine him using this to further terrorize his daughter by forcing her to touch the dead. He was a control freak; we know this from the descriptions of him by his neighbors and businessmen in Fall River. The motive for the killings was money. It was as simple as that. Yet, I felt Lizzie was also repressed, as were most women at this time, especially in the social milieu of New England society in 1892."

"We didn't get an opportunity to reveal any elements of Lizzie's sexuality in the screenplay, yet it was always there in the shadows. It was my idea to have Lizzie do the 'Lady Macbeth' nude sleepwalking gambit when she commits the murders, since this explains why she had not a trace of blood on her when the doctor and the neighbors arrive on the scene. If we could have done a follow-up of Lizzie Borden's life after the acquittal, you could really flesh out her character, especially after she meets Nance O'Neal in Boston. This would prove to be the undoing of her relationship with her older sister Emma, who moved out of the house in 1905, never to return. They died nine days apart after years of not speaking. It was such a fascinating subject you could really do two or three films about her and remain transfixed."

Curtis would never really get over this betrayal in his career, and even though he did manage to direct some TV movies and two more features, he remained as always an outsider in show business, too esoteric for the suits and yet too talented to be overlooked altogether. His final film, the self-financed *House of Usher*, would serve to forever remind us that like Roderick Usher, Curtis was too sensitive to survive in a world that had no place for artists anymore, unless they conformed to something he could not bear to be a part of. So he simply retreated into a shadow world of his own making, as Roderick retreated into the House of Usher, which in reality was Curtis' home.

Curtis's input still remains in key moments throughout the teleplay, in spite of Paul Wendkos's own style as a director (as evidenced in his later film, *The Mephisto Waltz*, in which he chose a similar movie-of-the-week atmosphere, with colored gels and disjointed dream-sequences). One of the most interesting moments in developing the love-hate relationship felt by Lizzie towards her father comes midway in the script when Andrew Borden savagely hacks Lizzie's beloved collection of pigeons to death with a hatchet, not unlike the one that would later end his own life. This entire scene is staged in a manner that reminded me of a similar moment in Harrington's *What's the Matter with Helen,* in which Shelley Winters does the same thing to her collection of white rabbits. The flashbacks to Lizzie as a child being forced to touch the dead in her father's "workshop" (in a very Harrington moment, young Lizzie accidentally bumps against the hose that is drawing blood from the cadaver, releasing a torrent of blood on both of them) allow the audience to begin to hate Andrew Borden, somewhat justifying his own gruesome demise. The suggestion of incest as a motive is also explored in these flashbacks as we witness Lizzie as a child receiving rather unfatherly attention as both father and daughter kiss each other on the mouth. The gifting of the ring from Lizzie to her father is also played out as a ritual between them; this is a relationship with subtext and shadows. One concept that keeps coming up is that Lizzie, in spite of everything, loved her father dearly.

The first murder of Abby the stepmother, was a passionate act of homicide, considering the savagery by which she was dispatched – multiple blows to the back and head. Lizzie realized after killing her stepmother that there was no turning back, creating a terrible certainty that her father had to die as well, since what she began was too horrible for him to ever forgive. It is my belief that money was the real motive here, since there is enough evidence to assume that Mr. Borden was about to change his will, cutting out both of his daughters in favor of his second wife.

There really is (as Curtis pointed out to me on more than one occasion) an entire film to be made out of Lizzie's life after the killings, with her move to Maplecroft, the mansion overlooking the town her family helped create, and remaining there the rest of her life, rubbing her crime into the very fabric of the community. Curtis also firmly believed that Lizzie had strong lesbian tendencies that were brought out when she encountered Nance O'Neil, an actress who loved to spend money and in Lizzie, found much more than a mentor. This would explain the older sister, Emma, pulling up stakes and moving out of Maplecroft, never to return. *Alfred Hitchcock Presents* aired one of their half-hour teleplays (*The Older Sister*) in which we discover that it was Emma all along who did the murders, with Lizzie covering up for her at the trial.

The fascination with this case has never let up in over a century. It has become a major feminist story with Lizzie Borden an iconic personality; a paradox of contradictions. Those close to the trial at the time could not help but comment on Lizzie Borden's eyes and the mystery they held within her gaze. She was, of course, high on morphine at the time, making her the true "Sister Morphine."

The Borden case has distinct parallels to the O.J. Simpson murders, since both cases have captivated the public around the world, and to this day the real facts in both cases are shrouded in mystery, although the vast majority now believe he did the deed, and this holds true with Lizzie Borden, in spite of several books that have been published with a wide range of speculation as to who else might have been responsible for the killings.

Jet Magazine once ran a cover photo of both O.J. and Elizabeth Montgomery from an earlier TV movie-of-the-week which seemed to foretell the future in ways no one could have imagined in 1977. The major difference in the two trials is of course the absence of forensic technology in 1892 in any of the evidence collected by the police in Fall River. Yet flash forward a century plus, and you are still confronted with inept police work contaminating the crime scene in the O.J. investigation that would later allow a killer to go free, just like Lizzie Borden, except in O.J.'s case, he left the community for good. The film industry has perhaps wisely left O.J. alone in trying to adapt his case to film, since the sensitivity issue is still very much present, but in Lizzie Borden's case all the principals are long gone; in fact, a recent survey has concluded that the majority of key people in the Borden case all died within 11 years of the 1892 trial.

So why has this fascinating case been ignored by the film world in general since the advent of the medium in the 1890s? The films about Jack the Ripper number in the dozens, as do most serial killers worth their salt, yet Lizzie's hatchet killings seem to attract the small screen with docudramas on the History Channel or vanity projects of the YouTube variety, the one marvelous exception being *The Legend of Lizzie Borden*.

In the 1940s, actress Lillian Gish starred in a play based loosely on the Borden murders, *Entitled 9 Pine Street*, with the actual names changed, but the circumstances being similar. Gish later took the project to her old mentor, D.W. Griffith, hoping to persuade him to direct a film version for Paramount with Preston Sturges producing. In spite of the talent involved, it was not optioned and quickly fell to the wayside of unrealized wonders in the could-have-been department.

Perhaps the closest thing in cinema history to mounting a full-scale Lizzie Borden film was a Robert Bloch-scripted horror film made to cash in on the runaway success of *What Ever Happened to Baby Jane* (yet another film about dysfunctional sisters, filled with violence and murder). Bloch had been fascinated with the Lizzie Borden case all his life, writing about it as early as 1946 in his early short story, *Lizzie Borden Took an Axe* (which was later broadcast on his national radio program, Stay Tuned for Terror).

William Castle's *Strait-Jacket* was in essence a modern-day retelling of the Borden case with everything omitted but the faux nursery rhyme and the axe. The legendary Joan Crawford lent her name and considerable acting skills to this penny dreadful, enduring fright wigs and emotional outbursts to compensate for the lack of talent in front as well as behind the camera. In

Joan Crawford follows in the footsteps of Lizzie Borden in
William Castle's *Strait-Jacket*.

better days at Warner Bros., this same material would have brought Joan another Oscar nomination; instead of which we get this bon mot from the Time magazine review: "It must also be the first horror film to boast that one of its diehard victims (Mitchell Cox) is a real life vice president of the Pepsi-Cola Company. As for Pepsi-Cola board member Crawford, she plainly plays her mad scenes "for those who think Jung". The script also allows for Joan to have another one of those unruly daughter relationships which would come back to haunt us all in the form of the spiteful and perhaps fictional account of her adopted daughter Christina in Mommie Dearest (which also finds a way to give Joan Crawford an opportunity to wield another axe for the entertainment of her public, forever demonizing a great star).

Lizzie Borden's fame was used fleetingly in other films, the most unlikely being the Moss Hart-George S. Kaufman Broadway comedy *The Man Who Came To Dinner*, which has a subplot dealing with the unhinged sister of the poor soul who winds up with Sheridan Whiteside as a very unwanted house guest. It seems the man's sister was a famous axe murderess from the past that had school children singing a certain nursery rhyme about taking whacks at her parents. More recently, rocker-turned-auteur Rob Zombie included a briefly-seen wax figure of Lizzie Borden in Captain Spaulding's wild ride in his debut film *House of 1000 Corpses*.

The jury may well be permanently out on whether or not the real Lizzie Borden did take that axe and give her parents those 40 whacks, yet as far back as most of us living today can remember, there has always been the shadowy figure of this certain spinster lady moving slowly down a darkened stairway clutching a shiny metal object in one hand, heading with demonic determination for that part of our collective imaginations where she may take her rightful place alongside Jack, O.J., and Lucretia as one of those human monsters whose crimes go unpunished in the courts of law but ultimately are judged in that higher court of public opinion. To take a line from the poster ads used during the initial run of *What Ever Happened to Baby Jane*: "Sister, sister, oh so fair... why is there blood all over your hair?"

Gloria Holden as *Dracula's Daughter*. Rare press picture photographed
by John LeRoy Johnson

8

Men Cried Out To Her At Dawn

Dracula's Daughter

I AM 11 YEARS OLD and it is late in the evening on a Saturday night. I sit cross-legged on the floor in front of the television set with rabbit ears watching the Shock Theater premiere of *Dracula's Daughter*. The scene unfolding in front of me takes place in a forest shrouded in darkness, the ground swirling in mist, the trees filled with fog. In the distance a wolf howls at the moon. In the foreground is a tall, aristocratic woman clothed in the blackest of velvet. A hood covering her head, she stands in front of a huge funeral bier blazing with fire. She lets the hood fall from her face revealing a chalk white beauty, then turns to her left and lowers her hand to the ground, seizing a large make-shift cross fashioned from two pieces of oak. As she raises the cross skyward, she turns her head away in fear, speaking these words as the flames consume the mortal remains of her father, Count Dracula: "Unto Adoni and Aseroth, into the keeping of the lords of the flame and the lower pits, I consign this body, to be evermore consumed in this purging fire. Let all baleful spirits that threaten the souls of man be banished by the spilling of this salt. Be thou exorcised O Dracula and thy body, long undead, find destruction throughout eternity in the name of thy dark unholy master. In the name of the all holiest, and through this cross, be this evil spirit cast out until the end of time."

I have seen this film countless times since, but the power of that moment has never diminished in its ability to bring an audience into a spider-webbed world of fantasy that was Universal pictures from 1925 until this film was wrapped in March of 1936, effectively ending the first golden age of horror in

American cinema. The film itself was always a curiosity in the genre, mainly because it lacked the star power of a Karloff or Lugosi to keep the flames of cult worship alive in the thousands of baby boomers that were being exposed for the first time to the first cycle of horrors flooding our TV screens in the late 1950s, where most of us would see films like *Dracula* and *Frankenstein* along with *The Mummy* and *The Wolf Man*.

Since the legendary star of *Dracula* Bela Lugosi was nowhere to be found in this sequel, the film has taken decades to find its audience. The actress who was given the role of a lifetime, Gloria Holden, was unknown at the time (1936) having worked on Broadway and then radio, doing several weeks on the popular Eddie Cantor program. Once you finally get over the loss of the Vampire King, whose presence is seen ever so fleetingly in a coffin, fully staked by Von Helsing (still played by the stalwart Edward Van Sloan) in the lower regions of Carfax Abby, the film takes up exactly where *Dracula* left off – with the romantic team of David Manners and Helen Chandler walking up the staircase into light, and well out of camera range, dissolving into the end credit roll.

I am writing this during the very month the film wrapped 74 years ago, and since that time the entire cast and crew have gone on to their respective rewards. What makes this so relevant for me is that I received in the mail a soft bound book from a colleague of mine (who has been in and out of my life for the last 35 years) named Phil Riley. He has edited together an early draft treatment of *Dracula's Daughter* by John L. Balderston, and then the real find is a draft by R. C Sheriff that was submitted to the Breen office by James Whale when it seemed like the director of *Frankenstein* was going to helm it with an all star cast and a lavish budget. The cover has a faux poster of the film had Whale directed it, boasting Jane Wyatt as the Countess and Lugosi, of course, as the Count. Phil has done the genre a favor in bringing to light this particular bit of history that almost fell into the cracks of time and space. Now we can read for ourselves what might have been if James Whale had been given carte blanche while the production code looked the other way.

In 1981 I was working as a researcher for a number of writers including John Kobal, Kenneth Anger and especially Richard Lamparski who was still writing his very successful series of "Whatever Became Of?" books. I owe a huge debt to Richard for putting me in touch with the tragic "little Maria" whom Karloff tossed into the lake to drown in *Frankenstein*, and he would also connect me with the fabulous Countess Marya Zaleska, or at least the actress that made such a lasting impression – Gloria Holden, then Mrs. William H. Hoyt of Redlands, California.

I went the way of a mailgram to her home in the desert community where she had been living all these years, introducing myself and hoping she would not feel intruded upon and perhaps grant an interview, since nobody had gotten around to asking about her career, at least in print. Gloria Holden ended her Hollywood career after filming *This Happy Feeling* for director Blake Edwards in 1958. I received a typed response in which she acknowledged that she was indeed the Gloria Holden, but wanted to know just what I had in mind, and especially how I discovered her address and married name. This was more than fair, considering I was invading her privacy.

I sent her some copies of my work as well as a letter from Richard giving me a clean bill of health and assuring her I was not some crazed stalker bent on terrorizing her. Gloria responded with great charm and candor after that. She explained that her life in Redlands was a quiet one with a close circle of friends cultivated by her husband from his days of teaching at the local college. After the first letter came, another which explained her current state of mind, as well as why she had been reclusive for the last ten years. In 1970, her only son, Chris, had just graduated from Redlands University and, as a reward for such hard work; his parents gifted him a red sports car to begin his new life. On the way back from a post grad party at the college he drove by a hillside that dislodged a 60 pound rock on top of his car, crushing Chris Hoyt to death. Gloria was inconsolable, went into mourning, and never really came out of it. By the time I reached her, she was a fragile woman with a heart condition that made visits impossible, but she agreed to talk to me on the phone.

The first response from Gloria Holden was one of reluctance to break her silence, partly out of grief, but also, after so many years, who could possibly care about "some horrid old film best left forgotten?" It took all my powers of persuasion to make her think otherwise. I began to ask her about some of her other films like *The Life of Emile Zola* and *Strange Holiday*. She warmed to recollections of Paul Muni. "Muni was a beautiful man, a real artist, it was my pleasure to be in his company and I feel we did good work. I thought *Zola* was a wonderful film. I played Madame Zola once again on radio after we did our film."

On the subject of Claude Rains and the film *Strange Holiday*, "Claude Rains was, next to Muni, my favorite actor to play opposite, a total professional blessed with a magnificent voice. I wish our film together had been a better one as so few people actually went to see it."

When I finally brought up the Dracula film, she kept her comments frustratingly brief. "My one starring role in Hollywood came at a price and I was never allowed another opportunity to carry a film after that. My memories are rather vague, now as I think back. It was a two month insanity to film because the Laemmles were about to lose the studio. We changed directors, the script was never clear due to constant rewrites, our final director, Mr. Hillier, was nearly killed on the set when a light fell on him, putting him in hospital. Mr. Lugosi was to play Dracula, yet he never did. We met on set for

publicity photos and a beautiful lunch at the commissary with all the current Universal players in attendance. Lugosi was very shy, like me, and we
connected on a strange spiritual level. He was very protective of me, as if I
really was his daughter. I shall never forget his advice to me: "This part will
never end if you are not careful. It carries great power. Be careful what you
play next; a part like Dracula can be a blessing or a curse. For me it has been
a little of both." He seemed to me, at the time, to be so much a larger than life
personality. He really owned the role and he knew it, and perhaps as his life
turned out it was a curse after all. But not for me. I left it behind me once it
was finished and through the grace of God I was not typecast. I did play her
one more time in a sense for Tod Browning, who had done *Dracula* in the
first place. He asked for me personally to play this strange woman, a medium, Madame Rapport. His only direction to me was "to play it like *Dracula's
Daughter*. Mr. Browning admired my performance a great deal, which I took
as high praise considering the source. It was his final film as a director. I was
blessed to have had a moment with him."

Gloria sent me a letter after our phone call and had this to say: "I have
worked with so many of the film greats, and that experience was a valuable
part of my life. Yet it seems, looking back, too small a contribution to say it
was a life's work. I can at this time (1981) do no more than try to overcome a
serious heart condition, and keep the home fires pleasant and bright. I cook–I
write–I watch KCET 28/TV and read. Your attention to me and my work has
me amazed that things I did thirty years ago really matter anymore... I am
living in the world today. I mean, if I write a fine poem today, make someone
happy today, help someone today, and of course I pray for those whom it is
my duty and privilege to keep in mind and heart. When I get well and stron-
ger I will likely be more responsive to the outside world. Mostly I want to
work, complete so many unfinished projects. I am fortunate to have a good
strong husband who is a professor at a college; he is active and athletic. We
have good friends in his profession. I was always so incredibly shy and afraid
of people in my own profession. It is also strange and wonderful how Mr.
Lugosi is still bringing people into my life with his curse of the Dracula's. In
this case, may I say it was a blessing and not, thank God, a curse. Love Gloria
Holden Hoyt..."

During the time I was in touch with Gloria it became known that she
had resurfaced, not through me but from a married couple who were autograph hounds known for acquiring arcane signatures of the most oddball
kind. They have become infamous in fan circles for not taking 'no' for an
answer, which of course is not a good thing. They made a pilgrimage to Redlands, staying nearby and telephoning until Gloria finally gave them what
they wanted just to get them off the porch. A month or so after Gloria passed
away, they began selling her signature for $150. This is a primary example of

the "fandom" William Shatner was lampooning on *Saturday Night Live*, only it is not so amusing in real life.

The result of this situation for me was receiving a telephone call one evening from the most eccentric of the "undead cult" that surrounds the myth of Count Dracula – the President of the "Count Dracula Society" Dr. Donald A. Reed. If you wish to learn more of this weird little man with the high-pitched voice, I highly recommend "My life with Count Dracula" written and produced by the Oscar winning writer of *Milk*, Dustin Lance Black. This must have been one of his first projects, and to his credit he stayed with it to the bitter end where we as an audience follow this deluded passionately devoted fan to his grave. Donald could be charming in a morbid kind of way, if he was in a social situation like an awards ceremony, however I saw both sides now as Joni Mitchell would have put it, and it wasn't pretty.

Dr. Reed was determined that I give him the contact information on Gloria Holden since the autograph couple were not known to him directly and he depended on me, being a former member of the Society, to give it up since after all he was the President, etc. Well I stood my ground and he finally hung up after threatening me with excommunication from all things Dracula, which was just fine with me. A few weeks later he sent a notice in the form of a bulletin that Gloria Holden was to be the recipient of a life time achievement award from the "Academy of Science Fiction and Horror" and once more demanding I give up her phone number and/or address. I finally got in touch with her even though I knew her response before I ever asked. She pretended to be flattered but simply could not wrap her mind around the concept of intelligent adults gathering in a group to honor a half century old film about vampires. She asked me to collect the prize and forward it on to Redlands and to be sure and thank all those involved in its selection.

I remember this as if it were yesterday. I dressed in my best black suit and drove down to the location Dr. Reed sent me to, hopefully mount the stage and explain just how fragile Gloria Holden was at this time, and how grateful she was to be so honored. I also had a short thank you speech signed by her to give to Dr. Don as a sort of memento, even though he had been such a moron about the entire situation.

I parked my car and noticed there was no shortage of spaces. Then the 'coup de grace': the location was correct but it had been held the night before, not only that, but I was later told by an Academy member who was there that night: "Dr. Reed used the event to announce in a ballroom filled with industry notables as well as fan boys and such that Gloria Holden would have been here personally to collect her award, however a certain villain named David Del Valle was simply too selfish to share her with the fans that waited all these years to pay their respects." Well I was pissed to say the least, and time does heal all wounds as they say. To this day I cannot muster even a tear for the loss of such a pathetic yet fascinating creature of the night.

I owe a debt to Phil Riley for making the R.C. Sheriff script available for me to study. There is nothing in Sheriff's version that remains in the film as we have all come to know it. Having said that, I discovered a screen grab online last year that shows a tapestry that is on screen for less than a second but, upon closer examination, you can plainly see that this was created exclusively for the film when they thought Lugosi was still in the cast. It shows the Vampire King center stage at his banquet prior to the wizard's arrival, and the curse that makes him a vampire, at least in Sheriff's version of the prologue, that sets the stage for the original film where Dracula summons Harker to his castle to buy real estate in England. The tapestry was a mystery until I read this treatment. If only James Whale had been able to

Poster art for *Dracula's Daughter*.

direct this with the kind of budget he enjoyed on *Bride of Frankenstein*.

Those of us that admire *Dracula's Daughter* have little reason to sing to the choir. If you have not had the pleasure, let me enlighten you on a few things regarding the movie itself. Like all films of this period, they are not without their faults. This film suffers from what Gloria described as a film made during the collapse of a regime. It is ironic that *Dracula's Daughter* would be one of the most expensive of the lot, and yet it looks like a programmer compared to say the *Bride of Frankenstein*. The budget for *Dracula's Daughter* was taken up in writers fees paying Bela Lugosi $4,000 to stand about for photo ops, and at one point he had to sign a contract permitting the making of a dummy to be placed in the coffin at the beginning of the film, even though it looked nothing much like him. This would later help the Lugosi family in settling a longtime lawsuit with Universal over the rights of actors who create characters so vivid that the movie—going public can think of no one else in the role.

The set pieces for both *Dracula* and *Dracula's Daughter* are what one remembers for a lifetime….the staircase in *Dracula* with the huge cobweb Lugosi magically walks through, yet the web remains unbroken…the coach ride to Borgo Pass…the matte paintings of Castle Dracula… In other words, the first reel. In the second film, the forest scene I describe at the beginning of this piece, the stalking of her first male victim in the streets of Chelsea (really a redressed Universal village), the revisiting of Castle Dracula at the conclusion of the film. What ultimately holds both these films together, in spite of lackluster scripts and anemic co-stars is the leads, is Bela Lugosi, who commands the screen when he is on it, and the same is true of Gloria Holden. Her dignity and bearing, matched by her line readings, invested with sadness and tragedy of a life held in darkness, is movie acting at its finest.

The rarest moment in Dracula's Daughter, as it is seen today, and perhaps the rarest artifact in the golden age of horror from Universal, a tapestry is glimpsed for a second on camera of Bela Lugosi as Count Dracula imperially standing at the center of his court before the wizard transforms his court into swine and the Count into a vampire from the R.C Sheriff script.

A cult has developed around the infamous sequence in which the Countess's servant Sandor snatches a poor waif named Lili (Nan Gray – later to become Mrs. Frankie Lane) from throwing herself into the Thames, only to lead her to the Countess's Chelsea studio to pose. The entire seduction by the Countess of Lili is now legendary as the premier introduction in the sound era of lesbian seduction. The scene was cut from the original, so you never see the Countess actually touch her victim; there is a clever jump to a Devil's mask above the fireplace so that the next thing you see is Lili in the hospital being treated by Dr. Garth (Otto Kruger). The Countess, like the Doctor, is a master of mesmerism, using the power of an occult ring, a device used much later in *Blood For Dracula* which also has a subtext of lesbianism in its plot, only this time it is a mad female doctor who has obtained an amulet from Castle Dracula, perhaps another of the Countess's jewels left lying about for the unlikely traveler.

I must thank once again my colleague Phil Riley for providing me with a copy of *Dracula's Daughter*—from Bear Manor Media press [the forgotten version by RC Sherriff] which upon reading instantly rekindled the fire allowing me to write this long overdue tribute to a great actress, a loyal friend whose kind heart and generous nature touched me in ways I am still discovering. After all, "There are far more things in Heaven and earth than are dreamt of in your...psychiatry.

9

Paul, Aleister, Rex and Alice

The Magician

ONE OF THE MOST FASCINATING LEGENDS regarding the life and times of "the wickedest man in the world," Aleister Crowley, involves his attempts to evoke the great god Pan in Paris with the aid of his disciple Victor Nueberg. The result nearly drove Crowley mad. He was discovered unconscious with hoof prints marked on his forehead like those of a goat. The Crowley legend is filled with such tales involving rituals of black magic across Europe, his devotion to Pan well known among his loyal followers at the time. Pan, the son of Hermes, was the Arcadian god of lust, a symbol, if you will, of the libido; a seducer of both sexes, something that definitely appealed to Crowley, whose sex magic was infamous in his day with both his female as well as male disciples. Horror cinema has delved into this material at least once every decade, the first being Rex Ingram's film *The Magician*, adapted from a novel by Somerset Maugham.

Maugham had actually encountered Crowley during his heyday in London where the two men enjoyed (at least it seemed they did) each other's company, since Maugham had later remarked to friends that he found Crowley to be a fascinating conversationalist, and very well read. However the novel Maugham chose to write depicted Crowley as a latter day Svengali with a touch of Dracula in the mix. This homage so infuriated Crowley that he reviewed it in that year's *Vanity Fair*, calling it rubbish, which of course it was.

In 1926 Rex Ingram decided it would be an ideal project for his newly acquired studios in Nice, bankrolled by M-G-M no less, and to star his beautiful wife Alice Terry and the legendary Paul Wegener, the sensational creator of *The Golem*, as Oliver Haddo, the Crowley clone of the piece. Wegener was

Director Rex Ingram posed here with "Faun" Stowitts on the Hades set
from *The Magician.*

an ideal choice for the role since he was a larger than life character in his own right. One of the leading actors of his generation in Germany, he was perhaps their first bona fide auteur since he was much more than merely a star. He was also a writer and director whose talents paved the way for the fantastic cinema in all its aspects to evolve into the genre we know today. *The Student of Prague* was his pet project, and his love of trick photography was historic at the time of cinema's infancy.

This is not the film by which we should remember Rex Ingram, since his reputation was made on the international success of *The Four Horsemen of the Apocalypse* which catapulted Valentino into a screen icon for eternity. Ingram also directed the first version of *The Prisoner of Zenda* as well as *Scaramouche*, both with Alice Terry. *The Magician* came back into the limelight early in 2010 when Turner Classic Movies screened it on their Sunday silent film series, allowing countless horror fans to tape the beautiful print they ran and making the film at last accessible for study. While the film boasts a fantastic Infernal fantasy about 20 minutes in, where Haddo arrives unannounced at Terry's home and, through magic, allows her a glimpse into a Hellish tableau of dammed souls at the mercy of a faun, or is it the great God Pan himself, since Ingram was influenced by Arthur Machen's *The Great God Pan* as well. If not for the aforementioned sequence and the presence of Paul Wegener (who owns the screen whenever he appears—a true horror star in the Lugosi/Atwill/Karloff tradition) this film would hardly be worth recommending. The good news is that being able to see it without the disadvantage of bootlegs and fuzzy dupe prints, it holds up better than I would have expected. The tinting of the different sequences involving fire are now bright red, and one can really appreciate John Seitz's beautiful photography for the first time.

When I first came across this film, thanks to the late Carlos Clarens, he always remembered *The Magician* as we all have—from the stunning stills of one Hubert Stowitts (1892-1953), a premier dancer who performed with the legendary Pavlova, and whose tour de force as the faun/Pan figure is unforgettable. It has always been the still of Stowitts holding Alice Terry in his arms that was used to advertise the film, more so than its real star Paul Wegener, yet the other positively outré photo from that moment is Wegener with his hair made to look like horns and his eyes evil incarnate, seated under a burnt out tree in Hell as if he is the one in charge.

The Infernal sequence as it unfolded on TCM seemed a bit short, as did other elements in the print, especially the film's title cards. What remains, however, is a visual feast. One of the eye-witnesses to the filming was director Michael Powell, who also had a small part in the film. Powell revealed that the Hades footage was organized by the film's still photographer Harry Lachman, although I am sure the concept belonged to Ingram, whose Irish heritage was in full bloom during the making of this film. He even flew the Irish flag over the studio so all of the inhabitants of Nice were aware of his Irish pride. The locals were also aware of the semi-nude dancers seen cavorting about the Hades set presided over by Stowitts, who was a last minute replacement for the legendary dancer Serge Lifar whose commitments with the ballet prevented him from accepting the role.

Among the other artisans involved in the making of *The Magician* were Henri Menessier, a protégé of Nazimova, who did the art direction. He had been a part of Ingram's inner circle since the end of *Mare Nostrum*. The noted artist Paul Darde was responsible for the mammoth statue of the faun that Alice Terry is nearly crushed by in the film's opening sequence. The Sorcerer's tower was created near the village of Sospel in the mountains below Nice and is almost identical to the Frankenstein tower in James Whale's *Bride of Frankenstein* (it has been said that Whale screened *The Magician* several times while making *Frankenstein*.) This comparison is but one of many influences Ingram's film is noted for now that *The Magician* is finally available for study after decades of being a "lost film". Anyone familiar with the Universal horror films of the 1930's will notice the plot points later used in *The Mummy*, *Murders in the Rue Morgue* and *The Raven*.

The casting of Paul Wegener in his only American film seemed providential, since he remains one of the pioneers of the genre, not only as the creator of *The Golem*, but as a champion of the fantastic in all that is cinema. Ingram and Wegener were both enamored with writers like Poe and Hoffmann, not to mention their mutual fascination with Eastern mysticism and the occult. Looking at his performance by today's standards it seems more comic than horrific since Ingram chose to dress him in loud checkered suits which, by the way, is not unlike the wardrobe Sidney Blackmer's Roman Castevet wears in Polanski's *Rosemary's Baby*. Wegener is every inch the showman in his performance, so much so that Ingram sends him up with the card "He appears to have stepped out of a melodrama." One must appreciate Wegener's swagger in every gesture he makes, sweeping his black cape up into his arms at every opportunity. He reminded me a bit of Lugosi in *White Zombie* with his melodramatic gestures and intense eye movement. Perhaps the most obvious comparison is with the Satanic character Karloff plays in *The Black Cat*, which as we all know is yet another thinly veiled portrait of Crowley, however when Ulmer's writers named his character Poelzig, the connection to German expressionism came full circle since designer Hans Poelzig was an active force in that period of cinema, having worked on Wegerer's *The Golem* as well.

The unveiling of *The Magician* on TCM was for me very much like finally getting to see *London after Midnight* after decades of imagining what it was like based on all the fantastic stills we've seen published over the years. This of course sets us up for disappointment: as with all the films of the silent era, not every moment is a golden one, and *The Magician* is for the most part slow and confusing, with lackluster performances from the secondary actors leaving Paul Wegener standing tall, if not in a different film altogether. Alice Terry is not used to her best advantage, considering her fine work opposite Valentino and Ramon Navarro. I think I know the real reason for this since I had a chance to ask the lady herself in 1979 when John Kobal was in LA researching one of his photo books, and allowed me to join him in meeting Alice Terry in the flesh.

One of the disadvantages of youth is not taking advantage of a golden opportunity when it is presented to you, as my encounter with Alice Terry would prove in 1979. At this time in my life I was collecting movie material more than commenting on it, and in spite of meeting Mae West face to face, I never took her sage advice to keep a diary since, as she wisely pointed out, it might one day keep me. John was forever in the habit of interviewing Hollywood personalities from both eras. He had amazing luck, especially with legends like Louise Brooks, Marlene Dietrich and Rita Hayworth – with whom he did a biography. I was already somewhat familiar with Alice Terry as the damsel in distress in *The Magician*, and when faced with the prospect of meeting her all I could think of was this woman acted with *The Golem*! I knew very little about her body of work in silent films, or her importance as a M-G-M star.

In those days John always liked to have someone along when he did these interviews to carry his tape recorders and keep him amused as well as driving him around town since he hated to drive himself. I wish I could remember more details of that afternoon so long ago, and why I didn't bring my camera as I did when I stayed with him in London. As I remember it, John was working on a photo exhibit that included several images of Valentino and Ramon Navarro from films like *The Four Horsemen* and *Ben-Hur*. Alice Terry was a leading lady to both stars, as well as being a star herself, so John was very pleased she had consented to an interview to take place at her home in the most rural part of the San Fernando Valley.

On the drive up we speculated if she would be anything like Norma Desmond in *Sunset Blvd*, as John made the point that her husband's cameraman, John Seitz, photographed Billy Wilder's film as well. We drove for the longest time, getting lost several times in the process, until we finally reached the road that lead up to two large houses separated by trees and a driveway. Alice Terry was around 79 at the time, still handsome, with a regal bearing one would expect from a movie star, yet there was nothing of Norma Desmond in this woman, since she was without any vanity regarding her time in the spotlight. In fact she laughed a great deal during our time with her about both Hollywood and her role in it as a film star.

The first thing you noticed about her surroundings was just how much art figured into her world. She still painted, but was charmingly modest about her work, preferring to show off her collection of other painters, of which there was a good representation on every wall of the house. Her sister lived with her and made a brief appearance before drifting off to other parts of the house as John began preparing to show Alice Terry the prints he brought from the exhibit. You got a sense from her that the past was something she had put to rest with no regrets, yet her love and respect for her husband was always forefront when dealing with historians like John. When he displayed a print of Ramon Navarro she was visibly touched, saying he had been a close personal friend and his needless death in 1968 was still a subject best left untouched.

I had asked John to please include a question or two regarding *The Magician* and he kept his word, asking her during a moment when she was recalling her days with Ingram in Nice, which she described as being his most productive of their time together. My partner, Chris Dietrich, transcribed the following from John's tapes and this is the first opportunity I have had to share them, since John never got around to using the material himself.

Paul Wegener as Oliver Haddo, luring Alice Terry to Hades once again as the dancer, Hubert Stowitts, tempts her.

JK: What was it like working as well as living in Nice?

AT: It was a very creative period for Rex. I remember we lived in a wonderful hotel called the Negresco filled with the most charming and talented people including, at the time, Isadora Duncan. She was living at the hotel without any money yet the innkeepers never said a word about her bill because she was such an attraction – a true force of nature that the locals adored her free spirit. One afternoon Rex invited Matisse to lunch just to meet her and of course he was charmed. We all were…

JK: Could you talk for a moment about the film you made with Paul Wegener while you were there?

AT: You mean of course *The Magician* …well this was never a favorite of mine since I really had very little to do except either look mesmerized by Mr. Wegener or be frightened to death by what he was about to do to me…. The atmosphere of that film was rather otherworldly because Mr. Wegener was always somewhat in his character. Rex was quite taken with his face, which was remarkable; his eyes were positively demonic when he focused them on you. He was quite a star in Germany and of course we all had seen The Golem.

JK: Did you enjoy working with him?

AT: Well yes and no, I mean he was very kind towards me and took direction beautifully from Rex. Since they were both of the same mind about his character, their working relationship was good. Mr. Wegener was a great star in his native land and this was the only film he ever made outside of Germany. The crew was put off by his pomposity, especially John (Seitz) who photographed the film. Mr. Wegener was, shall we say, a prima donna who insisted on being treated with great respect. He lost his temper quite a bit, always dressing down his servant, and especially his long suffering make-up man who one could not help but feel sorry for. Mr. Wegener brought along his personal valet as well.

JK: Did this behavior ever bother your husband?

AT: Not really, you see Rex always knew what he wanted as a director. I mean he visualized the whole film well in advance. The structure of it was fully realized before the cameras ever rolled. He wanted Paul Wegener from the beginning and visualized it with his personality and especially his physical appearance, which was commanding at all times.

JK: Was the film well received?

AT: No it was not well received, not by Rex's standard not at all... His relationship to the author, Mr. Maugham, was non-existent by the time the film premiered. He did not like Rex's adaptation in the least. Rex found Maugham's novel lacking in many ways and thought to improve on it, and this drew a wedge between them that was never removed. The Magician was never a favorite of mine, nor did Rex think much of it afterwards.

I wish I had been more aggressive in asking John if I could do a separate interview, yet looking back on that afternoon, I think Alice Terry said about as much as she cared to on the subject, even as an eye witness to film history. She was more then content to let the past remain exactly that and simply move on with her life, which was as peaceful and content as I ever saw for anyone who had such an active part in the film making process on two continents.

Last year I saw yet another film taking on the Crowley legend, only this time the man himself was front and center as his unholy spirit is brought back into the 21st century by computer technology in a *Chemical Wedding*. The always-entertaining Simon Callow played Crowley to perfection in my opinion. It was unfortunate that the script he was given let him down. For me the project is not without its guilty pleasures, not the least of which was the name the screenwriter gave for Callow's character—Oliver Haddo.

10

Sex and Death in a Kingdom by the Sea

Night Tide

CURTIS HARRINGTON'S *NIGHT TIDE,* which opened the Venice International Film Festival in 1961, secured the director a reputation (already known like his colleague Kenneth Anger for an avant-garde style of filmmaking) as an auteur in the horror genre at a time when very little had been written about such films. Curtis himself was a pioneer in the field of film scholarship having written extensively on the subject as early as 1952. There were two directors that became influences on Curtis's work, the most important being Joseph Von Sternberg, to whom Curtis would devote an entire monograph for the Museum of Modern Art. The second would be Val Lewton, whose work at RKO on a string of B-horror films served as a blueprint for much of what we admire in *Night Tide* today.

There is an irony in having *Night Tide* open a festival in Venice, Italy, when the film itself represents a time capsule of a now-vanished era that was Venice, California, circa 1960. At that time the California version of Venice (complete with faux canals, used to great effect a couple of years before by Orson Welles in *Touch of Evil*) was inhabited by a sub-culture of coffee house beatniks, free thinking bohemians adrift in a sea of jazz and cigarette smoke. Curtis opens *Night Tide* in just such an atmosphere, staging Dennis Hopper's first encounter with Mora (a suspected sea siren played by Linda Lawson) in a smoky jazz club called the "Blue Grotto."

This introduction differs considerably from, say, Simone Simon's introduction in Val Lewton's *Cat People*, which takes place at the zoo where she charms Kent Smith. Yet the connection is the same, for both these women

Linda Lawson as Mora the Mermaid in *Night Tide*.

share a repressed dread of their inner selves; both are morbidly drawn to folklore regarding their backgrounds and neither can escape the past. This theme is also found in Lewton's other films, especially *The Seventh Victim*, which was one of Harrington's personal favorites. The psychosexual tension between Mora and her admirer, played rather timidly by Dennis Hopper (of all people) at a stage in his career where he was still untouched by what was to come so he is still able to convey innocence. Hopper is dressed in what has been described as a "Homoerotic sailor suit" by some in Harrington's inner circle since Curtis always told the story of how he went to a tailor and had a specially-designed costume for Dennis that was very tight and revealing in a way the Navy would never have sanctioned. The outfit was then re-dyed to an off-white so it would not photograph so bright; the result nearly got Hopper thrown in the brig since he was stopped one night after filming by the Navy patrol for being out in a dirty uniform. Curtis was very amused by Dennis telling him that he was propositioned by men several times during the filming—but only when he was wearing his sailor suit. Curtis would always end the anecdote by saying, "Well, I never really knew if Dennis ever took any of them up on it."

For the record, Dennis Hopper has gone on record saying that at this early stage in his career he did "flirt with homosexuality as just another life experience." Otherwise I do not share the theory held by some critics that *Night Tide* has a "homosexual agenda," just because of the director's orientation. Curtis brought this up with me once when I was interviewing him about another—James Whale. He reminded me that in the 30' and 40's these kinds of questions were never asked and as far as any of Whale's films having a "gay agenda," he replied, "Bullshit. Jimmy just made damn good movies, the only thing that might hold water in that regard was his camp sense of humor, which I share as well. In fact Harrington cast his films in much the same manner as Whale. In *Night Tide* for example we have the actress Marjorie Eaton as the fortune-telling Madame Romanovitch, very camp, dressed in such a way that she looks a bit like Dr. Pretorius in Whale's *Bride of Frankenstein*; in fact in close up she almost looks like him in drag.

Curtis explained to me the genesis for the film during one of our interviews done over the nearly three decades we knew one another. "As a boy growing up in Beaumont, California, there was nothing much to do except go to the library and it was there in the stacks that I discovered Edgar Allan Poe. After that I was hooked on the macabre for the rest of my life. I found more to read at the local drugstore that stocked all the pulp magazines of the day including "Weird Tales" and another one called Black Cat. They introduced me to H.P. Lovecraft, Robert Bloch and William Hope Hodgson. It was Hodgson's *House on the Borderland* that led me trying my hand at writing. One of my first efforts was under his influence, *The Secret of the Sea*, since much of his weird fiction involved the sea. I was always drawn to the ocean and of course reading Lovecraft at the same time gave me a sense of dread and horror about the sea since he used it as a metaphor for all manner of horrors. In any case this bit of writing paved the way for my first real screenplay, *Night Tide*."

Curtis had acquired some distribution grants through Roger Corman's Filmgroup. With that in hand he then found a partner in a young Armenian named Aram Kantarian. Soon the two of them managed to raise money (the total budget for *Night Tide* was about $75,000). Now they were ready to cast the film and Curtis remembered meeting a rising young talent at one of the local coffee house screenings for his experimental films; that talent was of course Dennis Hopper.

Hopper had scored some attention in small roles for director's George Stevens and Nick Ray and was now ready (at least in Harrington's eyes) to play a lead. As Curtis recalled, "Dennis was a bit of a firebrand by then, inventive, energetic, emotional and sensitive, all the qualities I needed for Johnny to be." The only person on set not to respond to these charms was Hopper's leading lady, Linda Lawson. Long before I thought about writing about this film I discovered that Linda lived about six blocks from me, having run into her at the local post office. I was invited over for a drink one evening and she had this to say about her co-star: "Dennis Hopper had a lot of issues both professionally and personally. I thought he was attractive enough yet there was something in those eyes of his that warned me off on some level. He was fine for the first couple of days and then out of the blue he shows up at my apartment saying to me, 'We need to relate better if we are going to work together, okay?' So he comes into my apartment and immediately goes into my kitchen and crawls under the table. I mean, it frightened me! He rolled up into a ball and refused to come out, acting like a lunatic. When I finally got him to get up and talk to me it was obvious he was on something. I knew very little about drugs then and now so I was not prepared at all to deal with somebody who was. The next day I confronted him on the set away from Curtis and told Dennis if this or anything like it ever happened again I would walk off the picture for good. From that point on we were clear with each other but my coldness towards him affected my relationship with Curtis, who began to dislike me and to this day he never attempted to get in touch for screenings or anything. As far as the film goes I still receive fan mail about it…If I am remembered for anything it will be for playing the mermaid Mora in *Night Tide*."

Perhaps the most fascinating character in *Night Tide* is that of Marjorie Cameron, the mysterious woman in black who speaks to Mora in the Blue Grotto. This is the famous connection between this film and Lewton's *Cat People*. In Lewton's film Elizabeth Russell, made-up to resemble a cat-woman, speaks to Simone Simon in a strange language referring to her as "my sister." Harrington pays homage to this moment having Cameron do much the same thing speaking to Linda Lawson in phonetic Greek, a task Cameron did by memorizing each word at Curtis's request.

Since nearly every review regarding *Night Tide* considers it a kind of remake of the 1942 *Cat People*, I think it is important to comment here that without the presence of Cameron as the "sea witch" the comparison simply does not hold water because *Cat People* is a legitimate horror film with a supernatural shape-shifter whereas *Night Tide* explains the supernatural away in the final reel as a ruse concocted by Gavin Muir's sea captain as a means to eliminate all of Mora's suitors. The wonderful thing about *Night Tide* is how Harrington creates a void for speculation since even the sea captain has no knowledge of the lady in black whatsoever. Cameron appears at key moments in Mora's courtship with Johnny. She appears to great effect during Mora's fever dance on the beach which ends with her collapse. More importantly in a sequence Curtis considered the best in the film: Johnny follows the lady in black across the seedy landscape of Venice until she leads him magically to the captain's front door (a location which turned out to be silent screen actress Mae Murray's old villa) and then disappears once again. Cameron even figures in Johnny's dream of Mora reclining on a rock with her mermaid tail; as Johnny reaches for her she dissolves into Cameron. Elizabeth Russell, the counterpart in Lewton's version, only appears at the wedding table to utter the famous "My sister" line. There is no need to see her again because the audience has enough visual proof that Simone does indeed belong to a race of cat women. Only in Johnny's dream while Mora is taking a shower do we get any sense that if Mora was to have sex with him she would then morph slowly from a mermaid into an octopus strangling him to death. Every supernatural event can be accounted for in Harrington's film except the lady in black—the elusive Cameron.

Marjorie Cameron was so much more than just a cameo in the lives of those who knew her. A woman of vast intellect and abilities she moved in both artistic and occult circles in Los Angeles and anywhere else she traveled during her lifetime. She appeared in films for both Curtis Harrington and Kenneth Anger, influencing both men for the rest of their lives. Cameron's appearance in Anger's *Inauguration of the Pleasure Dome* was a mind-bending experience for Kenneth as he saw in her the Scarlet Woman as described by Aleister Crowley. Cameron was accustomed to this title, having received it originally from her late husband Jack Parsons, who recognized her power early on. With red flaming hair and piercing green eyes she dominated all in her circle, so much so that she eclipsed the great Anaïs Nin as the dominant figure in Anger's film. In fact the two occultists would move in together after the film was done. Curtis devoted one of his short films to her, *The Wormwood Star*. The title alone is important as it represents a magical child created by ritual. Cameron and her late husband devoted much of their time to performing this dangerous ritual known as "The Babylon Working." Cameron is such an important figure in her own right that rather than try inadequately explaining it all here, I suggest you read the new book regarding her life, also entitled The Wormwood Star. Curtis's film documents her paintings for posterity since she burned them all after the film was completed as per the instructions laid down in the aforementioned experiment.

Night Tide is paced like a fever dream populated with eccentric well-meaning characters that attempt to save the young man from himself as the object of his affections moves closer and closer to her pre-determined end. This was a staple in Lewton's universe and it applies here as well. It would take Curtis a few more years to develop his style more along the lines of his idol Von Sternberg, which would culminate with the making of GAMES and later *What's the Matter with Helen.* For the time being Harrington's obsession with film history would take the place of his later obsession with decor and the grandstanding of diva-like personalities like Shelley Winters and Simone Signoret.

The other personality to emerge from this film was actress Luana Anders, whose grace and beauty made her a natural for the kind of films about to be made as the 1960s came unto their own. Dennis Hopper was taken with her straight away, using her much later in his own film *Easy Rider.* Curtis would also work with her again in his *The Killing Kind.* Luana recalled her time with Harrington with great joy as she sensed his abilities as a director from this first encounter. "Curtis knew his business and how to handle his actors. His knowledge was encyclopedic when it came to film history and more to the point he knew exactly what he wanted in each shot that was set up. We had a great cameraman in Vilis Lepenieks; he did all of the exteriors on our film with Floyd.

Crosby, then working with us on the interiors. I would work with Floyd again with Roger Corman soon after this." Luana would also attract the attention of Jack Nicholson who would go on to employ her whenever he could.

Curtis would most likely not have shared Luana's view of his directing skill with actors. At the time of shooting *Night Tide,* as he admitted to me on several occasions, he shared the same plight as Roger Corman did in his early days of directing films, which is a total lack of understanding of the acting process. Both Dennis Hopper, and then later on Shelley Winters, were versed in Actors Studio and the process known as 'sense memory.' Both Corman and Harrington would go to acting workshops like Jeff Corey's to learn more about how to handle their actors. The result of course gave them both insight, although Roger would later rely on hiring actors that already knew their business (like Vincent Price), allowing him to do what he did best which was to produce. Curtis Harrington was never a producer but learned to guide his actors, pro and novice, into doing their best work for him in his later films. Dennis Hopper was only 24 years old when they did *Night Tide* and yet he trusted Curtis to present him for perhaps the only time in his career as the embodiment of youthful energy and optimism.

One of the great assets in *Night Tide* is the score by David Raskin, who came onboard as a personal favor to Curtis. The result is a musical evocation of the Venice beach culture with its coffee house poetry and jazz under-

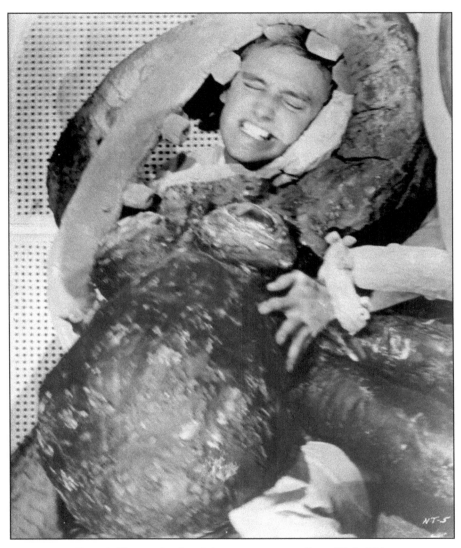

Dennis Hopper in the nightmare sequence from *Night Tide*.

scoring when necessary the danger that shadows Johnny as he pursues his siren into the depths of the ocean to the seedy underbelly of Venice itself. Raskin, known for his score of the classic film Noir LAURA a film which is referenced here by Curtis's casting of Gavin Muir as the old sea captain who may have discovered a lost race of Sea people" of which Mora is a direct descendant. As played by Muir he resembles Clifton Webb's Waldo Leydecker from *Laura* more than the father figure he is meant to portray. Curtis had wanted to cast Peter Lorre in the role, which would have brought him closer to working with another of Von Sternberg's stars since Lorre had made *Crime and Punishment* with the great director in 1935. Lorre would have provided a real manic obsessive character to the table, rather than the decadent, effete personality as played by Gavin Muir.

Curtis once told me a story of running into his idol Von Sternberg at a screening of *The Devil Is A Woman* at the County Museum where the great director asked him why he kept coming back time and again to see a film he already knew by heart. Curtis replied, "Well, Joe, why do you listen to great music over and over again? The answer is because it gives me pleasure," and this is how I feel about the films of Curtis Harrington. I have seen *Night Tide* many times and each and every screening allows me back into the sinister chiaroscuro landscape of his films. He always tried to broaden the poetic meaning of all his films no matter how absurd the premise might be. Curtis always lived a supernatural aesthetic. One visit to his home spoke volumes about his personality and his art. The *Trompe L'oeil* moulding that laced the ceilings of every room in his Art Nouveau retreat, props from his films, an evening slipper worn by Dietrich, and framed prints of Vampire bats (of which I now have two—a gift from George Edwards, Harrington's oft time producer). You literally stepped into the house of Poe, or better still, the house of Harrington.

Night Tide is probably one of the most evocative representations of Edgar Allan Poe in a film to date even though it is not formally based on any one literary work of the divine Edgar. The atmosphere and tone are Poe's as is the fatal woman our sailor lad Dennis Hopper pines to be with. Whether she is called Morella, Lenore, Annabel Lee or even Mora she is still the radiant maiden whom the angels called by name.

Curtis Harrington might have been marginalized in his lifetime; however his legacy as an avant-garde, esoteric occultist film director can no longer be ignored. To the end he dedicated his life to self-expression of the highest order and I for one will remain in his debt for the remarkable body of work he leaves behind forever more in this kingdom by the sea.

11

Wig of a Poet

The Tenant

THE EXPERIENCE OF CINEMA—people in a dark room losing collective touch with reality via a glowing screen—is part of the mystery at the core of human behavior. Sometimes we can even experience fear and dread at what we see on that screen and remember it for the rest of our lives. The poster art for *Le Locataire* and the English version *The Tenant* (1976) display the same quote: "No one does it to you like Roman Polanski." A veiled reference to the director's infamous sexual prowess, it also suggests his ability as a director to create suspense within the framework of his well-crafted films.

This is to my mind the last of his masterpieces prior to what many have described as "his decline from the success of *Chinatown* (1974) and *Rosemary's Baby* (1968). *The Tenant* was not well received when it was originally released, but it has aged exceedingly well and now critics have added it to what they like to call Polanski's "apartment trilogy" alongside *Repulsion* (1965) and *Rosemary's Baby*.

A film sublimely French in it's execution and theme, *The Tenant's* source novel, Roland Topar's novel *Le Locataire Chimerique* (1964) is steeped in surrealism and a direct product of the Panic Movement; a group of theater performers, writers and artists inspired by the mythic "great God Pan," the Movement was an artistic rejection of all that culturally came before in the visual arts, preferring to champion irrational behavior and obscenity, subverting classical iconography. It is no wonder this material attracted Polanski, long an admirer of surrealism from his early days in Poland.

Roman Polanski as Trelkovsky.

Polanski is a past master of translating novels to film—his adaptation of *Rosemary's Baby* is perfection, following every word in Ira Levin's book—so when it came to adapting Topar's novel into a screenplay he attempted a similar adherence, but the problem is that in the novel the protagonist, Trekovsky, doesn't really exist. The ambiguity of the novel is very difficult to translate to the language of film. Polanski adapted the material faithfully however, still allowing us plenty of clues, especially towards the end when we must determine if he's paranoid or the other tenants are really out to kill him or drive him insane. The final moments in the hospital may be the last word in film absurdity.

The film is at face value a study of alienation and displacement since Trekovsky is a Pole living in Paris. He is a little man, a man who will suppress his feelings to make other people comfortable; he is also a fool. It is to his ultimate folly in believing he is somehow a Parisian just because he has adjusted himself into a lifestyle in which he never truly belongs It shares a similar landscape with *Last Tango in Paris* as far as using the unnerving experience of apartment hunting in Paris as a launch for strange encounters. Both films display a very different aspect of Paris than the one's we've grown accustomed to in American films, i.e. rather than flowers and sunshine, we get pre-war plumbing, prostitutes, and despair.

One of the flaws even Polanski recognized in making the film was the short period of time in which we are watching Trelkosky (played by the director) before he abruptly descends into absolute paranoia. Polanski needed more situations to explain the behavior, whereas the novel has the power to relate all this in a fashion film simply cannot. This is why I see this film as Polanski's Rorschach test since the spectator has many options in interpreting whether or not this is delusional or, as I like to believe, an occult encounter involving spirits of ancient Egypt, hinted at in the novel but under Polanski's direction and cameraman Sven Nykist's intense focus allowed to infuse every shadow in that spidery building with ancient evil. The forlorn toilet as viewed from Trelkosky's window is filled with all manner of oddities from a severed head to a full figured mummy.

Trelkosky is not unlike Jack Torrence in Kubrick's *The Shining*, hallucinating phantoms in an equally isolated environment wherein we have no idea what's real and what's vividly imagined by the crazed characters. The Egyptian themes are not without interest as we pursue the idea of souls being transmigrated from body to body. Maybe Simone Chule left enough of herself behind to bring the next tenant full circle into her hospital room making as all tenant's in a parasitic society.

Trelkosky as played by Polanski reminds me of a protagonist in Sartre—or better still Camus—since he is tragic on one level and profoundly funny at the same time. The French during periods following war seem to find humor in the most absurd places and so does Polanski in this film. He is darkly comic while he is in drag checking himself out in the mirror voicing the idea "I look like I am pregnant" with jungle red nails and lipstick. Even his very hard to watch death scene is filled with silly bits that prevent us from taking in the utter morbidity of his visions involving conspiracy among the apt dwellers to cause his death. Are they Devils mocking his fall into the pit? Or is he hallucinating a private hell for his own perverse enjoyment?

There is a sublime moment in *Repulsion*, where Carol (Catherine Deneuve) is sitting in on a bench, watching the sunlight streaming in on the bench across from her. After a moment she reaches over and tries to brush the light away, the sort of thing one might observe someone doing in a park and

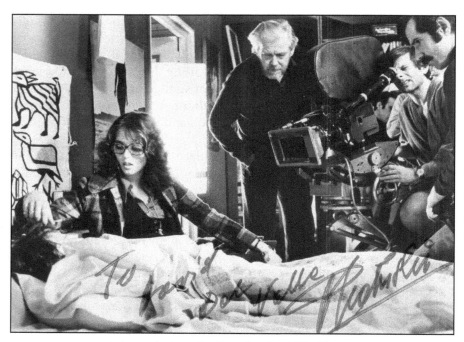

Autographed production shot from *The Tenant*.

instantly know there's something not quite right behind this pretty blonde surface. A similar park side scene occurs in *The Tenant* where, having had enough of a nearby screaming child, Polanski walks over and does the most politically incorrect thing possible and slaps the kid. That the one aggressive act by his character in the whole film turns out to be against a child is shocking and uproariously funny.

The film uses some locations in and around Paris (even though the main set the Parisian quarter was recreated on a soundstage) and the atmosphere is decidedly bleak and grey. Paris is a melting pot of races where your class determines how you are going to be treated. Trelkovsky is tolerated by Paris only while he has money it can drain. The feeling of being an outsider here in a city packed with alienated souls never leaves us, or him. A mood piece that has stood the test of time, Polanski has admitted that The Tenant has its flaws, yet the more one views the film the more its poetry manifests. After one gets used to seeing Isabelle Adjani looking less than stellar —-rather frumpy actually, she becomes one of the only likeable characters in the film. Shelley Winters is way over the top but it works in context with the other malevolent figures on the landscape, with Melvin Douglas as sour as they come with a forked tongued (literally!) to draw even more parallels with *Rosemary's Baby* and the tenants of the Bramford, i.e. the Dakota in New York.

One thing that did occur to Polanski while filming was that he fell in love all over again with Paris. He has lived there off and on ever since. I think this and his *Fearless Vampire Killers* are remarkable films, considering Polanski had to be both an actor losing himself in the role, forgetting about the camera and crew long enough to create a character, but never losing the edge that only a world class director can accomplish. So remember: "Nobody does it to you like Roman Polanski."

Barbara Steele as the mute killer in *Silent Scream*.

12

The Silent Scream of Barbara Steele

The Silent Scream

WHEN BARBARA STEELE, (the star of quite possibly the greatest Italian horror film ever made, *The Mask of the Demon*, {aka *Black Sunday*}) vowed "to never crawl out of another coffin again," she would have been wise to have included attics and hidden rooms in her pronouncement. The reason I make this distinction is the current release on DVD of a film that marked the only screen appearance for the Queen of horror for the year 1980. For years this film existed only on botched VHS releases and one attempt on Laser disc, fans that were far too young to have seen it first run had to make do with this situation. As one who knew a bit more than most about how this box-office gross-er came to be made with Barbara in the first place, I was more than mystified as to its new status as a "classic" slasher film in the tradition of *Halloween* (1978). As far as I was concerned, the one and only reason to sit through this catalogue of clichés was to see an icon at work. She appears only at the film's closing moments and she is worth the wait. With no dialogue Barbara uses her amazing face to register every emotion required and then some, dominating every frame she is in. As I sit in the glow of my computer screen, reading all these online reviews, I have to smile. Read on and see why....

The name of this classic bit of hokum is *Silent Scream*, made by the late Denny Harris at the crest of the 'slasher' craze that began with the superior *Halloween*. I know something about this film, since I was the one who got Barbara Steele the part and negotiated the contracts as her agent at the time. This was the only feature film she did in 1980 after three disappoints in a row, beginning with Louis Malle's *Pretty Baby* (a film Barbara first suggested to

107

Malle during an affair in Italy in the 60's that took place during her reign as the Queen of Terror when her beauty and fame was at its zenith). I had just gotten to know Barbara when this film opened in Westwood, with all the attention focused on the underage Brook Shields. Barbara had shot for weeks in New Orleans in this controversial film by a world-class director, hoping it would bring her back to the screen with dignity. However, the shoot turned out to be a rocky one, with Barbara hiding in the background, having made it clear to Louis that Susan Sarandon was not on her wish-list of co-stars to be filming with for weeks in an old house in the Big Easy. Apparently Sarandon was having a fling with Malle, which just rubbed our Barbara the wrong way. She did however make friends with Antonio Fargas and most of the other "ladies of the night" in the cast.

After *Pretty Baby* premiered she lamented, "If only Louis had given me just five more minutes of screen time I might have emerged as someone this town would employ." The next film to come along was *I Never Promised You a Rose Garden* by Anthony Page. In this, Barbara was cast as a figment in the imagination of a young girl suffering from mental illness. Barbara looked amazing in her fantasy costume with an elaborate headdress. Unfortunately the whole sequence was cut prior to the film opening, so this became another lost opportunity in the re-emergence of the Queen of Horror. The last film at least kept her front and center and was directed by the fannish Joe Dante, who knew her work but made no attempt to help her look her best. In fact he paid no attention to her until the end of the film where she has the last line and the final close-up; but in a film entitled *Piranha*, the gesture was more akin to throwing pearls before swine.

I began working in earnest with Barbara immediately after the Dante film since we had discussed her lack of visibility in Hollywood after she returned from the Texas locations where *Piranha* was shot. Placing Barbara in the Academy Players Directory, which in those days published two books a year, was the first step to get the word out that she had U.S. representation and was actually living in Hollywood rather than Europe (The Academy Players Directory is a comprehensive list of actors and actresses containing pictures and contact information, often used by casting directors). In those days before cell phones and lap-tops, actors had to make the rounds of the studio casting offices regardless of who they were. The big stars were, of course, offered scripts through their agents, but for my clients at Del Valle, Franklin and Levine, I had to rely on the daily Breakdown Service to give me the lowdown on what films and parts were coming up on any given day. Looking back, I sent Barbara on some pretty lame projects for a woman of her ability and grace. I tried episodic television at first, sending her to Bert Remsen and his partner, Dick Dimman, as well as Bobby Hoffman over at Paramount. She actually read for things like *Barnaby Jones*, if you can believe that! It was humiliating for me to do this and I still remember receiving a call from her after the *Barnaby Jones* reading: "David, I went to this thing looking, if I do say so myself, rather good. In fact, I got whistled at as I walked across the street to the casting office." One of the issues in those days was an actor's TVQ, which in layman's terms meant, "How many shows have you had done?" and "What were the ratings of each?" This was then tallied into a score and that was how they rated you. Barbara read for the part of Morgana in the TV movie *Dr. Strange* with Sir John Mills, only to lose the part to Jessica Walters who had a much higher TVQ than Barbara.

The first project I tried to involve Barbara in as her agent was a made-for-TV movie with the ridiculous title *Devil Dog: Hound of Hell*. The only reason I felt this might help her is that number one, it was being directed by our mutual friend, Curtis Harrington, and secondly, it might at least start to build a TVQ rating for Barbara, who had up till then done very little American television. The film turned out to be a new low for Curtis, whose reputation did not need to go down this road in the first place, since the network gave him no opportunity to display his talent other than to direct the train wreck put before him. The part that suited Barbara to a 'T' on paper at least was that of the high priestess to a coven of witches. The part was no more than a cameo but it was work and I wanted her to have it. All went according to plan and Barbara went down to read for Curtis at the offices of CBS. Later in the day I received a call from her, laughing about the whole experience. "David, there I was standing in front of Curtis and some 20-something casting director trying to summon a sense of urgency to lines like, 'O Satan, appear before us. Let us offer you this puppy for your infernal desires,' or some shit like it. I mean, give me a break; I began my career summoning the Devil. I mean, I just give up, David."

I will always remember one of the perks in knowing Barbara was to be privy to her off-kilter sense of humor, which saved many a situation like this one. I assured her that she didn't need to worry, Curtis would cast her on reputation alone for a part like this....Well, I could not have been more wrong. The part went to our dear friend, Martine Beswicke, whom Barbara had known in Rome at the start of both their careers in movies. Martine's behavior always amused Barbara, who described her to me once as, "A double Long Island Iced Tea disguised as a teenage nymphet." Martine had always been the Bond glamour girl while Barbara proclaimed her disdain at "climbing out of anymore fucking coffins." As fate would have it, Martine was having a "White Party" in Santa Barbara the very next weekend and both of us were invited along with Curtis Harrington. Martine lived at that time with her manager/agent Robert Walker and at least three of his other clients, in a large, rambling house in a joyful commune atmosphere...at least that was the way Martine described it at the time.

I was a bit down for the occasion as I was still focused on getting Barbara some work and not much in a party mode; however, the crème of the jest was about to take place. The day before the party a group of Italian film journalists had arrived in Hollywood to interview the "Queen of Italian Horror," and Barbara wasted no time in inviting them as well to what she described as "her" celebration on the park-like grounds of her Santa Barbara friend...neglecting to mention it was Martine's affair. The afternoon of the White Party, all went as planned. Curtis and the rest of us turned up for cocktails and a buffet in this beautifully landscaped park by a pond. Barbara looked amazing (as always) in white, but of course so did Martine, who was also celebrating her new role in Curtis' TV movie. At the end of the day Curtis stood up from his little group of friends and said, "Excuse me, I must say hello to a very special lady." He then walked over to Barbara and explained that he could just not bring himself to cast her in such a demeaning role and hoped in the future they could work together in a project worthy of their time.

A few weeks later Barbara received a copy of the magazine spread from Rome which heralded the event, "La Strega di Roma," entertaining her friends on her Santa Barbara estate." Martine of course was not amused, but later on laughed it off because after all this was Barbara Steele we were dealing with here, and to take a line from Charles Vidor's *Gilda*, "If I was a ranch they would call me the bar-nothing." After all, there are no limits to the Queen of Horror.

Having exhausted the acting breakdowns during most of 1979, the idea came to me to create our own vanity project with her fan base in mind. Vampires have always been a successful commodity in the cinema, with Dracula in any incarnation a compelling draw at the box office. Frank Langella had brought the character back that year both on Broadway and then as a film (with Olivier as Van Helsing, no less). One of my personal favorites of the Universal Golden Age of horror films has always been *Dracula's Daughter*, a direct sequel to the Lugosi film and yet underrated at its time of release. It became obvious that Barbara Steele was the perfect choice to play the Countess Zaleska, following in the footsteps of Gloria Holden, who made such a lasting impression in the original.

My idea was well received by Barbara so we set about to put together a treatment setting the whole thing still in the 1930's, not realizing how expensive this was going to be if we ever did get a studio interested. The whole concept was to update the story only in terms of censorship, which prevented the original from addressing the sexuality of the Countess directly. Our version had the Countess seducing a beautiful cocaine addict named Lily, to be played by her old friend Martine Beswicke. In the script Lily chooses to become a vampire to end her addiction and begin life as an undead with Dracula's daughter. The ideal director for this was to be Curtis Harrington; at least in this he would not have to work with children, pets or Shelley Winters.

Reflective pose of Barbara Steele between takes of *Silent Scream*.

Looking back I can blame the whole thing on the boogie. We never could get such a project greenlit in the Hollywood of 1979 with a star that was only revered in Europe and a director who was doing episodic television. All this was so unreal for someone like Barbara Steele, who could still remember when films were offered to her over an elegant lunch near the Spanish Steps, and it was her decision whether or not to accept. Now those days of La Dolce Vita were all but a dream as she and I contemplated our futures over margaritas at El Coyote. No wonder Denny Harris's offer seemed so well-timed and providential.

I was desperate to find Barbara a decent part in something and then it happened. One morning the breakdowns came into my office with this notice at the top of the second page: "Denny Harris Productions is looking for an actress in her forties with a horror-movie following. Dark hair, dramatic personality." I took a resume and photo personally to Denny's office and within a day Barbara went over for a meeting, signing the contract the same day. I got her special billing and $5,000 for the week she worked on the film. The best news for her was the fact she had no dialogue to memorize. It was a walk in the park for the Queen of Italian Horror. The whole thing was a bit of a holiday. She wore very little make-up, her wardrobe consisted of a worn-out pink robe and a butcher knife, and when she wasn't sticking some-one with the knife she cuddled a teddy-bear…her idea, since she was playing a traumatized teenager gone-to-seed in the mansion's attic.

The second day on which Barbara worked, my partner, Chris Dietrich, visited her between takes of mayhem. I treasured a photo of the two of them which is now lost, in which Barbara is standing over Chris, who is doing his own silent scream, as she appears to be getting ready to stab him with her bloody butcher knife. Chris was always her biggest fan, having seen *Black Sunday* as a child in Danville, Illinois. He became her close friend and at one point lived with her on Lasky Drive, babysitting her then-eight-year-old son Jonathan. I think Barbara really enjoyed working before the cameras again, playing a silent force of nature, allowing her to act as if she were making a silent film, which we know is the truest form of cinema.

In the tradition of one of her previous films, *Young Torless*, Barbara was cast after the film was made and then her sequences were added to it. In *Young Torless* it was to give the young lead a sexual outlet, which gave his character more depth. In the case of *Silent Scream*, Harris had shot the film once in 1977 and then scrapped the better part of the footage, recasting it with recognizable names like Cameron Mitchell and especially Yvonne De Carlo. Barbara loved working with Yvonne the most. She would call me after she left the set and describe Yvonne's arrival on a Harley with a leather-clad boyfriend half her age. "I want to be just like her at that point in my life, do-ing just what turns me on."

Barbara's sequences were all shot on a soundstage dressed to look like the attic-in-question, with claustrophobic walls leading in and out of her hidden room, which was created like a teenage girl's boudoir from the 1950s, with a re-cord player that played 45s. The most tragic moments occurred when Victoria sat before the mirror of her dressing table, reflecting on the loss of her youth. It is a testament to Barbara's ability that this cameo set this otherwise pedestrian film in a class by itself. In spite of all the internet ramblings about this being a sleeper hit or a genre classic, don't you believe it for a moment; this film exists for one reason only, and that is the presence of an actress whose legend has grown more potent as time goes by. And in the years since 1980, more and more fans have sought out her classic Italian output to watch her at the top of her game as a cult figure, which as of 2009 is more available than ever.

The Scorpion release of *Silent Scream* is anamorphic, with a commentary by the writers who went on to do *Pitch Black*, which gave Vin Diesel a career… something *Silent Scream* didn't accomplish for any of its leads in 1980.

13

Hello, I'm Butch

Theatre of Blood

THE MOST DEFINING MOMENT for me in what may well be Vincent Price's signature film, *Theatre of Blood*, comes towards the end of the second act when Coral Browne arrives to get her hair done with a policeman in tow, since half of her Critics Circle has been gruesomely dispatched by a very irate actor named Edward Lionheart, played to perfection by Vincent Price. Coral as 'Miss Moon" seems to have missed her appointment at first, or so says the rather gay-looking young man (Diana Rigg in drag) complete with a shaggy moustache on duty at the reception booth.

However 'Butch" is available and it appears to be her lucky day because "Butch is very chic, does Princess Margaret's hair and chicks like that." Miss Moon is persuaded, and at that moment, ascending a spiral staircase is Butch, a rather tall man with a fuzzy Afro hairdo wearing a white blouse emblazoned with very Tom of Finland male nudes. "Hello, I'm Butch. Hey, dishy-dishy hair, can't wait to get my hands on it."

The film is overwrought with black humor and gay humor like this.

During her appointment, Miss Moon has her hands tied as Butch remarks, "This is something new from 'Gay Paree," for what will become her final hairdo. "Oh, I wish you would let me do something camp with the color, Darling, I mean, like flame with ash highlights." Price then proceeds to fry her to oblivion while quoting the Bard's 'Henry IV, Part One.'

The real genius of Antony Greville-Bell's screenplay is how seamlessly he weaves Shakespeare's most violent moments with clever bits of homage to Vincent Price's long career onstage and in films. For example, the first time

113

Vincent Price as "Butch the Hairdresser" in *Theatre of Blood*.

we see Price he is made up to look like a policeman. Vincent's very first appearance on a stage was that of a policeman in the play *Chicago*. "I won that role by being the only one around at the time in London that really knew how to chew gum." His reputation as a gourmet cook is exploited in the sequence where he exacts his revenge on another one of the nine critics; this time it's Robert Morley playing a flamboyantly gay reviewer, in pink suits with two poodles, both wearing bows in their hair. "This is your dish, Meredith Merridew." Price is faux-French with a goatee. The two actors would later appear on Vincent's televised cooking show *Cooking Pricewise*, which aired in the UK not long after this film wrapped. Morley is disgustingly done-in by revising the text of Titus Andronicus so that Queen Tamora is now a decidedly different Queen, devouring large portions of poodle pie until he chokes to death on his "babies."

Antony Greville-Bell only wrote three screenplays (the other two being *The Strange Vengence of Rosalie* and *Perfect Friday*), both quite different in design from this film, which is without question his best work. At first glance the concept for *Theatre of Blood* does indeed look like a cash-in on Price's former success with *The Abominable Dr. Phibes* and its sequel, *Dr. Phibes Rises Again*, since both films deal with revenge –this time around in exceedingly spectacular ways. But these films, as directed by Robert Fuest, bear little resemblance to what would follow, since Fuest's visual sense always came first, creating an Art Deco fantasy landscape where little if any blood is actually shed on camera. He perfected this on the hit TV series *The Avengers*, which never duplicated any real violence or bloodshed during its long and successful run. If Robert Fuest had directed *Theatre of Blood* the result would have been visually stunning but it would not have had the Jacobean cruelty Douglas Hickox gave the proceedings.

One of the delights to be found in *Theatre of Blood* is of course the elaborate ways in which Lionheart uses Shakespeare's text to exact his revenge. The only one of the celebrated actors not to be put to death was Jack Hawkins, who is instead made to follow Othello's lead and strangle his wife played by the much loved Diana Dors,(one of the UK's reigning sex symbols of the 50's, she remained a favorite by turning to character acting with great success). There is a six degrees of separation at work here because Hawkins, who was battling throat cancer at the time of filming, had his larynx removed so it was necessary for an actor to dub his voice for film work. The actor chosen for this job was Charles Gray (widely known for his role in the *Rocky Horror Show* as the narrator as well as the Bond villain in *Diamonds Are Forever*).

Charles was also a close friend of Coral Browne, having appeared with her on stage and screen. Charles Gray was most certainly introduced to Price during the making of this film. The three of them would work together less than two years later when Gray joined Vincent and Coral for what would be their first appearance on stage together in the West End performing Jean Anouilh's *Ardele* at the Queens Theatre. This production, while lavishly produced with these three respected actors, should have been more successful than it was, especially with the lukewarm reception Price received from the critics. It would take the life of Oscar Wilde to finally place Price back into the, spotlight of the theater world he abandoned so many years ago for Hollywood.

I had an opportunity to question Vincent Price about this film during our time together in San Francisco where he was being honored at the Palace of Fine Arts. He was staying at the Clift Hotel for the duration and invited me up to his suite for one of our many taped interviews regarding his career. A portion of this interview is available on my DVD, *Vincent Price: The Sinister Image*. For many years Price always cited *Tomb of Ligeia* as his personal favorite, however time can alter many a perception so that afternoon he amended that by making *Theatre of Blood* his most enjoyable experience in filmmaking.

"I always knew something wonderful would happen to me before I turned 65," he said. When Price made the film in 1973 he was at a crossroads both professionally and personally as well. His contract with American International had long since soured to the point of no return; *Madhouse* had been a disaster, which was a shame since the concept of a horror version of both *All About Eve* and *Sunset Blvd.* was enticing to be sure. His off-screen hostility to actor Robert Quarry could have been an asset if the powers at AIP had not rushed the production with shoddy production values, not to mention cutting the film during its editing stage until it made little sense.

"I didn't want to do *Theatre of Blood* at first since I had just been offered a summer season at the Rep Theatre in Missouri. They offered me a chance to play Becket in Elliot's *Murder in the Cathedral* as well as O'Neill's *Long Day's Journey into Night*. This always seemed to happen to me when I had a chance to return to the real craft of acting, something to feed the soul." Price had to decline the engagement in order to make the film. His apprehension melted away when he finally sat down and read the screenplay. "The script was absolutely brilliant with wonderful dialogue. I simply could not wait to play this character of Edward Lionheart. I mean, what actor would not jump at the chance to give back some of his own to the critics?"

The cast of *Theatre of Blood* was also a factor in Price's enthusiasm for the project. Hickox had assembled the crème-de-la-crème of the British stage for extended cameos as the nine critics Edward Lionheart dispatches with the aid of the Bard's text. Aside from Coral Browne and Robert Morley there were also Jack Hawkins, Arthur Lowe, Dennis Price, Robert Coote, Harry Andrews, and Diana Dors. Vincent's co-star was Diana Rigg, whom Price adored from the very first meeting. "Diana is one of the best actresses in England as well as being a great deal of fun to know...She worked in drag during portions of our film, during the scene where I murder the lady that was to become my wife, Coral. Diana came on set wearing these tight trousers with a large sock stuffed in her pants. I roared with laughter, as did the crew. They loved her, as do I."

The father/daughter chemistry between Price and Diana Rigg helps establish his character as more sinned against than sinning even in his most gruesome moments of mayhem. Her death scene towards the end, taken from Lear, is quite moving as she lies in Price's arms reciting the lines she had

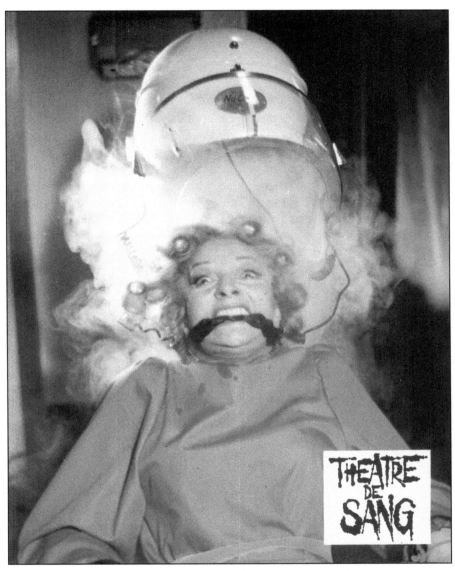

Coral Brown as "Miss Moon" is in for a "bit of a shock" in *Theatre of Blood*.

played ten years before under the direction of Peter Brook with the great Paul Scofield as Lear.

Price would go on from this project with the support of his new wife to finally return to the stage where he would triumph with his magnificent one-man-show *Diversions and Delights*, playing Oscar Wilde, the role his late friend Laird Cregar also played back in the 1940s.

Both men were under contract to 20th Century-Fox at the time. Vincent did the eulogy at Cregar's funeral and then replaced his friend in *Dragonwyck* playing the Gothic character he would later perfect in HOUSE OF USHER. Price had enjoyed resurgence in his career after the success of these eight Corman Poe films, which firmly established him in the film world as the new master of the macabre.

It would however be the unexpected critical success of *Theater of Blood* some ten years later to restore his confidence as an icon. Vincent remained over the moon during the duration of the filming of *Theatre of Blood*, for here he was, at last surrounded by his peers, all respected actors in the theater, being directed by a young and talented man, with brilliant dialogue allowing him the opportunity to speak some of Shakespeare's most profound lines while basically being Vincent Price as well. His soliloquy from Hamlet, spoken in front of all these wonderful actors while billowing curtains fly around him as he moves outside along the railing of the high-rise offices of the Critics Circle, is a tour-de-force beautifully played by one of America's most underrated actors. In this moment, both the personal and profession lives of Vincent Price became one, allowing his audience who had remained faithful for five decades to finally see him reach beyond the cardboard castles of Roger Corman's Poe-scapes into a Brave New World of both Gods and monsters.

14

"Get Out My Pendulum, Kiddies. I Feel Like Swinging!"

Beach Party

THE NIGHT VINCENT PRICE DIED, television stations across the country ran the pendulum scene from *Pit and the Pendulum* as a collective memory his audience would instantly recognize as the screen persona of Vincent Price. This is as it should have been because if any film could act as an homage to Price's popularity, not only as a "Horror Icon" but a pop culture icon as well, this was it. It was more than likely that his producers at AIP felt the same way, since he lampooned the role not only in the aforementioned *Beach Party* film, where he does a sly cameo as "Big Daddy", but literally revisits the set in the first of two appearances as the title character in the Dr. Goldfoot films of 1965.

The dual role of Nicolas Medina and his evil father Sebastian left a lasting impression on anyone who saw it, as the on screen incarnation of all things Edgar Allan Poe. This was especially true of 12 year olds and movie fans with only a passing reference to the literary Poe. In his first performance in a Poe adaptation, *House of Usher*, Price hardly spoke above a whisper as the hypersensitive Roderick Usher within his bleached out visage and white hair. In *Pit and the Pendulum,* Price is totally over the top creating his most extravagant performance with all his soon to be trademark facial tics complete with wide-eyed cringing in terror at the many cobwebbed set pieces thrown at him by Daniel Haller. Vincent received some truly nasty reviews from the critics of the day and for once he actually sat down and began to write a letter to one of them only to tear it up when he finished, knowing by then it was all in vain to try and explain your style to someone who never

119

Unpublished candid of Barbara Steele and Vincent Price on the *Pendulum* set.

acted in their lives. It is somewhat ironic that Price would endure bad no-tices for Pit when the critics would only have to wait another year to have real cause for concern when Price was cast as Richard III in *Tower of London*, which may contain Vincent Price's worst screen performance.

I can still remember the first time I saw this film as a 13 year old at the old Fox Theatre in Sacramento; they built a giant makeshift pendulum which was made to swing back and forth above the Marquee. All this bal-lyhoo made for an unforgettable experience for a monster in kid in the making; however it was watching Price at the films climax dressed all in black with that hood masking his face (which was for me the intimate in evil), possessed by his torturer father, Sebastian, confusing poor John Kerr with his late brother who had been put to death for his adultery with Sebastian's wife. This was such an all powerful image watching Vincent Price manipulate those chords which lowered the pendulum itself lower and lower until it drew blood on John Kerr's chest; no wonder that night of October 25th 1991, America chose to remember this actor with a scene like this one; a tour de force by one of the country's leading masters of the macabre.

Several years before, Vincent and I were taping my Sinister Image show dedicated to his career in Horror films. We watched the pendulum scene together on a small monitor on the set. Vincent stared at himself saying lines like "You are about to enter Hell the neither regions, the abode of the dammed" he looked over at me and said "this is just too hokey for words, David." We both laughed since I did not disagree except in telling him that it was that very "hokeyness" that made his films remain contemporary and fun decades later. As far as I am concerned the main reason the Poe films directed by Roger Corman are still remembered today is primarily because of Price and his baroque acting style. If you can imagine all eight of the Poe films directed by Corman but starring say, Ray Milland instead, would we still be watching them with the same degree of enjoyment? I think not, yet Milland's only Poe film, *The Premature Burial*, is not without its charms but one still regrets Price not being able to do it in the first place.

It is fascinating to me that Vincent's co-star in *Pit*, the equally iconic Barbara Steele, would only work together with Vincent the one time. It was like a bad joke that whenever Barbara found the perfect muse or mentor for her persona in films, she quickly moved as far away from success as possible. I mean, after she is launched by Mario Bava in *Black Sunday,* she never again places herself under his direction whether by choice or design. Now she finds the perfect on screen partnership with Vincent Price in these Poe films and still refuses to be in any of the films that would follow. I know she was offered *The Raven* and perhaps *Tomb of Ligeia*. Corman told me he remembered asking her to be in the non-Price Poe film as well.

I did find a moment to ask Barbara about making this film and she had this to say. "At the time, everyone I spoke with in Hollywood told me I would enjoy working with Vincent, yet nothing prepared me for the man himself. He is one of those unique personalities. Definitively an old soul, cultivated, intelligent, sensitive, exuding an occult presence on film which, of course, is why Vincent became such an icon to this particular genre. More importantly for my taste, Vincent possesses a wicked sense of humor, which got us through the material we had to work with panache and style. My entire part was nearly silent, filled with reactions of either shock or horror. Roger was on a roll at this time, having had such success with the first Poe film and this one would prove no exception. The sets were draped in cobwebs and mold, which suited Vincent to a tee. Corman is a bit like Bava in that he is private, shy and unobtrusive with his actors, yet demanding in terms of the crew. When Roger is on the floor he is the master in charge. Roger was patience itself. When it came time for my confrontation with Vincent in the castle dungeon, as he lay there in the dust, we did the most takes trying to find just the right emotion for my character. Vincent's concentration is total when the cameras are rolling. When he grabs me by the throat and then kisses me, I no longer thought I was acting, as he began in earnest to choke the life out of me. When the scene was finished he immediately returned to being Vincent Price again, genuinely concerned for the remainder of that day's shooting. I am glad you saved these contact sheets from the film to show me now because I could not have remembered as much as I have without them. I can now recall the pendulum chamber which was a work of art. During our few breaks between set-ups I would tell Vincent about these amazing Italian lunches at the local trattoria we enjoyed while working on the Bava film. One afternoon Vincent dropped by the make-up room and suggested we have an "Italian lunch" together, which translated into two bottles of red wine and a loaf of his homemade bread along with wonderful cheeses. We both got delightfully plastered right there in the pendulum chamber while a photographer recorded the event, none of which has seen the light of day until now, David! I remember Vincent escorted me onto the set by saying "isn't this the most phallic thing imaginable?" It was his saying this as I was staring up at this long pendulum that seemed to reach beyond the set itself, that just reduced me to gales of laughter and, mind you, it was mostly the way he delivered those lines. He managed to top even himself by taking advantage of the moment to add "Don't worry, my dear. They will put a rubber on it for our moment when dear John is under it."

"Not long after the dungeon incident Vincent and I were doing yet more publicity stills on the castle staircase overwrought with cobwebs—the staircase being in reality nothing more than a mock up of less than 50 steps. I was in full regalia in my well-worn, risen from the casket shroud while Vincent had on his floor length silken dressing gown." During a break from the two of them lying in every imaginable position of disarray on those steps, Vincent rose to his full height and then lifted his gown to display a pair of shocking pink socks. "I have them in baby blue as well...this helps me from getting a bit too morbid while doing these kinds of films. I believe you cannot be too careful; one could easily take yourself so seriously that you wind up walking down Hollywood Boulevard in a cape!"

Barbara loved working with Price as these comments point out. Later I was able to ask Vincent about his memories of working with her. Vincent recalls, "Barbara Steele was a natural for this particular role as my evil wife

Elizabeth. I remember how shy she was the first day of work. Barbara arrived on the set barefoot and ever so Malibu. She had a quick mind and knew something about art, so we passed the time between takes discussing that, not that there was really that much free time on a Roger Corman set to begin with. The scene where she taunts me into madness down in the vaults took some time to block out properly for the cameras, and I am sure she never forgot what happened. When we actually shot the thing, I had a moment where I did, unfortunately, get a little too carried away while in character, so when I grabbed her by the throat and then planting this violent kiss right on her mouth, I really did start to strangle her in earnest...all the while Roger is sitting there watching all this go down without making a sound. Then he looked at us very oddly, I might add finally calling out "Cut! Print it." As soon as I realized what I had done I began apologizing to her immediately and as I remember it, she asked if we needed another take. She was certainly a pro after that. I recall asking Roger to give her more to do in the film, since she was photographing like a character out of a Goya painting with that amazing face. She had a true sense of the macabre, which is as I well know essential to making this kind of film work."

"We shot stills all over the place. Vincent really did try to strangle me towards the end of the film and I was so paralyzed with fright during the whole experience that I forgot we were making a movie. Vincent was so sweet after. He came to his senses, of course. I had bruises on my throat for a week. I must confess I kind of got off on the whole thing which of course shocked our young director who was so straight laced he could have passed for a CPA (Certified Public Accountant).

The on-screen chemistry of Price and Steele was instant, since both performers have this connection to the extravagant; this makes the fact that this would be the only time these two icons would ever work together. Years later Barbara was asked by Channel One in Italy to do a documentary on her status as the "Queen of Horror." The producers used my apartment to film her scenes and they brought all the equipment to do a feature film, i.e. laying down tracks to run a camera on, etc. I phoned Vincent to see if he could be persuaded to come down for a reunion of sorts. The producers were over the moon because his name alone could get them better exposure outside of Italy. When Price thought about it he finally said "no" because, from his point of view, they really did not know each other outside of her four days on the film and felt awkward trying to connect with her after so many years. I was disappointed that I could not make this happen, especially for Barbara. Later on I discovered that Price had been very close to Barbara's ex-husband, screenwriter James Poe, whose first wife was also named Barbara and they both were part of Price's inner circle during his long marriage to Mary Price. I imagine now that Vincent felt Jim might feel somewhat negatively if he did something like this, although Barbara Steele was still years away from meeting and then marrying James Poe when they make *Pit and the Pendulum*.

One of the fascinating things about watching *Pit* several times is the way the two personalities of Price and Steele seem to subvert one another. It is almost as if Barbara's character, Elizabeth, only exists in Price's mind, since all her scenes with him, until the finale, are in soft gelled flashbacks that seem so much like a dream. It is also obvious that Price's role as her husband, Nicolas, has never consummated the marriage, thus making Elizabeth's motivation to sleep with Dr. Leon even more understandable. This situation comes up again in *The Haunted Palace* where Price is also in a dual role as Debra Paget's husband, Charles. He never touches her, so when he becomes the warlock Joseph Curwen, one of the first things he tries to do is bed his ancestor's wife. Her reaction to this speaks volumes about their relationship and, once again, we have a Vincent Price movie where he plays an emasculated man; weak and unmanly…another bizarre, outré performance in a catalogue of work that goes all the way back to his contract days at 20th Century-Fox playing similar roles in *Leave Her to Heaven* and *Shock*. All these films have a fascinating neuroticism about them that is due, in part, to the persona of Vincent Price himself. The crème of the jest would come in 1962 when Price would play perhaps the most foppish role of his entire career as Fortunato Lucresi in *The Black Cat* segment of *Tales of Terror*. In Richard Matheson's script, the overwhelming gay wine connoisseur is a total "ladies man", wooing and bedding Peter Lorre's lonely wife played by the ever camp Joyce Jameson. A complete reversal of stereotypes, Price would not attempt to play an openly gay character until he impersonated a hairdresser named "Butch" in *Theater of Blood* in 1973.

This film has more than stood the test of time and repeated viewings yield more insight into where the cycle of Poe films would go from there. The six films that came after all benefited from not only the world wide box-office success of *Pit and the Pendulum* ,which in reality created the persona that established Barbara Steele as a Horror star in Europe and not the popular belief that it was *Black Sunday* that launched her career. Barbara had always made a point of saying she filmed her scenes in the ill-fated Elvis film, *Flaming Star*, which was done after, not before *Black Sunday*. It was her work in *Pit and the Pendulum* that created the buzz that led to her making more of these films in Italy. For Vincent Price, this film forever cemented his name with that of Edgar Allan Poe; his tour de force performance set the standard for how far the actor could go in a horror film as long as you really *were* Vincent Price. In fact, it is not unlike what happened to Antony Perkins with his signature performance in *Psycho*. The two men shared a florid acting style that in certain films could always be relied on to deliver the goods. In Ken Russell's outré production of *Crimes of Passion* we can see a certain homage to Price in Perkins' histrionics' as the demented reverend who channels a bit of Sebastian Medina in the final reel.

Vincent Price strangles Barbara Steele "for real" in *Pit and the Pendulum*.

Pit and the Pendulum is a nearly perfect example of what has come to be known as a "Corman-Poe film" with its bizarre landscape of melancholia, catalepsy and red candles illuminating dank corridors leading to crypts containing prematurely buried ancestors; a dominion where bedeviled noblemen dine in great halls while suffering thunderstorms through stained glass windows enhanced, of course, by a decidedly lavender decor. All this showcased by the overwhelming presence of Vincent Price, a screen actor of perverse energies and flamboyant gestures so perfectly suited to this kind of film that it has taken us a full decade after his death to realize just what an undisputed master of the macabre he really was… unique and one of a kind.

15

"Another Black Sunday With You"

Black Sunday

THE FIRST TIME I EVER SAW *BLACK SUNDAY,* the American version of the Italian horror classic "La Maschera Del Demonio," was at a drive-in with (I believe) *Konga* as a double feature. The year 1960 was a particularly banner year for genre films, when you consider within that 12 month period we would not only see Hitchcock's *Psycho* and Corman's *House of Usher* but this really intense black-and-white nightmare from first-time director Mario Bava. Imagine being 11 years old while witnessing a woman being tied to a stake and then impaled by a hooded muscleman using a hammer to attach an iron mask filled inside with spikes to the helpless woman in bondage. Even in black and white, the blood that spurts out from the face after the hammer strikes is as shocking as the shower sequence in *Psycho*, and this comes within the first ten minutes of the film!

Black Sunday is not without its faults; the acting of the male lead John Richardson is lackluster since he was hired for his beauty, not his skills as a leading man. The supporting cast fares better. Except for Richardson and his leading lady Barbara Steele, the rest of the cast are seasoned Italian actors who know their business.

It is with Barbara Steele that the cult surrounding this film really begins. She was a Rank starlet from England, as in fact was her leading man John Richardson. She had been groomed by Rank for starlet roles that never really seemed to suit her unusual beauty; even in glorified walk-ons in English programs like *Bachelor of Hearts*, Barbara stood out like a spider on a valentine. What Mario Bava achieved in casting her was nothing short of

Barbara Steele poses in front of a screening of *Black Sunday*, especially for a
German film crew in downtown Los Angeles (1995).

black magic because he understood at once that her bone structure, matched
with those enormous eyes, would be nothing short of iconic in the guise of
a vampire/witch lusting for revenge while trapped undead in her marble
casket.

I have been very lucky when it comes to meeting personalities that I
admired from my youthful drive-in days in Sacramento and *Black Sunday*
would be no exception. Barbara Steele has undoubtedly figured into many
youthful male fantasies over the decades, especially for those of us that saw
this film in 1960 at the impressionable age advertised with a warning in the
American ad campaigns: "No one under 12 will be admitted without an
adult." This was almost never enforced, I assure you, as most every male fan
I have ever encountered in the half-century since *Black Sunday* premiered in
the States saw it alone or with his peers.

The film made the totally unknown Barbara into a star, at least for the duration of the 1960s, in her newly-adopted home of Italy. During this time, Barbara dined with Gore Vidal, was seen reading intellectual books at sidewalk cafes with Antonio Moravia between shooting her scenes in Fellini's *Otto e Mezzo* (8½). The downside of all this attention was, of course, the false sense of being at one with the intelligentsia of Rome and far above the Technicolor graveyards that beckoned from every corner of the European film industry. They saw in her persona exactly what she had become under the direction of Mario Bava: a fetish horror queen who possessed an otherworldly beauty that glowed with occult possibilities. Barbara, still in her 20's, was seen as a very neurotic, willful eccentric who broke hearts and contracts in equal measure. She turned down everything that was offered her in the horror genre until she realized that not every film offered had a pedigree like Fellini's. In reality she did a baker's dozen gothic horror films in Italy between 1960 and 1967.

I would finally meet this diva of darkness in the summer of 1976 through the efforts of my soon-to-be partner Christopher Dietrich. Chris was another of her fans that saw *Black Sunday* at an early age and never, ever got over it. Barbara became an obsession of Chris's from that day forward. He told me that the first time he saw the film, he remained in the theater all day long, seeing the film four times before finally leaving after the final performance. This ritual was being repeated in cinemas all over the country. It was not until the 1980s that I would understand how widespread this obsession had become with young men who had all seen *Black Sunday* when they were 12 years old. Around 1985, the American Cinematheque honored Mario Bava with a retrospective. During the first evening's screening of *Black Sunday,* I was sitting in the theater which was filled to capacity with (I kid you not) an entire theater totally devoid of women, with 30-something bearded men (and a few without facial hair) all reliving this childhood grief in concert, a brotherhood of Bava/Steele devotees.

My first meeting with Barbara Steele took place in a two-story house in the Westwood/Wilshire district of Los Angeles. Chris had already met with her in Malibu earlier in the year, as she was in the process of divorcing screenwriter James Poe and moving back into Beverly Hills, where she would remain to this day. Barbara had a son, Jonathan, who was about seven years old at the time of our first meeting. I had fussed for days trying to organize this first encounter. I discovered that she was close to Stuart Whitman, who was the godfather to her only son, and his ex-wife Carolina was one of her best friends as well. As luck would have it, one of Stuart's sons, Tony, was an acquaintance of mine so I asked him to join our little group, hoping this might elevate the encounter to a notch above an autograph convention. In those days I was still such a fan and meeting someone like Barbara Steele, who had always seemed so remote and otherworldly—well, you just never thought of her going to the DMV like ordinary mortals. However, that attitude was about to change and forever. The night of the first encounter was so exciting, as I had no idea what she would be like; plus, since all of her films had been dubbed, I really did not know what she would sound like in person other than a very brief phone conversation which allowed me to hear that somewhat odd British accent for the first time.

It all seems like a bit of a daze now trying to remember that evening. She arrived a bit late of course, with her boyfriend-of-the-moment, a handsome TV actor named Anthony Herrera who had just played a detective in the TV movie about the Manson/Tate murders with Steve Railsback as Manson. Barbara was everything I could have hoped for in person: she was bright, funny, modest and very shy about her career. She loved the attention she was getting from my assembled guests and soon let her hair down after we collectively finished off about six bottles of champagne. The first thing I noticed was her relief that we were not wildly overzealous horror fanatics (at least we didn't come off that way to her, thank God). Barbara was at this time convinced that if she could secure a role in a non-horror film, she still might crack the Hollywood system of typecasting that haunted actors like Christopher Lee and, of course, the iconic Bela Lugosi. I went to great pains to reassure her that it was her persona in the Fellini film that we all adored, not giving way to the truth—which, of course, was none of us present had ever gotten over her screen debut with those otherworldly eyes of hers staring out of her coffin with a glass window fixed above her face so the cross placed above it would prevent her resurrection, her glance promising the pleasures of Hell. No other actress in the history of cinema ever had such an introduction to the world stage of personality like Barbara was given by Mario Bava. The late director had given his share of interviews explaining his side of her appeal. Bava always felt that she never understood what he had done for her, launching her as no other actress had ever been into this exclusively male world of horror icons. "Fellini spoiled her and as a result of this she thought she was too good for such films." The truth about Fellini is that there are no stars in a Fellini film other than Fellini. The exception to the rule was always Marcello Mastroianni who remained a star with or without Fellini's attention. Marcello would write his own memoirs a few years later, citing Barbara as a prime example of Fellini's indifference to his actors. "Poor Barbara never had a chance after Fellini's attentions gave her the wrong impression as to her importance in the film, cutting her scenes until she had very little left in the final film." Fellini was also well known for not really launching any of his discoveries beyond the film they were doing for him at the moment. Case in point: whatever became of the male leads of *Amarcord* or *Satyricon*? Mario Bava would never work with Barbara again, although the two names are forever connected by the film that made them both worldwide icons of the horror genre.

After that first meeting, Barbara seemed to open up more and more regarding her feelings about trying to exist in Hollywood when her heart and soul, as she kept telling me, was in Europe. "I am a European, David. I need to smell the antique decay of those avenues in Paris." She did not have the same feelings for England, however. "I see those vacant eyes staring back at me whenever I ride the underground. All those people there are in a state of grief for a country that no longer cares what happens to anybody that is not rich and upper class." As far as her recollections about the making of *Black Sunday*, it was somewhat like trying to discuss the first *Dracula* film with Chris Lee; she respected the fact that her entire fan base came from that one film and that it was stunning to look at, but horror films to her could never approach the intellectual high she had achieved with Fellini, and living in Italy at that time, she was wined and dined by all the great directors of the day, including having a very complicated relationship with Louie Malle. Malle finally gave Barbara a part in his *Pretty Baby* out of respect for her having turned him on to the book in the first place. "If only Louis had given me 10 more minutes of screen time I might have salvaged my career."

Barbara's relationship with admirers and horror fans has always been a bit bizarre. When she was at the height of her fame in Italy, an invitation arrived by messenger from the newly appointed dictator of Libya, Muammar Gaddafi, to join him for an informal brunch. Barbara recalled that the entire affair was lavish but a bit off-putting since each chair had an armed guard stationed by it, fully equipped with submachine guns. Hers was a glamorous life, there is no doubt. In those days she had tea with Noel Coward, midnight walks along the Thames with Charlie Chaplin and a long term affair with Antony Quinn in the process. By the time I got to know her, she was well into the horror fan stage with weekly requests for autographed photos of herself from *Black Sunday*. While we were preparing for her first convention appearance at Chiller Theater in New Jersey, she received a request from one young man from Wisconsin named Jeffery Dahmer, who specifically asked for an autographed photo of her with the holes in her face from the infamous prologue of her most famous film. Of course he got one and she saved his letter. Enough of these and Barbara could start her own black museum. This kind of attention from demented fans caused her to remark on Clive Barker's BBC program, "I don't know who these fans of mine think they are addressing? They place a kind of persona into my image that has nothing whatsoever to do with me as a person in real life. I think they are all suffering from some childhood grief and in some way, I address that aspect of their repression and fear."

One of my favorite of her stories regarding *Black Sunday* is the one she liked to tell about her make-up girl who diligently prepared her for the dual roles she had to play, (whether or not she did the most famous make-up, the one with all the holes in her face left by the mask of Satan which was pounded into her, remains to be seen). In any case, as Barbara explained to me, "This poor girl was involved with a very abusive boyfriend who beat her and felt she was cheating on him with all the men on or off the set. She would come to work with bruises on her neck where he tried to strangle her. It was just insane. One day she did not come on set at all and I became very concerned, so I went to the producers and expressed my fears to them. As it turned out the girl was found later that week shot to death by this madman, and what was so wicked about the whole affair was he shot her in the vagina!" Whether this story is really true is something I will never know for sure, but it is so typical of Steele's off-kilter way of looking at the world. She also told me that during the last scenes where she is tied to the stake as the evil Princess Asa, her dress caught fire for real and she could very plainly hear Mario Bava telling his cameraman to "Keep filming no matter what!" As many biographers have discovered in interviewing Barbara over the years, she loves to tell stories and will sometimes color her recollections in favor of what month the film was done. For years she maintained it was in the coldest of winters, yet production records have shown it was in the late summer of 1960, so at this point you have to decide what to believe. She was all of 23 when she made the film and that was now over half a century ago. I have watched the film with her at least three times over the years and she has finally come to terms with it being her legacy, yet remembering what it was really like to film is like—as she puts it—"Remembering details of my first prom."

When Barbara and I did sit down and try to analyze her most infamous film, she made the point of describing the atmosphere that she encountered in Rome that year as "optimistic, joyous and bright. I felt so connected and endorsed by the Italians, yet it was underscored by this uncanny dread and fear that the Italians have lived with for centuries. I felt like I was becoming a character in a D'annuzio novel." I remarked that she was never very effective playing virgins, which of course made her laugh. I felt that her characterization of Princess Asa ranked right up there with Count Dracula and Lady Macbeth in terms of a monster. What makes Barbara Steele's persona so unique among other things is the fact that no other actress in the cinema is known for playing such a role. Most of the women known for appearing in horror films are regarded as "scream queens"; in other words they are for the most part all victims of a force or monster rather than ever becoming one. The only notable exception is Gloria Holden in *Dracula's Daughter* and of course she never made another one like it for the rest of her career. I have shown this film to Barbara and for a time we dreamed of her remaking it, since Holden was like her cinematic mother in many ways.

Barbara always refers to Mario Bava in very respectful terms and yet we will most likely never really know what transpired between them that summer in 1960, except to say they made an impact on one another that, for reasons known only to them, would never be repeated. I had heard rumors

Barbara Steele as Princess Katia. Photo by O. Civirani.

that Bava had wanted her to play opposite Christopher Lee in the director's *The Whip and the Body*, a role that ultimately went to Daliah Lavi. It was a part Barbara could have really taken to the next level in Sadian cinema, had she chosen to accept. Bava complained at the time that Barbara was "always late arriving on the set." He found her difficult and unresponsive to things like wearing fangs, etc. However, in her defense, Bava never really wanted to make a vampire film per se because the vampire myth is not really an Italian thing to begin with. Bava was really creating a ghostly fairy tale within a centuries-old class struggle between the "padrone," the aristocrat who lives in the castle lording over a village like Burt Lancaster did in Visconti's *The Leopard*. These lords were vampiric in the way they drained the lifeblood from the people. The two evil vampire creatures that come back to life in *Black Sunday* are far more vibrant and cunning than their ancestors that now inhabit Castle Vajda. The current prince is weak and filled with a dread he has no chance of overcoming. The role of Princess Katia is also a bit of a bore, as she is in a constant state of anxiety or is unable to consummate her feelings for the handsome doctor who catches her eye in the ruined abbey when we first see her. Barbara would never have become a star if this was all she played in the film. I often wonder how it would have been if she had played only the evil princess and some other ingénue had played her ancestor. Barbara would have been the first all-out vampire priestess in a film since Gloria Holden's tour de force in 1936, ironically a year before Barbara Steele was born.

After a lifetime of watching this film, its faults glare out more apparent as I grow older. Now that the European cut of the film is available it will never seem quite right to me, since I grew up with the AIP cut of the film, including the Les Baxter score and dubbing that seems right. By comparison, the European opening credits reminded me of one of those K. Gordon Murray revamps of those Mexican horror movies we all saw on television back in the day, as age overcomes the youthful innocence that first allowed me to sit in the dark and dream of this dark world in which life and death could be divided in black and white. Mario Bava is finally given his proper place as a poet of the horror genre, with several of his films regarded as classics of their kind. Bava created such a unique funerary glow around the lens of his camera, framing his diva against gothic tapestries, infecting the camera with a tangible sense of anxiety and dread. He took Barbara Steele's unique face, a combination of wide glaring eyes combined with high cheekbones which seemed to inform her persona with erotic seduction and vengeful Sadism in equal measure; Bava literally turned her into perhaps his greatest special effect.

One night after a dinner party at Barbara's, we sat in her living room, which contains in one corner a giant cross she bought in Mexico, complete with a crucified Jesus (which, she being Barbara, festooned with red chili pepper lights, creating a somewhat unholy Christmas tree). It was in this atmosphere, fueled by countless glasses of red wine, that I asked her if she ever believed in the Devil or vampires. She gave me one of her best horror queen looks with one eyebrow raised, the way she liked to do in films like *Castle of Blood*. "David, you are such a goblin, aren't you? Well the answer is yes I do. One day, when I was still in my make-up as Princess Asa, I sat down in front of my dressing table and looked into the mirror and froze as if ice were put down my back. For one moment I cast no reflection whatsoever in that mirror. It is always unwise to use movies as your guide for reality." With that she threw her head back and laughed like the Devil...

16

Edie's: A Cocktail Bar on Figueroa

SOMETIME DURING THE SUMMER OF 1982 I found myself at Duke's Tropicana Café, then located on Santa Monica Boulevard. Duke's had become a Hollywood rock-and-roll institution since both Jim Morrison and Janis Joplin had nursed many a hangover within its greasy walls and booths during the summer of '68, when Duke's first opened its doors. On this particular morning (a Saturday, if memory serves) the joint was jumping with a cross section of Hollywood and rock-and-roll personalities. In the corner booth sat a very familiar-looking older gentleman with two other men around the same age. Now at this point I must tell you I am really good at recognizing former film stars and the like and on this Saturday morning I was staring at one of the only surviving stars of *Casablanca*, the actor/director Paul Henried, the famed Warner Bros. leading man and then TV and feature film director. If Paul had never directed anything he would still deserve my attention but this man who worked with Bogart also directed one of my all-time favorite guilty pleasures, *Dead Ringer*, one of the macabre films Bette Davis made in the wake of her *What Ever Happened to Baby Jane?* success. Paul had been the co-star on *Now Voyager* where he famously lit two cigarettes and then handed one of the lit ones to Davis at the film's teary finale. As I watched Mr. Henried begin to collect his things I knew I had to do something fast to let him know I was aware of who he was, but how? At this point in time I still smoked and the guy I was with that morning also had the habit, so I waited until Paul Henried had made his way up to the cash register and then I made

Bette Davis playing twins for the second time at Warner Bros, the first time
around was for *A Stolen Life*.

my move. He sort of noticed that I was grinning at him as he walked over to
where I was standing, still waiting for a booth, and at that moment I took two
cigarettes out of my coat pocket and yes, I did exactly what you are thinking
I did: I lit two of them and handed one to a startled Paul Henried, who as it
turned out was a real sport, accepting it with such panache. By now a couple
of the customers caught on to what was going on at the cash register and with
all eyes on the two of us applauded the situation.

I was so impressed with the grace he displayed at what could have been a real moment of embarrassment for both of us if he had not been so gallant about this blatant display of Hollywood nostalgia. I took the moment to introduce myself and then told him how much I enjoyed his films at Warner Bros., especially *Now Voyager*, and then I brought up his film *Dead Ringer*. He smiled and while he paid his check he gave me his card and then said to me, "I enjoyed making that film probably more than you did watching it… Bette is such an enormous talent that it was a pleasure to direct her in anything."

This was the first time I was able to articulate just how much this film has stayed with me since seeing it as a kid at the drive-in and then again countless times on television. The fact that I would bring up what is acknowledged by most film buffs as a highly enjoyable piece of camp from a totally over-the-top Bette Davis riding the crest of her popularity from *What Ever Happened to Baby Jane?*. Her co-star Joan Crawford was doing exactly the same thing that year, starring in her own variation of *What Ever Happened to Baby Jane?* mania with *Strait-Jacket* over at the Columbia lot with William Castle.

The "divine feud" between Joan Crawford and Bette Davis has been well documented elsewhere but in discussing *Dead Ringer* it always amused me that even though Davis's film was a first class Warner Bros. production photographed by Ernest Haller with a suitably macabre score by Andre Previn, with a hand-picked collection of top Hollywood character actors, the fact remains Joan Crawford's trashy low-budget William Castle howler (with Joan playing at being both 25 years old and 55 within the same film) did twice the business *Dead Ringer* did that year (1964) because Crawford went out and sold it in major cities across the country. Bill Castle knew how to sell a horror film but he had no idea how much wattage a star like Crawford could put out when it came to her career.

When I first met Bert Remsen he was moonlighting as a casting director with another actor Dick Dinman. The combination of these two became Remden Casting, and very successful at it they were. Bert was a great guy and loved to talk "Hollywood." He told me that Bette Davis had cast approval on *Dead Ringer*: "The first time I met her she was in make-up sitting in her chair in front of one of those very theatrical mirrors with light bulbs all around it….She had just taken one of her huge eyes and lifted it the lid until she looked positively freakish glaring at me with one eye lid extended….Without missing a beat she said, 'Can you mix a cocktail and stay on your mark?' I laughed and told her, 'Most definitely I could do both and sing Irish while I'm doing it.' She laughed that famous cackle of hers and told the producer, 'He's in. I like him just fine,' and that is how I got the part of her bartender at Edie's. During the filming she came in one day with a copy of the Hollywood

Reporter and was really excited. She said to me, 'Bert, have you seen the crap Crawford is up to over at Columbia? I mean, she is doing Lizzie Borden in blackface!' and with that she just broke herself up laughing. I was then convinced that the Crawford/Davis feud was an ongoing concern with no holds barred..."

The first thing I realized with *Dead Ringer* is how old-fashioned a film it is for 1964. It adheres to many film noir conventions, yet was marketed as a horror film, which it decidedly is not. The murder of Margaret De Lorca by her sister Edie is so bloodless as to register disbelief that she was actually shot in the head in the first place. Much attention is placed on Edie removing her dead sister's stockings and jewelry before donning her sister's widow's weeds and making her hasty exit from the poverty that was her life on Figueroa Street.

While her rival was over at Columbia filming "crap" and beheading most of the cast in the process with an axe, Bette was at that same moment being expectedly photographed by Ernest Haller with much attention to.

Noir shadings in the opulent surroundings of GREYSTONE, the Doheny estate which had been used in films a varied as *The Loved One* and the 1991 remake of *Dark Shadows*. Gene Hibbs was assigned to do Davis's make-up and he managed to give the star a streamlined "glamour" look that took at least 10 years off her appearance in *Dead Ringer*, something Joan Crawford could have really used in her Columbia fright flick since *Strait-Jacket* required her to do flashbacks (sadly ineffective) as her 25 year-old former self.

The original title of *Dead Ringer* had been the noir-ish *Who Is Buried In My Grave?* They even retained this title into the advertising stage of the promotion as several posters were released prior to the release date from the studio with that title before Warners decided that the only way to go with a Bette Davis film after *What Ever Happened to Baby Jane?* was to milk the connection for all it was worth: In *What Ever Happened to Baby Jane?* the poster art maintained the catchphrase "Sister, sister oh so fair, why is there blood all over you hair?" Now with *Dead Ringer* the phrase was "Mirror, mirror on the wall, who's the fairest twin of all?" It is a supreme gesture that after the well-publicized feuding that ultimately ended the Davis/Crawford partnership on *Hush, Hush Sweet Charlotte*, which also came out in 1964, Davis realized that the only actress with whom it was worth sharing the screen was herself, and that is exactly what we have here with *Dead Ringer*. Except for some minor upstaging by the wonderful Jean Hagen in what became her final screen performance as Margret De Lorca's flighty high society confidant, Davis is free here to act herself literally off the screen. The support she gets from top-flight character actors like George Macready and Estelle Winwood only enhances her own performance even more. The standout performances from Karl Malden and Peter Lawford never get in her way. The most poignant character in the film is played beautifully by Cyril Delevanti as her butler Henry, who knows the score from the moment Edie leaves the De Lorca mansion at the onset until Margaret/Edith is taken away by the police for poisoning her husband. It is Henry who sees the goodness in Edith and maintains his silence until the bitter end, giving Davis one of her most heartfelt lines: "And I thought I was all alone." Davis understood the importance of such moments and made sure her co-stars were solid in her support.

It was always my impression that *Dead Ringer* was designed to follow Bette Davis's success in *What Ever Happened to Baby Jane?* and to a certain extent it was. However there was another version based on the source novel *La Otra* that was filmed in Spanish around 1946 showcasing Dolores De Rio. After that the script sat dormant for years at Warner's until the studio dusted it off as a possible vehicle for Lana Turner, whose work for producers like Ross Hunter made her a natural for this kind of film. Turner had achieved a certain reputation by then by way of the scandal sheets that had a field day after the murder of her lover Johnny Stompanato by her teenage daughter. This was most likely the reason Lana Turner turned it down, not wanting to do another murder mystery, even one in which she got to play opposite herself. Bette Davis had been offered a role in the "Rat Pack" western *Four For Texas* and withdrew to make *Dead Ringer*. Her co-star, the Oscar-nominated Victor Buono, was also in the cast of this film, making it a reunion of sorts for them. One can only imagine the quality of scripts that were being sent to both Bette Davis and Joan Crawford if *Strait-Jacket* is any indication at all.

The motif of famous actors playing twins is a long one and just this week seeing Dominic Cooper in *The Devil's Double* play both Uday Hussein and his double was a reminder just how well it can be done now, yet the real test rests with the actor and in Cooper's case it has made him a star. Bette Davis was already a legendary actress by the time *Dead Ringer* came her way. She had played twins once before in *A Stolen Life* (1946) and this may have been a factor in why it took so long for Warner Bros. to convince Davis or any other actress to tackle such a project. When Davis made life such a living hell for Joan Crawford that she left the location for *Hush, Hush Sweet Charlotte* after filming nearly half the film, Crawford was later replaced by Olivia De Havilland, another actress who had some experience playing twins in *The Dark Mirror* (a well-done thriller made by Robert Siodmak, very similar in theme to *Dead Ringer*; this film also had two sisters, one homicidal, the other less so).

The best of all the films involving famous actors playing opposite themselves has to be (in my opinion) the 1988 *Dead Ringers* with Jeremy Irons

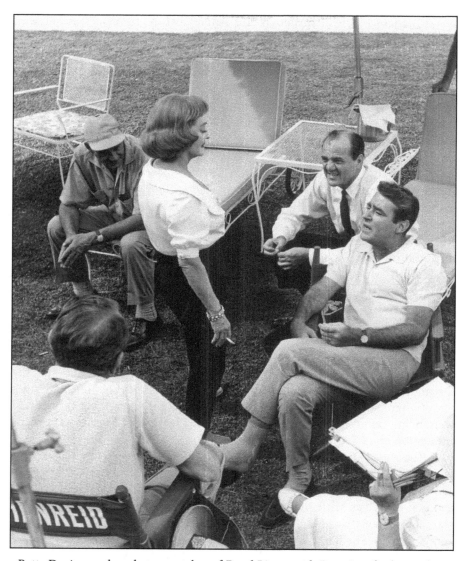

Bette Davis seen here between takes of *Dead Ringer* with Peter Lawford seated to whom she gave a role in this film a promise she made Peter for his hasty departure from appearing in *Whatever Happened To Baby Jane*. co-star Karl Malden and director Paul Henreid in director's chair look on.

in a tour-de-force performance under the direction of David Cronenberg. Recently I watched Edward Norton, another fine actor, play twins in a much underrated film *Leaves of Grass*. The list goes on with special mention to the creepy "Grady daughters" in *The Shining*, Tony Randall in *The Seven Faces of Dr. Lao* and of course Jack Lemmon in *The Great Race*. Bette Davis does not have to suffer her twin more than the first reel since she summons her to Edie's cocktail bar right after their tense encounter at the De Lorca mansion where she shoots her sister in the head…reminding us all of the tagline from *What Ever Happened to Baby Jane?* ("Sister, sister oh so fair, why is their blood all over your hair?"). In the case of this film there is no blood, period, and even when Edie has to see Margaret's body at the morgue it is a very dead but altogether perfect corpse. The lack of gore and blood in *Dead Ringer* simply confirms its status as an LA noir masquerading as a horror film—at least in the advertising.

In spite of the "Addams Family" harpsichord that does its spidery best to keep informing us we are in a macabre situation there at the Doheny estate the film is decidedly a thriller with noir overtones. The great Dane "Duke" that could not stand Margret De Lorca takes up with her sister which proves the undoing for glamour boy Peter Lawford. Now his death scene is as close as we ever get to a classic horror film moment in *Dead Ringer*. I have always been fine with that considering we already had a full-throttle performance from Davis that same year with *Charlotte*. Davis clawing her way down the stairs as the swampy remains of Joe Cotten stands above her as a living corpse is classic Grand Guignol.

I have believed one of the reasons a film like *Dead Ringer* stays in one's memory so vividly is the staying power of one of the cinema's most enduring stars. In her earlier work in films like *The Star*, Davis proved once again that she would take on a role that was unflattering and risky only to walk away with another Oscar nomination for her bravery. In *What Ever Happened to Baby Jane?* she appeared in clown make-up that I doubt any other actress of her generation would ever have dared to do. Bette Davis deserves her iconic status alongside Joan Crawford and Olivia De Havilland. De Havilland has always given Oscar caliber performances in her work on the screen, and even in her moment of despair making *Lady in a Cage*—an unfortunate misfire and not her fault—she still gave a stunning performance. The film itself is just too nasty for its own good.

I still have not seen the remake of *Dead Ringer*, done around 1986 as a made-for-television affair entitled *Killer in the Mirror*. I remain confident that it will have little effect on my admiration for the 1964 version which still, like all cult films that you revisit time and again, is "Like seeing an old friend" to life, which is another line from Baby Jane, when Crawford finally is allowed to read her fan mail…this was a remark made by a fan of Blanche Hudson after watching *Moonglow*…a fictitious title for one of Crawford's early films for M-G-M.

Both Crawford and Davis had their careers revitalized after *What Ever Happened to Baby Jane?* Davis fared a little better for the rest of the 1960s, whereas Joan had to suffer for the likes of Herman Cohen and Bill Castle.

Davis did not get out of this unscathed either; Joan may have bowed out in a cave in England with *Trog* as her swansong, yet never knowing when to quit seems to have died with Garbo because Bette Davis just had to make *Wicked Stepmother* before saying goodbye to her adoring public. We must forgive them both since it was never about the money, it was just one more curtain call—or as Edie would have put it, "Where I am going to spend it—outer space?"

17

Riccardo Freda's *L'Orrible segreto del Dottor Hichcock*

The Horrible Secret of Dr. Hichcock/Raptus, 1962

VICTORIAN PERVERSIONS

Raptus, the alternative title of Riccardo Freda's *L'Orribile segreto del dottor Hichcock* (*The Horrible Secret of Dr. Hichcock*, Italy, 1962) is certainly apt, as its effect on individuals attracted to the macabre is not unlike a rapture or delirium of cinematic pleasure. The atmospheric visuals of Riccardo Freda's masterpiece of sexual alienation and necrophilia stands without precedent in the Golden Age of Italian Horror that virtually seized the Roman film industry from 1956 to 1966.

With more than a nod to the literary influences of Ann Radcliffe and the 19th Century that informed them, *L'Orribile segreto del dottor Hichcock* is a catalogue of Victorian repressions regarding desire and death, the marriage bed and the grave. The perverse behavior of our "hero," Dr. Bernard Hichcock (Robert Flemyng) – much like that of Scottie Ferguson (James Stewart) in *Vertigo* (1958) or Verden Fell (Vincent Price) in *The Tomb of Ligeia* (1965) – results in the creation of a fetish-object of desire and death from each of his wives. The screenplay removes Dr. Hichcock from moral convention entirely and, as the surrealist critics observed, with no narrative rationalization, his actions can be savored as a nightmare fantasy dramatically enhanced by Rafaelle Masciocchi's scarlet lighting. The film's funeral sequence in particular led esteemed critic Raymond Durgnat to comment on how effective such lighting could be, capable as it is of giving horror a visual poetry unique in the cinema.

The good doctor and his first wife, Margherita (Maria Teresa Vianello), are dyed-in-the wool Victorians whose sex games have tragic consequences. Margherita is a willing participant in those nocturnal rituals which seem only to satisfy Dr. Hichcock, a man whose lust remains insatiated unless the body in question is as cold and lifeless as possible. Margherita's role during these episodes seems to be to close her eyes and think of England; apparently a perfect wife would do this and more to keep her man at hearth and home. How all of this finds its way into an Italian landscape of black cats and Roman Catholic guilt is one of the paradoxes wherein *L'Orribile segreto del dottor Hichcock* is regarded by many film scholars to be the penultimate example of Italian Gothic horror, equaled only by Mario Bava's seminal *La Maschera del demonio* (*Mask of the Demon / Black Sunday*, 1960).

STEELE'S SUSPICIONS

L'Orribile segreto del dottor Hichcock was completed in an astonishing 16 days in April of 1962. Freda, a notorious gambler, made the movie on a wager that he could create a period film in two weeks time. The submissive sexuality and mysterious subtext was partly a result of the director's decision to toss out a dozen pages of Ernesto Gastaldi's screenplay, reasoning that there was no time to delve into the motivations of the main characters.

The object of all this sexual tension is the queen of Italian gothic cinema, Barbara Steele. Her reputation rests on the series of films she appeared in between 1960, when Bava made her an icon of fetishism in *La Maschera del demonio*, until her swansong *Un Angelo per Satana* (*Angel for Satan*), directed by Camillo Mastrocinque in 1966. Here, Steele enjoys a change of pace as her role of Dr. Hichcock's second wife is not a villainess but a victim of her husband's obsessions. Cynthia is the new lady of the manor, and like Joan Fontaine in the Hitchcock films (*Rebecca* [1940], *Suspicion* [1941]), she begins to suspect her husband of poisoning her as well as being haunted by the specter of his first wife.

Steele recalls the making of *L'Orribile segreto del dottor Hichcock*:

> Freda I liked very much. He had energy and intelligence. He is the one director out of all the Italians that I felt a true connection with even though he was very autocratic. I liked him enough to feel an obligation for him to win his bet and buy this particular horse he wanted very badly. *Dr. Hichcock* was done while I was still shooting *8 1/2* [1963] for Fellini. I did it strictly for the money. We were working 18 hour days and believe me, you don't relish a close-up after that kind of suicidal pacing and trauma. Oddly enough, I actually liked those deranged working hours. It's difficult to keep the momentum on a picture like that when you have these phenome-

nal pauses between takes. But Freda prevented this by maintaining absolute control at all times with no preparation. You have to feel safe with the director and Freda knew exactly how to keep me in a state of crisis long enough to get what he wanted. I wish we had done more pictures together.

MORE CAST AND CREW

Freda had ushered in the first of the Italian horror films in the sound era with *I Vampiri* (1957), and *L'Orribile segreto del dottor. Hichcock* was the brainchild of the two producers of that earlier picture, Luigi Carpentieri and Emmano Donati. Although *I Vampiri* was not a financial success, the pair decided to make another horror movie under the banner of their jointly-owned company, Panda Films. Freda believed that one of the reasons *I Vampiri* failed was that Italian audiences could not accept the idea of Italians making these kinds of pictures, so on *L'Orribile segreto del dottor Hichcock,* they anglicised the names of all concerned with the exception of the three principal actors, Barbara Steele, Robert Flemyng and Harriet White. Only the film's composer, Roman Vlad, retained his correct name.

Carpentieri and Donati then secured a true specialist in the genre, Ernesto Gastaldi, just 25 years old at the time. He had already written the screenplays for *Il Mostro dell'opera* (*The Vampire of the Opera*, 1961), *Lycanthropus* (*Werewolf in a Girl's Dormitory*, 1961) and *L'Amante del vampiro* (*The Vampire and the Ballerina*, 1961). Gastaldi's career would span four decades, making him the chief architect of many of the classic gothic horror films and *gialli* that are so well-regarded today.

Gastaldi's genius here was to invoke the master of masters, Alfred Hitchcock, and not only through the film's title character. He extended the homage to the very theme of the film, the obsession for a love that has died (referencing *Vertigo*), a perverse *amour fou* between Steele's character and the former Mrs. Hichcock. References to other Hitchcock movies are weaved into the fabric of *L'Orribile segreto del dottor Hichcock*, beginning with the housekeeper (Harriet White), who is a cipher for Mrs. Danvers (Judith Anderson) in *Rebecca*; the portrait of the first Mrs. Hichcock, also from *Rebecca*; the glass of milk from *Suspicion*; the skull that Cynthia finds in her bed, from *Under Capricorn* (1949); not to mention that all four of these Hitchcock films deal with threatened wives.

The role of Dr. Hichcock was interpreted by Robert Flemyng, a staple of the British film and television industry who appeared in various productions until his death in 1995. His most notable roles were in George Cukor's *Travels with My Aunt* (1971) and Stephen Soderbergh's *Kakfa* (1991). His only other genre credit was Vernon Sewell's *The Blood Beast of Terror* (1968), opposite Peter Cushing.

Barbara Steele in *The Horrible Secret of Dr. Hichcock.*

Flemyng was interviewed by the late film historian Alan Upchurch in March of 1992 regarding his work in *L'Orribile segreto del dottor Hichcock*.

My agent sent for me and asked me to meet with the producers. Carpentieri was in London, and I met him, and he said that he spoke Italian, and very little English. He gave me the script. And I rather liked him. My agent said, "Would you like to do it?" and I said, "Well, I want to go to Rome, yes!" The script was in English, called *Raptus*, and it was hilariously funny. On the first page it said, "For some people, sex and death are indissoluble." I thought, "Oh, good gracious me!" By the time I got back to Brighton, I found out the script was about necrophilia! Freda knew how to compose a picture and how to move it, how to cut it and all that. He was a very talented man. The film was made on a shoestring. I think I got, oh, a thousand pounds or something. Barbara may have gotten a bit more. I just hammed away at it and hoped for the best.

The Hitchcockian housekeeper, Martha, was played by veteran actress Harriet White Medin, who was hired even before the director as she was known to be a fine English actress as well as a dialogue coach for Gina Lollobrigida. In the summer of 1995, Medin and Steele were reunited at a cocktail party at this writer's home in Beverly Hills. They had not seen each other since the filming of *Lo Spettro* (*The Ghost*), Freda's 1963 sequel to *L'Orribile segreto del dottor Hichcock*. Harriet recalled,

Barbara was very much the star in those days, and I remember seeing her years later in New York at a screening of *8 1/2*. On *Hichcock*, I remember getting a call from Mr. Flemyng asking me if I read the script. I said yes, isn't it terrible, and we agreed to act as badly as possible to make sure they would never take it out of the vault! Of course, Freda made sure he got the best from each of us regardless. Freda was a very unpleasant little man, always shouting at people and screaming at the crew for one thing or another. Barbara was always late and it drove him crazy. It reached a point that I did not enjoy going to work. I was somewhat new at all this, and I kept doing things that he did not like, yet Freda knew his craft and was good at his job. I much preferred working for a man like Mario Bava. Until your party, Barbara and I had no time to get to know each other. On both of those films, she was always being made up and had to worry about the lighting and the columnists that came on the set. There was no time for much of anything but the work.

One of the guilty pleasures in viewing *L'Orribile segreto del dottor Hichcock* is the brooding, highly dramatic musical score of Roman Vlad (who is also responsible for the compositions in *Lo Spettro*). Here, Vlad infuses the Technicolor images with a force that intensifies the obsessive and ghastly secret of Dr. Hichcock. His other genre scores include *The Mighty Ursus* (1961), *Caltiki the Immortal Monster* (1959), *Hipnosis* (1962) and the film that started it all, *I Vampiri* (1957).

Barbara Steele reunites with Hichcock co-star Harriet White Medin in the home of David Del Valle.

CONCLUSION

As we have passed the 40th anniversary of the making of *L'Orribile segreto del dottor Hichcock*, it has withstood the test of time and the criticism of those involved in its creation. Director Freda passed away 20 December 1999 with the knowledge that he was a pioneer in the field of Italian *fantascienza*, in the company of Mario Bava and Antonio Margheriti as the architects of the Golden Age of Italian Gothics. All three directors were captivated by the presence of Steele in their films. Since *L'Orribile segreto del dottor Hichcock* is the crown jewel in Freda's canon, we may conclude with his description of the Queen of Italian horror:

Barbara Steele! Remarkable! Her eyes are metaphysical, impossible, like the eyes of a Chirico painting. Sometimes, in certain kinds of light, her face assumes an aspect that doesn't seem quite human, and would be impossible for any other actress.

18

Bonding With Sister Hyde

Martine Beswicke

I WAS RAISED IN A "NO, YOU DON'T" world overrun with rules, to lift a line from the "woman in the moon" from the second remake of *A Star Is Born*; so imagine if you will what it was like for someone like me to be living in Hollywood during the Disco era of the late 1970's when one could reinvent oneself in a glittery world of "Yes, you can"–anything you want is there for the asking. It would then be no surprise to find yourself partying with larger-than-life characters that once dazzled you on the silver screen.

There is one very special woman of all the show business characters I encountered during my decades in Babylon. She became in time more like a sister to me, sharing most of my ups and downs in the process. Martine Beswick came into my life like a bolt from the blue. The signs of the Zodiac were in full swing and Jupiter aligned with Mars that night in the summer of 1978 when I blissfully walked into the Blue Parrot (a long-ago watering hole on the corner of Larrabee and Santa Monica in West Hollywood, named after the bar in *Casablanca* run by Sydney Greenstreet) to meet my friend, Steve Tracy (an actor soon-to-be somewhat of a household name as a semi-regular on *Little House on the Prairie*). Steve and I went way back to my college days in San Francisco when he got his start in the first 3-D soft-core gay film, *Heavy Equipment*, with Jack Wrangler and Al Parker. Steve was a curly-haired guy with a great sense of humor who stood about 5'4." Everybody loved Steve. It would be hard to believe that in a few short years (1986) we would lose him to HIV. Steve loved Hollywood so much that he requested his ashes be scattered under the Hollywood sign. To this day I always think of him whenever I pass in its direction.

Now, the mad British director Ken Russell figures into this as well, since I was carrying with me that evening a set of 11×14 photos taken by David James, from Russell's *The Music Lovers*. By the time I arrived, the bar was in the process of filling up, so Steve and I found a place by the window facing the boulevard, where I could show off my latest treasures. As we examined the photos, another attractive curly-haired guy was watching us with great interest (which in the Blue Parrot was not unusual). Looking back, this would prove to be a life-changing moment. The curly-haired guy finally came over and introduced himself as Mark Baker, asking if he could see the photos and recognizing them instantly as from a film by Ken Russell. Steve looked at Mark for a minute, then asked, "Weren't you Candida on Broadway?" I then gave him another look and said, "I just saw you at a cast-screening of *Swashbuckler* in Westwood last week!" Mark played Peter Boyle's boy-toy, complete with long silver nails that dripped poison. Well, it turns out that our boy Mark knew Ken Russell far better than any of us, because he played a small role in *Valentino*, acting alongside the great man himself.

Steve and I had a couple of drinks with our new friend before he drifted off into the night, leaving Mark and I to our own devices. This was a Friday night so Mark stayed with me until Sunday morning, where we then met actress June Gable (who appeared on Broadway with Mark) at Joe Allen's for brunch. It was during that brunch that Mark insisted I hook up with another friend of Ken Russell's, Leonard Pollack, giving me his phone number on the spot.

The afternoon that I first met Lennie was another of those life-altering moments as I instantly got who he was and knew I wanted this talented man as a friend. Lennie was packing to go off to London the next day so our first visit was cut short; but with Lennie ten minutes can be illuminating, so during my first glimpse of his flat (which was decorated with his designs, artwork and photographs) I noticed a double-exposure of a very Art Deco woman posing with a beaded scarf around her neck. Her hair was almost Afro in design. I later learned the entire concept, make-up and hair, was Lennie's. Lennie told me that she was Martine Beswick, an actress he observed sitting in an outdoor cafe in London while he was working on *Valentino* for Ken Russell. He thought she would make an amazing Nazimova so he approached her for contact information, which he then passed on to Ken. Lennie took that photo of Martine in the manner of Nazimova; the results were fantastic. When he said her name I knew instantly who she was as I had long admired her work in films like *Dr. Jekyll and Sister Hyde* as well as *Prehistoric Women* for Hammer Films of England. Most movie fans would know her from the two James

Bond films she appeared in, *From Russia with Love* and *Thunderball*. I would later discover that Russell would have loved to use her but United Artists insisted on a "name" actress in the role so he gave the part of Nazimova to Leslie Caron, who emoted quite well, but it would have been a tour-de-force if "La Beswick" had been given a chance.

I made such a fuss over Martine once I realized he knew her that even though we had just met, Lennie gave me Martine's phone number, explaining that she now lived in West Hollywood and would most likely enjoy having a drink with me. After leaving a message for Martine on her answering service introducing me, my new friend was off to the UK, having done me a kindness neither one of us could even begin to appreciate until much later.

The first encounter with Martine was simply a Mardi Gras of the mind, and leave it to my other new friend of the moment, Lennie Pollack, to have known simply by his remarkable instinct for connecting people that it would turn out that way. I first spoke with her on the phone, explaining how amazed I was that she was living in Hollywood, to which she replied, "Darling, one simply has to be where it all is happening, don't you know? And right now that place is Hollywood. After all, you're here as well, aren't you, Darling?" I invited her on the spot to come over to my Beverly Boulevard abode for drinks the next evening and so she did. My first glimpse of La Beswick was equally unforgettable. She arrived wearing a tricked-out Minnie Mouse combo of red and black; her black-and-red jeweled top was sleeveless, her mini-skirt was black with a bright red heart for a buckle and a matching heart in her hair, which was up. When I opened the door she looked me up and down and then said, "Well, Darling, as you can see, your phone call gave me a heart-on so here I am wearing mine just for you!" I was hers from that moment on, and the rest of the evening was one huge admiration society for all things Beswick.

This first meeting was around the end of 1977 and Martine had just done an episode of *Baretta* with Robert Blake. She played a belly dancer who entices guest star Strother Martin into some intrigue involving a stolen jewel, as I recall. She loved working with Martin, who told her she was an eye-full, and from that moment on they were a double act on-and-off the set. When I visited her place the following weekend she had a poster of herself made up as the belly dancer tacked on her bedroom door. Her charming apartment at that time was filled with flowers and hearts with a cat residing on its own pillow of pink and red. Martine was always filled with an optimism that came from an inner beauty she possessed, probably all of her life. When someone like Martine is born, invested with great beauty, some things in life come easy and this can lead to a certain hauteur or cruelty towards those not quite so blessed. In Martine's case she was never too self-involved not to be aware of other people's feelings and never in the twenty-plus years I have known her have I ever seen her be vindictive or unkind to anyone in her orbit. This is a quality she shares with Vincent Price, who also fell in love with her on the set of *The Offspring* some years later when I was the unit publicist for that film.

Looking back now after all these years it is providential why we clicked so well. I think we both felt comfortable with each other; then came a trust that good friends have that allows a certain bond to develop. Up until I met Martine I tended to be the guy who always looked at a bottle that is half full and thought it half empty. After a lifetime dose of Beswick it was always to be half-full, and for that I am in her debt. One thing we shared in common was the love of talking on the telephone, and remember, this was well before cell phones, so we behaved like those teenagers in *Bye Bye Birdie*–always filling each other in on all the gossip that hovered over Hollywood like the smog it is so well known for. One of the first serious conversations we had was, naturally enough, about her career. I was stupefied that she was not already a huge star in Hollywood with that glowing personality she possessed, not to mention being gorgeous. It was her belief that her exotic quality, which separated her from the rest of the women she came up against for parts, played against her. Sometimes I think she simply overpowered the casting directors she read for and many of them were sadly lacking in imagination, so parts went to other less flamboyant actresses. This dilemma she tried to solve by consulting a numerologist, who suggested she add an extra letter to the end of her name so the gods of chance would once again smile on our Bond girl. Hence "La Beswick" became "La Beswicke."

From the time Martine won the title of Miss Jamaica, winning a car (which she then sold to go to London and begin her career), her looks opened the door and then it was up to her to do the rest. Of course, luck always plays a role in there somewhere. Her first turn in a James Bond film was appearing in the credits of *Dr. No*, and this followed with a speaking role as one of the gypsy dancers that vie for the attention of James Bond in *From Russia with Love*. Martine loved to tell the story of how much the other exotic woman who played her adversary hated her, leading up to the fight itself. The rehearsals went without incident but when the cameras started to roll this woman really put her claws into Martine and what you see onscreen is a bona-fide fight to the death. Her next experience with Bond proved to be one of the highlights of her early career. As Paula in *Thunderball* she is given a bit more to do and never once had to perform a catfight again onscreen. *Thunderball*'s director, Terence Young, liked her very much, making this a delightful time to be Martine, who was now officially a "Bond Girl." Martine remembers the attention she received, which became so intense that the car she was riding in during filming was almost overturned by fans screaming for the "Bond Girl." The set was overrun with millionaires wining and dining cast and crew in a style not seen since.

The kind of La Dolce Vita lifestyle Martine was leading in the days during and after the Bond films became what is now known as the golden age of film making in Europe. She became romantically involved with actor/model John Richardson while they were filming *One Million Years B.C.* for Hammer Films, a studio Martine would also work for a bit later down the road. Their relationship was so intense that many, including Hammer star Christopher Lee, thought them married even years after they parted company.

Martine explained that being with John was always filled with drama, both high and low, because he was constantly being hit-on throughout their relationship, which she found to be quite a turn-on. While he was filming *One Million Years B.C.*, he was required to wear a full beard. She remembered how the day he no longer needed it he would shave a portion of it off and then they would make love for awhile and then he would shave off a bit more and repeat the lovemaking. "I loved helping John remove that beard!" John had also starred opposite Barbara Steele in *Black Sunday*. Both Barbara and Martine were well-acquainted with one another by then, and Martine was frequently mistaken for Barbara on film sets since they both were dark-haired and exotic. Martine used to make me laugh with her impersonation of Barbara by folding her arms over her head and then pretending to be a Venus flytrap opening her petals for the unwary fly. They were night and day as people but they both found themselves cast as dark divas in horror films, although Martine never got as typed as Steele because of her connection to the Bond films. They kept her more action-oriented than Barbara, whose one and only film for Fellini gave her a more art-film allure at the time.

"During the making *One Million Years B.C.* I became quite friendly with Hammer executive Michael Carreras and his wife, so as the film was coming to an end he approached me with this idea of doing a kind of spoof of B.C., which eventually became *Prehistoric Women*. His pitch to me was, 'Martine, you will play the Queen of a tribe of dark-haired amazons who falls for an English explorer who wanders into her domain.' I of course said, 'Absolutely, Darling. I am your Queen.' We did this film very quickly with Michael directing, which was very much like making a home-movie Hammer style. Once again my leading man, Michael Latimer, was less than my idea of bliss but whatever. My character was such fun to play it didn't matter. At one point my director brought out this enormous prop of the white rhino sporting a huge white tusk. Without really thinking about it, he suggested that I worship the tusk by rubbing my hands up and down it while invoking some chant. I simply looked at Michael Carreras and burst out laughing. 'You really want me to do that? I mean, really Michael, I've been asked to do some outrageous things in my time but giving a 1200-pound rhino a hand job has to be in a realm of its own.' The film is a cult classic today and while I was living in Hollywood I would get asked about this film almost more than any other. In fact I was at a party at Curtis Harrington's one night that was being given for Helmut Newton and his wife. Helmut was such a fan of bad movies that he made a deal with me that if I got him a tape of *Prehistoric Women* he would love to photograph me for one of his projects. I of course was happy to oblige."

"The other Hammer I did was of course *Dr. Jekyll and Sister Hyde*, which is a cult film as well. The interesting thing about that one was the actor who played Dr. Jekyll, a lovely fellow named Ralph Bates who sadly is no longer with us, began the film looking nothing like me at all and yet as the film progressed we really began to resemble each other in some strange way that only the camera picked up on. I mean, our hands began to look alike, etc. We did some publicity stills where we did look like brother and sister. The director on this one, Roy Ward Baker, was a seasoned pro to be sure, so we got along fine. However the producers kept after him to do more nudity than the script called for and at that point I had to put my foot down. I mean they even had second unit guys putting cameras under stairwells and such to try and get some extra bits, but it was all for nothing and in the end I think we did a classy film considering what they were really after."

Martine's only attempts at making an art film came with mixed results. Her first, entitled *Last Tango In Zagarol*, was as you can imagine a take-off on the Brando film, only as a comedy. The only drawback was her leading man, Franco Franchi, was no Brando; in fact he was a comic who was simply not funny. During the filming Franco attempted to seduce Martine in the crudest fashion. After having had enough of his groping, they had a scene in a bathtub, so in front of the entire crew Martine climbed into the tub and lowered her hands into the water as if she were looking for Franco's private parts. After a moment she looked over at the crew and in Italian said to them, "Where is it Franco? Oh, there it is! Oh my, it's so SMALL!" breaking up the crew while putting the sexist actor in his place for the duration of the shoot. The other film known as *Il Bacio* (*The Kiss*) proved a bit better, at least in terms of wardrobe. Martine was fitted for an elaborate Cocteau-inspired bra made out of disembodied hands, that took three hours to apply. Her role was that of a hedonistic sorceress. Her co-star, the wonderful Valentina Cortese, was playing a drug-addicted countess inspired by the real-life Marchesa Casati, who cast spells. They were required at one point to do a lesbian love scene so, to break the ice, Valentina took Martine to lunch where both ladies got a bit tipsy. When they returned to the set they surprised even themselves with the results, some of which made it into the film. Martine responded well when working with pros like Valentina. Later on she would make her only western, *A Bullet For The General* with Klaus Kinski, which also became one of her best films. She told me that in spite of Klaus's reputation they got on very well, and if circumstances had been a little different they might have had a fling. " There was definitely a connection there with Kinski and me."

By 1974 Martine found herself in Canada filming SEIZURE, a low-budget horror film marking the debut of director Oliver Stone and starring Jonathan Frid, still basking in his *Dark Shadows* fame. The original title for this was *Queen of Evil*, which was Martine's character in the film, however Oliver thought better of it, if for no other reason than avoiding the possible fallout from a film being called *Queen of Evil* that starred Jonathan Frid.

The production was a family affair from day one with cast and crew living commune-style in the old house that served as Frid's spooky old house in the film. Mary Woronov is among the cast, as is Herve Villechaize. Both became close with Martine as they partied together during the filming that lasted nearly a month. A few years later I would reunite Jonathan and Martine at my place in Beverly Hills when Frid found himself in a road company revival of *Arsenic And Old Lace* in Los Angeles. I knew Frid slightly by then and called him during the run to see if he would come by and surprise Martine, whom he had not seen since the film. He agreed straightaway to come by on a Sunday afternoon, which he did, and we had about 45 minutes to catch up before Martine's beloved black VW (which she named "Pearl") began to park in front of my patio. As soon as Jonathan saw her get out he remarked, "Well, we will not get a word in from now on, David. La Beswicke has landed." I wish I had videotaped the event because these two characters relived the whole shoot in my apartment. Frid remembered having to raise his voice to a bellow at one point when the off-set drama was too intense between cast and crew. Martine reminded Frid that she decided from the first day of shooting to romance the DP simply to keep him sober long enough to get the film made, and how strange Troy Donahue was acting all the time, speaking with a whisper on-and-off camera when he was not totally in the bag himself.

At this point in time Stone was in denial about the film, refusing to discuss it, but all that changed by the time the DVD finally made its appearance. Martine was quite taken with the young director during filming but from what I was hearing she had her hands full with all the in-house melodramatics that seemed to plague the set. Frid was charming throughout the afternoon, explaining with little regret on his part that his career never really took off after Shadows; he was really a stage actor at heart and had found his niche doing plays and readings across the country when the spirit struck him. It was in moments like this when I caught a glimpse of what Martine must have been like back in the day in Rome or London, when she was working on the films we have all come to know her from, and yet she could reminisce about it all without the least bit of regret.

The end of the 70's brought more and more TV work her way and by the time I knew her she was doing at least one guest appearance every other month. One of her favorites was an adventure show called *Cover Up* which brought male model Jon-Erik Hexum into the limelight, and he was not only

Martine Beswicke in 1995. Photo by Dan Golden.

one of the nicest guys around but drop-dead gorgeous. Martine was crazy about his voice, telling me what a tour-de-force they would have on-camera when their unique voices could share a scene. Sadly that was not to be because, as we all know, Hexum was killed onset in a freak accident. I was in London at the time and found out about it on the news. Martine did two episodes of the show with his replacement, Anthony Hamilton, a classically-trained ballet dancer-turned-model. I remember Martine calling me after the first day on the show feeling very down because her love scene with Tony was falling flat and she could not figure out why, since they really hit it off when they met before taping! . It did not take long for her to discover that Tony was gay, and that accounted for the lack of fireworks in their first initial scenes together. Well, once she knew this, they worked it all out and became great friends off camera as well, to the extent of spending weekends together with their respective boyfriends. Hamilton was on a short list to play James Bond when Pierce Brosnan could not get out of his Remington Steele contract. The tabloids got hold of a shot of Tony out partying at an after-hours bar called Probe, which was infamous as the gay bar immortalized in *American Gigolo*. The result was no James Bond for Hamilton; he did however continue to work right up until his death from AIDS in 1995.

During the spring of 1980 Martine accepted an offer from Cannon Films to be the third actress to play Xavier Hollander in *The Happy Hooker Goes Hollywood*, stepping into the footsteps of Lynn Redgrave and Joey Heatherton to give her spin on the fun-loving madam. Cannon films were then at the height of their productivity with dozens of films being made around the world (I covered this aspect of their productions, including HOOKER, in the January 2008 Camp David column A CANNON-BURY TALE [1]). Martine was optimistic from the beginning about this production since she would be the star sharing bon mots with scene-stealers like Phil Silvers and Richard Deacon. However her leading man was to be played by Adam West, whom she thought too unlikely a choice for scenes involving her character to be in lust with him. This was even more problematic when they began filming as it took all of Martine's suspension of belief to get this scene on film. She told me, "I really went the distance with Adam West on HOOKER, since I was required to have two on-camera orgasms with a man I would not be attracted to otherwise, but that's why they call it acting." Fortunately during the production Martine was happily involved with a very handsome boyfriend which more than evened-out the chores of lusting after an aging Batman.

The Happy Hooker Goes Hollywood opened nationally a few months later and we all went down to the local cinema on Hollywood Boulevard to see its first run on the big screen. Martine, looking adorable wearing a cowboy hat, arrived with her boyfriend in tow. Afterwards we all returned to her place for champagne and giggles about her giving Adam West a climax in the movie. In spite of her misgivings about West, and the producers' attempts to add soft-core when her back was turned, I thought she did well in an exploitation film that was never anything more than a tease in the first place. It reminded me somewhat of the old AIP beach-party flicks, except this time people actually got laid in a tasteful fashion for 1980.

One of the more difficult assignments for Martine during this time was playing a semi-regular on the soap *Days of Our Lives* which meant waking up at 3am and having to run lines right up to going on camera live in front of millions of people. The stress was of course enormous and yet Martine seemed to thrive on the energy of it, at least for a while. I used to tape her appearances for her and I remember her calling me towards the end asking me to tape a certain day to see if she survived the shooting. When I asked what this was all about she explained that if the camera panned down and there was a long shot that showed her body she might survive for another paycheck. I dutifully recorded the moment when her character was gunned down, and no, the camera did not pan down, and that was the end of Martine on *Days of Our Lives*.

"I have been very fortunate during every aspect of my career in the sense of knowing what I am capable of doing as an actress. I mean, one must work with the face and body you were given and in my case my looks always got me through the door. In Hollywood it takes far more than just being beautiful because the town is filled with stunning-looking men and women every day of the week. I made the decision to leave Europe and come to Hollywood because this is where you must be if you are really interested in having a career. I have made some unforgettable friendships here that will stay with me all of my life, so I will never regret the time spent in Hollywood because I have had a ball."

There are so many memories I share with her that I cannot possibly recount them all; I mean dancing to the Disco heat at Studio One with Calvin Lockhart, or watching in dismay as I dropped my dancing partner mid-air in front of an amused Anthony Hopkins at the Variety Arts during his opening-night party for *The Tempest*, or getting hopelessly lost in Chinatown with John Carpenter in tow.

The list goes on. I am however proud to have been the one to divert her attention to doing memorabilia conventions, so for over a year she and I traveled to New Jersey and back doing Chiller Theater as well as several other venues. I was officially her manager, securing the bookings and taking care of the cash. These were the best of times: waiting for her to collect me in the early morning hours when we did them locally and heading to the Ray Courts autograph show, her ritual of summoning the "great spirit" to give us a positive and hopefully profitable day. The public for these shows were usually respectful and for the most part fun. We did have our share of crazies, including some rather rude questions about her sex life. On one occasion someone asked, "Just how big is Sean Connery's cock?" I must say she handled the situation beautifully, without a hint of anger; just a laugh, which is all one can do in these situations.

One of the most memorable conventions was the one we did with Udo Keir in San Jose, with our friend Mary Woronov as well, although we flew up from LAX with just Udo who, under any circumstances, is a handful. The convention was a bust due to the weather so all of us just sat out the convention part of it and spent our time chatting away with the other child stars from yesteryear until 5pm, then went down to the cocktail lounge to blow off the experience as best we could (I have already written about one of the other encounters we enjoyed in the May 2008 installment of Camp David entitled "THE HILLS HAVE EYES...AND AN OPEN BAR").

By 1998 Martine had somewhat retreated up to a small community near Santa Barbara, where for a year she ran a restaurant (appropriately called

Martine Beswicke as Sister Hyde in *Dr. Jekyll and Sister Hyde.*

Delilah's). As with everything she does she put her heart and soul into this venue, only to discover that she was working day and night with no time off since she was the boss. After a year Martine made the decision to return to England to be closer to her Mother and sister. I knew this was a difficult choice for her since her extended family, all her friends of the last two decades, were all here in Southern California.

Once she made her mind up the only thing left to do was organize a farewell party and that she did in short order. I received this invitation by mail:

THE GRAND DUCHY OF DRAGONIA
CORDIALLY INVITES YOU TO ATTEND
A JUBILEE IN HONOR OF HER HIGHNESS
THE DUCHESS OF DRAGONIA
ON THE OCCASION OF HER RETURN TO THE MOTHERLAND
(GOD SAVE THE QUEENS)
BY ORDER OF THE COURT THIS REGAL DAY OF
MERRYMAKING SHALL COMMENCE
MARCH 17TH 1998
FROM 4PM UNTIL THE DUCHESS IS SPENT

The merrymaking did indeed last all through the night with guests like Tab Hunter and most of her many close friends from days gone by under the Hollywood sign. I could never really say goodbye to someone like Martine because she will always be in my heart, which is so right for a woman who made hearts her signature. Martine's heart was always open, allowing love to find its way in.

Memorials

Dan O'Bannon (back to camera) directs Clu Gulagher and James Karen in *Return of the Living Dead*. Photo by Dan Golden.

19

In Hollywood No One Can Hear You Scream

Dan O'Bannon

THE RECENT PASSING OF GENRE WRITER/DIRECTOR Dan O'Bannon caused me to unearth my picture file on his directorial debut, *Return of the Living Dead*, which since its first screening has steadily built a substantial horror fan base as a classic zombie film in the tradition of the original *Night of the Living Dead*. This act created a Pandora effect, unleashing a flood of memories I thought long forgotten about my time on the *Return of the Living Dead* set during the months of May and June of 1984. When the Mike Dalling Company first asked me to cover this film for them I thought it was a vampire film, agreeing at once to go down to the Burbank location with my photographer, Dan Golden, and check out the scene.

Looking back I can better understand why Dan O'Bannon was so paranoid about the press in Hollywood, especially concerning his image, since he was after all an outsider, a maverick railing against the system he so wanted to be a part of. Yet he refused to play the game. It is very telling then that when I asked him what his favorite H. P. Lovecraft story was he replied, *The Outsider*, a short story filled with the intense longing to escape from a desolate castle into the outside world only to discover at the climax that he, too, was a monster unable to take his place among the living. When I asked about his favorite work of Poe he chose the poem *Alone*, a piece in which even Lovecraft could see himself in the words, "From childhood's hour I have not been as others were." Neither Dan O'Bannon nor his literary idols could see themselves as part of the mainstream no matter what endorsements came their way in terms of praise or success. Dan wrote blockbuster screenplays like *Total Recall* and *Alien*, yet never achieved the kind of mega-success of, say, a Joe Eszterhas, who could turn in a treatment and receive a million-dollar advance for rubbish like *Showgirls*. The last time I spoke to Dan was about the time of his second directorial effort, *The Resurrected*, ironically an adaptation of Lovecraft's *The Case of Charles Dexter Ward* (filmed once before by Roger Corman as *The Haunted Palace*). Dan had chosen to frame the tale in the present-day with a neo-noir motif and, to his credit, it was somewhat successful as a stand-up Lovecraft film with Chris Sarandon giving a creepy performance in the dual role of Charles Dexter Ward and his evil ancestor Joseph Curwin. Dan was, as usual, at odds with the company who produced it, as they cut his film without his approval, de-fanging the film of its blood and gore and trimming away his vision yet again. Dan would get his revenge at the end of his life by writing his own adaptation of Lovecraft's most famous creation, *The Necronomicon*. Dan himself was always an outsider, first as a child his parents did not understand, then arriving in Hollywood after film school only to find the same situation on a larger scale, failing to adapt successfully in what he regarded as a nest of vipers cannibalizing themselves in franchise film-making.

Sometimes these on-set encounters can be fun, since you get to not only engage with the director and crew while they are at work but (as with this film) also lunch with the actors and hopefully stay long enough to observe some cinema magic in the process. My first experience on the *Living Dead* set was anything but fun since I arrived just in time to witness actor Clu Gulager square off with his director in a verbal shouting match that left the crew silent and tense. Now, before I go on with this it is important to know that both Clu and Dan, who would lock horns several more times before this film would wrap, came out of the process the best of friends and remained so until Dan's death this past December.

After witnessing this encounter I stayed away from both men until lunch broke. As I entered the area set aside for the cast and crew to eat I saw Clu heading straight in my direction, whereupon he greeted me like a long lost relation. "You are the journalist from the Mike Dalling office, are you not? I am Clu Gulager. Please just call me Clu." He then walked me over to where the food was being served and together we took a table and sat down to our lunch. Clu was concerned about what I had just witnessed and was determined to deflate any bad press that might come from it. He explained that what I observed was a very heavy scene in the film where his character was supposed to react with rage and frustration over the hopelessness of the situation his character was in and at that moment someone had walked into his range of vision causing him to lose his concentration altogether, which in turn caused him to lose it for a moment since, in his view, the director is supposed to keep the set free of distractions, among other things.

It was impossible not to like this man. He and I became fast friends during that first lunch and I for one understood how that might just be the straw that would break the camel's back at that moment. I later discovered that Dan had made more than a few enemies on this shoot and he knew it. O'Bannon was a product of USC Film School and was at that moment practicing the auteur theory they teach so well at that institution. In other words the director has a vision and in order for that vision to reach the screen he has to take command of every department, telling each and every crew member and technician their job so they can do it better, thus making a better film all the way around. Most of the other actors found Dan to be somewhat difficult but it was all for a good cause since he was, after all, the very talented screenwriter who wrote *Alien*. Almost everyone on the set was in agreement about one thing and that was Dan O'Bannon had written a great script for them to make, which accomplished the difficult task of making a horror film funny. It was a parody of George Romero's film and that was exactly what was needed.

The next time I went on-set was to watch the scene where the yellow cadaver played by Terry Houlihan comes to life and causes all kinds of havoc. Terry was covered in this yellow body make-up with a bald cap in place so he all but resembled a mannequin from hell. The set was filled with faux toxic fumes from the gas leaks that set the stage in the script for the living dead to return in the first place. This made the whole set smell like black flag insect spray. It was never a comfortable shoot under any circumstances, both in temperament and design. There was a tenseness going on with Dan as he was under great pressure not only from the producers but from his special-effects people, including make-up which had to be checked and doubled-checked as so much depended on every aspect of the zombies looking just right. I remember that the producers were worried about the zombies moving way too fast in some scenes to match what they thought an audience had come to expect from their zombies onscreen. If only they could have imagined the end result, everybody would have just chilled and really dug the scene.

As I watched Terry the yellow cadaver come to life, check his marks once more, then go back behind the door, there was a break for some tech stuff and I had my first chance to speak to Dan face-to-face. He was polite with me but there was always a distance since I was after all the press, so watch out! I kept thinking all during the rehearsals for this scene that it was so like that scene in Howard Hawks' *The Thing*, where all the men are watching the door knowing that at any moment a bloodsucking thing was going to break in and kill them. I had this scene running in my head so I mentioned it to Dan and bang! It was like a bell went off in his head, and he looked at me as if he had just discovered my existence. "I fucking love *The Thing*! Hawks is like one of my heroes. You know, I was hoping for that moment with this scene as well, and now you have confirmed my thoughts. This is great! Thank you so much for noticing." From that moment on Dan O'Bannon liked me and respected the fact that we both were film buffs. I was no longer the dreaded press but a colleague. This was as good as it got on the set of *Return of the Living Dead*, and a memory I will always hold dear when I think of Dan.

Dan O'Bannon arrived at this point in his career with an enviable resume of credits, the most exotic of which was his involvement with Alejandro Jodorowsky's ill fated adaptation of Frank Herbert's *Dune*. Dan flew over to Paris where he literally wowed Jodorowsky with his talent and creativity. He was put in charge of all the special-effects, working for six months before returning to LA to do more work on the project. This all came to an end when Dan received word from Paris that the money failed to materialize, ending a magical experience with the dean of avant-garde filmmakers. His career from his days after USC, beginning with the filming of *Dark Star* alongside John Carpenter, are well documented elsewhere so let's just say that Dan had more than enough background to direct. He just needed this baptism of fire with *Living Dead* to understand that a good director hires the right people from day one, allowing them to do their job while you as a director involve yourself, keeping it all in focus. Dan was never much of a "people person" and this led to much of the animosity felt by cast and crew during the making of the film. There were moments during the filming like the day Dan was set to film the weird little guy they brought on set to play one of the misshapen zombies. One of the more unpleasant requirements was that he actually eats calf brains on-camera. Well the crew was up in arms about this and Dan, to his credit, walked over and ate some calf brains in front of everyone present, remarking afterwards, "I would never ask an actor to do anything on camera I would not do myself."

James Karen remembered the shoot as being very physical from his standpoint because his character was so manic and did so much jumping around. But there is one thing on which both Jimmy and Clu both were in agreement, and that was how good the script was, really funny and edgy in ways a zombie film had never been allowed to be; even *Zombies On Broadway* left their zombie to react by the book, relying on the two comic actors to add the humor (which on that film was in short supply, making Lugosi the only reason to remember it now). I will always be grateful for *Return of the Living Dead* as the film which brought both Jimmy and Clu into my circle of friends where they have remained all these years later.

It is well known that Tobe Hooper was set to direct *Return of the Living Dead* when his schedule changed abruptly, allowing Dan, the screenwriter, to take over. Time has been more than kind to this film, allowing it to turn into a classic first-of-its-kind punk-rock zombie flick, and this in turn caused a change in Dan himself as time went by. He actually got involved with the fans' grass roots campaign to get *Return of the Living Dead* out on DVD, sending the internet fans flocking to dozens of websites devoted to the film

Dan O'Bannon at home in Santa Monica (1985). Photo by Dan Golden.

to write and email their demands to the studio directly, the result of which was the deluxe edition of *Return of the Living Dead*. The real pleasure of this DVD is Dan O'Bannon's personal observations about the film while he was still well enough to make them.

Soon after the film was completed I was invited to spend some interview-time with Dan at his small house in Santa Monica where he greeted both me and photographer Dan Golden in his bathrobe because his stomach was bothering him that day. Looking back it is now clear Dan suffered far more than he let on about the illness which would ultimately take his life. Away from the set Dan was more laid back and reflective about the experience. I think he was beginning to feel he had created something that was unique, although at that point there was no way of knowing just how popular the film was going to be. Dan was like a proud dad, showing off his "outer office" which contained floor-to-ceiling scripts, drafts and treatments of his entire output as a writer. In rows divided by shelves, he had every draft of *Alien* from the early *They Bite* right through to the *Star Beast* and beyond, to the version we all have come to know as Ridley Scott's masterpiece. Dan was always savvy enough to acknowledge Ridley's contribution which sort of reminded me in a strange sort of way of how Robert Bloch regarded Hitchcock, the only difference being Dan O'Bannon was a far more accomplished screenwriter than Bloch. Bob was really a novelist with a real talent for the short story. His screenplays were always rather routine in comparison to his writing.

The afternoon went by pleasantly enough with Dan regaling us with tales of Jodorowsky and a couple of rather wicked observations on John Carpenter, not to mention producer Tom Fox. At one point I asked if we could do stills of the two of us together and then some portraits of just him. Dan reflected for a moment and then asked if we could hold back printing them for a time since he really wanted to enjoy being private a bit longer, reasoning that it was just a matter of time before his fame would overwhelm his life to the extent that he would be mobbed in public once his fans knew what he looked like. And you know what turns out to be sublimely funny about Dan O'Bannon? He really meant it.

20

Where Has My Easy Rider Gone?

Dennis Hopper

As I sadly watched the frail figure of 73 year old Dennis Hopper make his way to the podium on Hollywood Boulevard to modestly accept his long overdue star on its walk of fame, he seemed like a man falling from a great height, and his entire career began to flash before my eyes. From his humble beginnings as a star struck youth from Dodge City, Kansas, to the back lots of Warner Bros where an 18 year old Hopper would sign his first contract, Dennis Hopper always had a destiny to fulfill, not just on the silver screen but more importantly as an artist.

When Dennis's family relocated to San Diego in 1949, his artistic life was about to take root with his very first contact at the La Jolla Playhouse, which turned out to be Mary Price – the second wife of Vincent Price. Price would prove to be a lifelong mentor to the young man, allowing him his first contact with artists like Jackson Pollack, Franz Kline and Richard Diebenkorn. Price also introduced Hopper to his personal collection of art which influenced Dennis in time to his own style of painting – abstract expressionism.

As Hopper's artistic life began to unfold, so did his acting career, and soon he secured a seven year contract with Warner Bros beginning with, ironically, a small part in *I Died A Thousand Times*. This would lead to the life-altering encounter with James Dean in the legendary *Rebel Without a Cause*. It would be with Hopper's role as "Goon" and his now famous first line of dialogue, "What are we going to do with him", that his second mentoring would begin in earnest with his devotion to James Dean. Dean taught Hopper the imaginary line: the difference between what was "real" – the life of

Dennis Hopper in *The Last Movie*.

crew behind the camera, and the "unreal" make believe – acting in front of the camera. Dean told him to abandon gestures and simply react to situations as you would in real life.

Hopper's lifelong pursuit of photography would begin on *Rebel Without a Cause* as well. Dean had opened the door not only to Dennis's acting style, but gave him perspective in never cropping a photo, always going for the full frame. It was James Dean who first told Hopper he would direct films somewhere down the line. The next film they would work on together would also be their last. While filming *Giant* for George Stevens, Dean died in the now infamous car crash that killed a man but created an icon. *Giant* was a turning point for Hopper, as his performance was considered Oscar worthy, and soon he was on his way. Dean's death seven days after Hopper did his last scene devastated him in ways he did not realize at the time. Warner Bros put him in several projects until his volatile encounter with director Henry Hathaway on the film *From Hell to Texas which* would lead to his expulsion from Hollywood.

The ghost of James Dean had influenced more than Hopper's acting style, as he was now branded as "difficult" to impossible to work with as an actor. This in turn allowed him to pursue his other talent in photography in which his star would shine as brightly as it ever did on film, something Dean was also aware of in his young protégé. Eventually Hopper would make his way to the East coast in 1961 where the "method" was in full swing under the influence of Lee Strasburg's actor's studio. There he would learn the phrase "sense memory" for the first time, adding to Dean's advice. Hopper could now tap into the reality of any acting scene by simply using his own life experience, to recall things, which is what method acting is all about.

When Dennis Hopper finally returned to Hollywood, he was married to Brook Hayward, the daughter of Leland Hayward, the producer of Broadway blockbusters like *The Sound of Music* and *South Pacific*. Dennis and his bride took up residence in Bel-Air and began to live artistic lives in what was becoming the swinging sixties in Hollywood. A fire in mid 1961 would see Hopper's home burn to the ground and with it all of his abstract expressionism. Not one painting would survive the flames. His photography, however, was spared because Dennis was in the middle of showing his work in a gallery at the time of the fire.

By 1963 Dennis Hopper was a well-established photographer and artist with many friends on both coasts. This was also the year he would meet Andy Warhol, introducing him to the Hollywood art scene with a series of parties and exhibitions. Dennis would also appear in what is now regarded as Warhol's first movie, *Tarzan and Jane Regained...Sort Of*. This 16mm production involved Hopper wandering through the rotting canals of Venice, California looking somewhat bewildered while at one point taking off his shirt and beating his chest a la Tarzan. Hopper would also make a life defining purchase at this time by paying $75 for a Warhol Campbell's Soup Can. Hopper's collection of art would achieve epic proportions as time went on, and this was something he worked on even through his darkest days of substance abuse, which almost ended his artistic as well as his earthly life at one point after the success of *Easy Rider*.

In 1967 Hopper would stop taking photos for the next decade as he began to pursue his dream of directing films. It would be while working on Roger Corman's *The Trip* that Hopper would be given his first chance to direct a scene as well as second unit along with co-star Peter Fonda. This film was important to Hopper's artistic vision as well as a lifestyle, since the country's youth was undergoing a radical transformation that would forever be known as the "counterculture movement," the Love generation, or perhaps the more lyrical Age of Aquarius. *The Trip* was also written by Jack Nicholson, who would create the trio that would later make *Easy Rider* the signature film of a generation.

The second opportunity for Hopper to test his directing skills would come in the form of a biker flick known as *The Glory Stompers* for which Dennis directed several scenes. This and *The Trip* made a great sounding board for what was to follow in 1968 when Bob Rafelson and Bert Schneider agreed to finance another "biker" film, this one named *Easy Rider*. The title comes from an old bawdy Mae West line "Where has my easy rider gone?" that stayed in screenwriter Terry Southern's mind and then made its way into legend.

In the sixties, the public of the day turned away from Hollywood because the studio system was ill-prepared to grasp the paradigmatic alteration that was currently in the process of overwhelming the arts as a whole. The counterculture was flexing its newly found muscles with the "new kids on the block" – Kubrick…Nichols…Penn…Altman and Polanski, with Dennis Hopper climbing to the top of that list with *Easy Rider*. One can look back at all of the cinema of that era and begin to revaluate Dennis Hopper's three films as a director as a "trilogy," *Easy Rider* is really somewhat inspired by Kenneth Anger's *Scorpio Rising*, as well as being the bastard son of Brando's *The Wild One*, with a dash of Conrad's *Heart of Darkness* grafted on, as Fonda and Hopper ride their coke filled Harleys into hell. Instead of going west young man they go east to their predestined doom. In *The Last Movie*, set in Peru, the Cocaine capital of the world, Hopper creates an environment filled with Brechtian devices so that we, the audience, can take a front row seat for the demise of Western culture as well as the American dream.

The western genre itself is ravaged by homage through Hopper's camera lens while presided over by one of its auteurs, Samuel Fuller, basically playing himself. The film is on one level a tripped out riff on *The Treasure of Sierra Madre* with Hopper's on screen persona – the stuntman – staying behind after filming is over to search for gold and drugs. The specter of James Dean hovers over this set as well, with Hopper setting up a store front and naming it "Jimmy's place," and rightly so since in Hopper's universe James Dean will also have a place and a time to influence Hopper's art. The legend of Hopper wearing a ring on set given to him by Dean is of interest here because it represents an energy, an occult power for Dennis to draw from. The bronze and silver Aztec artifact was always on his finger, where he was seen rubbing it for luck, or to draw some of its supposed power. Dennis dreamt of making a film with his mentor, Vincent Price, playing what else but an elder magician, with Hopper as his apprentice who owns the ring but keeps it locked away since he already knows its power and has no need to wear it. Price is killed at one point and the ring stolen, but Hopper wins in the end by using its power with the knowledge left to him by his master. I had hoped one day Dennis would actually make the film, but now it is yet another lost horizon in a long career.

The third film, *Out of The Blue*, is more or less a punk era extension of *Rebel Without a Cause*. Hopper took this film over in mid-production, altering the concept into his own dark vision, with the inspired addition of Neil

Young, not to mention the punk rock take on the proceedings. During each and every one of these productions Hopper still maintained his high level of interest in art and painting, making him even more unique as a filmmaker/artist working within the system in America. He would continue this examination one step further when he directed *Colors* later, his take on the urban scene in LA with street gang violence, thanks to his star Sean Penn, who suggested he direct the film.

Dennis Hopper has made more than 120 films, during which time he collected art from such longtime friends as Warhol, Jasper Johns, Edward Ruscha, Marcel Duchamp and Bruce Conner, whose style inspired the editing of *Easy Rider*. He has worn the four hats of expression with vigor, being an actor, painter, director, and photographer while achieving fame in success in each and every one.

I chose two of his films in particular to try and explain how much his acting has worked its spell on my imagination over the years. While I am a fan as well as being vastly entertained by his voice and off kilter personality, he remains very much like Klaus Kinski, an actor who has stared into the abyss and something has indeed stared back. After years of substance abuse Hopper got clean and sober by the time of *Blue Velvet*, yet ironically this was his most druggy, out of control performance ever, and also one of his greatest. The creation of Frank Booth is a tour de force by which all such other manic attempts will be judged. What sense memory could Hopper have channeled to bring this character into being? When David Lynch gave Hopper the part, he was told by the actor that he really had no other options, since Frank Booth was Dennis Hopper's evil twin; at least in that dark universe David Lynch tends to inhabit.

One of the mysteries of *Blue Velvet* is just how much was cut prior to its release? I have seen stills of the infamous pool hall sequence, which was apparently cut to shave the running time, with yet another murder left on the cutting room floor. There was, however, another moment which I am sorry is not in the final cut and that is the sequence when Frank takes Kyle and the Blue lady on a nightmarish joy ride to what Brad Dorf's character describes as "pussy heaven," a place our young lead may or may not have gone before. Now when Kyle punches Frank you would have thought this was it; Frank would kill him. But as Hopper revealed at a press conference I attended to promote *Blue Velvet*:

"When he punches me that is when I take him out of the car and put lipstick all over him.... What actually happened was I put all this lipstick on Kyle, then force him to take down his pants where I draw a lip-line all around his ass and then sodomize him. When he wakes up in the field the next morning his pants are down around his ankles and there's lipstick smudged all over his ass. That was the scene, my friends, but David decided not to go with it...

you know *Blue Velvet* was easy for me to do because David is not only a director but he is also the writer and, more than that, a painter. He knows exactly what he wants visually. This is a perfect working relationship. Every single thing in the film I did was scripted....wonderful experience from day one."

When Hopper was working on *Apocalypse Now*, he was far from sober and it showed, yet his performance was so intense he owned the screen whenever he was on it. After years of wanting to work with Brando, by the time it came to pass, Hopper was still too out there for Brando's taste, so his only request to his director was "Francis, please keep Dennis away from me if at all possible." As soon as Hopper wrapped on the film he flew directly to Spain to play – what else – a drugged-out junkie named "chicken" in a film that can only be described as a mess, entitled *Las Flores Del Vico* or *The Sky Is Falling*...a vague reference to the Chicken Little fable, I suppose. This film also stars Carroll Baker as 'Treasure,' a washed up star from Hollywood, which is pretty much what she was at that time, having fallen from grace after HARLOW as well as the fab *Carpetbaggers*, which is her best work in my humble opinion. Anyway this film is a must for anyone following the career of Dennis Hopper because it is a textbook of Hopperisms that would flourish to greater effect a few years later in *Blue Velvet*. A hard film to find but one that is worth the effort once you have, this film also is badly edited, photographed, you name it, which is surprising since the director is Silvio Narizzano who gave us *Georgy Girl* as well as *Blue Velvet*, that really cult western with Terence Stamp, and last but not least *Die, Die My Darling* with Tallulah Bankhead. How could a pro like Silvio make such an abomination? Well, only Silvio knows, and so far nobody has ever gotten around to asking....

One of the first projects Hopper signed on for after his stay in rehab during 1986 was the long awaited sequel to Tobe Hoopers ground breaking classic *The Texas Chainsaw Massacre*. This sequel became the cornerstone in the three picture deal Hooper made with Cannon films, the other two being a remake of *Invaders From Mars* and *Lifeforce*. As Dennis himself said at the time "My agent begged me not to make this film, he warned me that it would destroy my career all over again. I listened to his advice as well as some of my friends all saying basically the same thing and then went down to Texas and made it anyway. I am here to tell you I made more money on that film than I did on *Blue Velvet*."

Dennis Hopper also celebrated his 50th birthday on the set of *Texas Chainsaw Massacre II* with a party telling the press at the time doing this film made it possible for him to play lots of golf with his pal Willie Nelson. As far as his performance, Dennis may have been clean and sober but his acting in this film does not disappoint as he emotes way over the top yet again preaching the Lord while wielding a mean chainsaw.

Dennis Hopper as Frank Booth in *Blue Velvet*.

The film was at the time a severe disappointment to the fans of the original; however, this is no longer the case today. A new DVD special edition "the Gruesome edition" has come out ranking *Texas Chainsaw Massacre II* as a neglected cult classic whose black comedy was misunderstood at the time of its original release. While it borrowed shamelessly from *Motel Hell*, it has Tom Sarvini special effects to recommend it as some of his best work. One look at Rob Zombie's *The Devils Rejects* and you can see the influence was more than homage as Zombie lifts chunks of plot from Hopper's film into his own script. As with most of Dennis Hopper's film work one has to keep coming back to fully appreciate his legacy. While this was one of Hopper's rare excursions into the horror genre, it certainly paved the way for his tour de force as Frank Booth.

The lasting image which first began my awareness of Dennis Hopper was a still Curtis Harrington shot of him, reflected in a broken mirror. This was, I believe, his first lead, playing the young sailor in Curtis's homage to the films of Val Lewton, *Night Tide*, which, like the Warhol short, was filmed in the canals of Venice, California. I spent one evening a few years ago with the leading lady of that film, Linda Lawson, and her memories were clear but not too flattering regarding her relationship with Hopper at the time of filming.

"Dennis was very talented and so excited about playing a lead in Curtis's film, which was done for no money at all, so we all pitched in to make it work. I invited Dennis over to run lines one afternoon, and when he arrived at my apt he walked in and went straight back to my kitchen and climbed under the table and would not come out. He was really scary when he chose to act like this. Afterwards we worked together only on location or with Curtis present. I warned Dennis that if he acted that way again I would walk off the film. The end result was Curtis really did not like me that much in any case, and we never saw each other again once the film was wrapped. It is bittersweet now since I get so much fan mail about that film, and now it is a cult film with articles being done about it all the time, but it was not a pleasant experience for me because of Dennis being in such a weird place emotionally..."

It is only fitting that after all these years Dennis Hopper now resides in Venice, California, where so much of his early life as both an artist and an actor took place. His legacy is still a work in progress yet his impact is ageless and will continue to inspire future generations of artists who will ponder the question, "What are we going to do with him?"

WITHIN A MAN OF LIGHT..THERE IS LIGHT
WITHIN A MAN OF DARKNESS...THERE IS DARKNESS

21

The Randy Gnome of King's Road

Aubrey Morris

THOSE OF YOU THAT HAVE BEEN FOLLOWING my exploits are probably aware of my endless fascination with British Character actors and it has been my good fortune over the years to have made the acquaintance of some of the most eccentric as well as the most talented in Show business. However once in a blue moon an actor you have admired from afar turns up in your life and through a series of seemingly unrelated events becomes your worst nightmare instead of a warm and fuzzy edition to your memoirs.

Such is the case with the incomparable Aubrey Morris, a staple in British television and films since the late 1950s. Mr. Morris looks and sometimes acts a bit like Freddie Jones but never had the opportunities which place Mr. Jones in the stratosphere of the elite in the acting profession. Aubrey Morris is perhaps best known for his perverse turn in Stanley Kubrick's *A Clockwork Orange* where he manages in just a few moments of screen time to be creepier than Keith Moon as the lascivious "Uncle Ernie" in *Tommy*. As Mr. Deltoid the "guidance counselor," Aubrey's body language and line readings indicate a more homoerotic subtext in guiding young Malcolm McDowell into the nearest bedsit for a quickie.

While the Kubrick film may be his finest hour upon the silver screen for most fans, I came to know him best from countless British television shows like *The Avengers*, *Danger Man*, *The Saint* and *Return of The Saint*. Aubrey was also in the legendary BBC production of *Cold Comfort Farm* with the fantastic Alistair Sims. I really began to appreciate his work when he started to turn up in horror films during the late sixties, early 1970s like *The Night*

Aubrey Morris in *The Wicker Man*.

Caller From Outer Space, Blood From The Mummy's Tomb, and Tobe Hooper's bloated vampire Sci-Fi epic *Lifeforce*.

Since I lived half of my life around Hollywood and its varied locations it is certainly not a surprise to find many of your favorite actors shopping and dining about the neighborhood. And it was on just such a night around mid 2003 that I spotted our Mr. Deltoid in the flesh waiting in line for a prescription in the pharmacy section of *Pavillions*, an all night market in West Hollywood right on Santa Monica Boulevard. At first I thought about treating this encounter like a birdwatcher sans keeping a diary with entries like "Spotted Aubrey Morris in the pharmacy....hope whatever is wrong with him isn't fatal." My partner Chris Dietrich was with me that night and knowing how much I enjoy these sightings pushed me onward into making myself known since we all know being shy is not one of my hang-ups. Chris then said the magic words "why don't you do an interview for Films in Review. You know Roy would get a kick out of you running into him like this". So now that I had a purpose I got up and went over to where he was standing and spoke to him. "Mr. Morris? Yes...he said looking me up and down before speaking again "do we know each other? he said with a bit of that half smile he has down pat from years of mugging for the camera's. No we don't but I am a fan of your work and would love to interview you for Films in Review which is now online. On I went for about 10 minutes until they called him over to the counter for his order and by then we had exchanged phone numbers and I was expected to call and set up a meeting.

The following day I called and got his answering machine so we played phone tag for a day or so until I finally caught him at home. The very first conversation I had with him was slightly uncomfortable because of what he managed to say within the first few seconds of chatting.... "Oh before we go on are you planning to bugger me...I mean it's been so long since I've had really good shag." Well, I mean thanks for sharing but are you high or what?

I assumed he was putting me on and since I only really knew him from his films I just took it for what I always chalk up to being British as well as eccentric, not to mention Aubrey was after all Mr. Deltoid. I mean, really.

In spite of the little alarms ringing in the back of my head I invited him over for a drink at the guest house I was then renting in the hopelessly pretentious section of Beverly Hills you are so used to seeing on TV shows like 90210. I was not too concerned about the randy behavior of our Mr. Morris because I was not going to be alone with him since Chris would be there to make sure I wasn't fucked to death by this oversexed gnome from across the pond.

Aubrey Morris arrived on time and since it was not easy to find the entrance to my part of the grounds unless you had been there before, I walked out to the front of the main house and walked him inside. I noticed that he was driving a new car and before I could comment further he explained that he needed a decent looking car to make the rounds of the casting offices or for auditions. Aubrey is not unlike most of the actors I've met from England, like Michael Gough for example, who always refer to themselves as "jobbing actors" which means these guys do not sit by the phone and wait for offers; they get out and make a difference.

Aubrey came in and immediately asked if we had any tea as he had a pill he needed to take....I was just about to offer him a cocktail and so this changed the program ever so slightly since I had tea but no cream. Aubrey, always polite, explained that he was the kind of Englishmen who always had his tea white; however, he needed something to down his medication so he made an exception. Having survived our first obstacle I then began to chat about his films. I had looked all day for some stills of him that I should have had in the archive and managed to find a really camp photo of Aubrey with his throat torn out from his Hammer film *Blood from the Mummy's Tomb*. When I showed him the still he made such a fuss over it that I simply made a present of it to him on the spot. He then proceeded to tell about working with the director of *Blood from the Mummy's Tomb*, the late Selt Holt. "I was onset the day Selt had his fatal attack. In fact he collapsed in my arms. Selt got a severe case of the hiccups which triggered his heart attack and Selt died straight away." Aubrey remembered being asked to arrive at the studio early one morning to choose a throat for his death scene. He was ushered into a make-up room that had an entire wall of torn throats to examine as the entire cast except for the stunning Hammer queen Valerie Leon all die at one point or another by this gruesome means. Jimmy Villars and I stayed drunk after Selt died and so I never bothered to see the finished film at all.

As we were in the midst of our interview Aubrey asked where the loo was and then took his leave…in a few moments he came back into the living room and nearly fell over. I asked what was wrong and he explained that he was diabetic and needed something sweet immediately, so Chris and I scrambled around the house finally finding some of those little packets of sugar which he ate at once. By this time he was looking really ill and both Chris and I felt he needed to rest. At that point he asked if one of us could drive him back home as he did not think it was safe for him to get behind the wheel feeling like he did. So we decided that Chris would drive him back in his car and I would follow in mine to bring him back. We managed to get Aubrey into his car and then I followed them back to King's road in West Hollywood where Aubrey lived in a complex of buildings that took up the entire block of King's road in the heart of boy's town.

Aubrey insisted we come in until he felt himself again. At this point I was frightened that he was going to die at any moment as he was at that time in his seventies and not in the best shape as well. Once inside his place it was at once comfortable and very much a bachelor pad in so much as it was filled with books and scripts with the basic clutter one accumulates having moved from another country. Hollywood never really feels like home for a lot of people in the first place. Aubrey seemed to be coming around to his old self and began to act as host showing us around his apt, giving both of us this weird little wink as he showed us his bedroom. I remember him remarking it was almost the largest room in the flat to have had so little in the way of activity…a line we just let slide away as I noticed he had a cabinet filled with video tapes. He quickly explained that these were his "show reels" and complete versions of some of his movies and tv appearances. I noticed one tape marked Suez 1956 and asked about it as I had no idea what it was. Aubrey took the tape out and said "oh lets watch a bit of it OK? I am very proud of this performance and if you are going to write about my work you will need to see this. I did this for the BBC in 1979 and I play Nikita Kruschev complete with the Russian accent...in fact I learned some Russian for the part as you will see.." The tape was a bit dupey but I am very glad to have seen it because Aubrey is outstanding in it with a cast that included Robert Stephens who had just married Maggie Smith and two Hammer stars, Michael Gough and Jennifer Daniels.

By now Aubrey was in fine form and as we finished watching his star turn as the leader of all the Russias, he asked if I would like to take anything back home to watch for the interview, so I chose his "show reel" which had his best bits from current shows like *Red Roses and Petrol* where he plays father Morton and a cable horror film *She Creature* which was also known as the *Mermaid Chronicles* which I like very much with Rufus Sewell.

One thing I began to notice is how almost all of Aubrey's Hollywood performances were alike.....he had perfected this acting persona of the eccentric old sage with a love affair with the bottle and seemed to play variations of it for most things he did in the states. Aubrey is not unlike, say, my other actor friend Reggie Nalder in that he may not be right for most parts, but when he is, there is simply no one else that can play it and Aubrey Morris has that quality in spades.

During this visit Aubrey kept looking for this scrapbook of his with all his reviews and photos and simply could not remember where he had stored it. Even to at one point phoning the managers office to see if any work man had been in his apt while he was out. He did find two photos of himself from Robin Hardy's now classic film *The Wicker Man* and insisted I take them and have them copied for the article I was to do and I agreed asking if I could make a print of one for him to autograph for me. At this point he seemed to be getting tired and we decided it was time for us to go as well....he was very nostalgic by now reflecting about his mother who he told us lived to be in her 90's and how he missed telling her about his acting jobs and how at the end he stood over her bed and held her hand telling her as she was drifting away how much he loved her and would always be her little boy.

As he talked I could see that in spite of his age Aubrey Morris was just that, a little boy that never really grew up much like James Barry's creation Peter Pan. All this reflection made me feel very sad and it was time to take our leave. Aubrey walked out to the packing garage and apologized for frightening us so and we left him by saying how much we enjoyed the time and felt like we were old friends even though we had just met.

The next day I received a call from Aubrey and he sounded a bit off and then he asked me the most extraordinary thing "When I began to clean up the place this morning I noticed one of my silver spoons was missing. do you think your friend Chris nicked it?" I was so stunned that I said to him you are kidding aren't you? I mean Chris does not steal and I can't believe you are saying this to me, after all we brought you home when you were ill and this is the way you behave? Aubrey got very quiet and said "well I am just asking and I can't find my scrapbook either. You didn't take that did you?" Aubrey are you mad or what? If you remember last night you could not even find it so how could I have taken it...besides you walked us to my car and we were in shorts. I mean think about what you are saying will you?

He finally just tried to change the subject but I was really pissed off at the old poof for being so nuts so I hung up on him. Afterwards he tried calling back and I simply decided that he was mad as they come and wanted nothing further to do with him at this point. Also this was the end of 2003 and little did I know that Chris had less than a year to live and I had more on my plate than to deal with a totally delusional wildly out of control actor. Aubrey had told us the night before that for years he had a severe drinking problem and used to get really in your face when he had a bit too much. He remembered being on a tour with a group of very famous actors, and they were traveling by train and he got so out of it with Richard Burton or someone of that caliber that he was put off the train and woke up the next day without a clue where he was or what happened.

This experience really spooked me and I began asking around Hollywood about Aubrey and soon discovered that he had a reputation for putting people off and it also was affecting his ability to secure acting assignments as he mistook things for insults or sexual connotations that simply were not there to begin with. He was fortunate to have in his corner actors like Patrick McGoohan who made it his business to see that Aubrey worked whenever he could find a project that had a small part for him. They went way back to what is perhaps the first film Morris ever did, *The Quare Fellow,* in 1962. Ian McShane also found work for Aubrey in his series *Deadwood* and they too went way back in time. Ian had him on his English series *Lovejoy* as well. During the time I knew him Malcolm McDowell made a personal appearance at a screening of *A Clockwork Orange* and Aubrey turned up and Malcolm made note of this and also found a part for his former acting partner.

After that phone call I began to remember other remarks Aubrey made that were strange like his recollection of Patrick Stewart when they were filming *Lifeforce* in London. Aubrey told me that Patrick ran out of cash one night while they were in the middle of a night shoot and asked Aubrey if he could borrow 20 pounds and he would return the money straight away...well according to Aubrey Patrick just forgot about it until one day Aubrey spotted

Aubrey Morris in *The Wicker Man*.

him getting into a taxi and went over and asked Patrick Stewart if he could please have his money to which Stewart apparently was so outraged at being asked in public to pay back a loan that he threw the pound note at Aubrey and drove off in a huff and the two actors never spoke again. I mean what an odd story to tell an interviewer since it was meant to make Patrick Stewart look bad especially now that Stewart is well known for the Star Trek series. Aubrey also did his share of Sci-Fi with *Space 1999* as well as the original Star Trek.

After my last phone conversation with Aubrey I decided to simply drop the whole notion of interviewing him even though if you look at the back log of Camp David's for 2003 you will see a column where I mention having met him and was planning to share an exclusive interview in the near future. It has taken five years for me to return to this material and certainly not in the way either one of us would have expected.

The final confrontation came about because by my not returning his call and such he began going around Hollywood into memorabilia shops looking for his scrapbooks and asking if I had sold the two photos of him from *The Wicker Man*. I knew then that I would have to see him one more time in person and return his two original photos which were now back from the lab with two additional copies for me which at the time I had wanted prints so he could autograph them for me....now I could really care less.

I finally called him up and he was like a different person altogether... laughing and sounding as if he and I had just come from a dinner party or something....anyway I suggested we meet across the way from his King's Road apt in a corner coffee bar. I had his photos at that moment I had planned to simply hand him the folder and say my goodbyes. When I arrived he was still at his place and so I went ahead an ordered a coffee and waited for the Wicker man's gatekeeper to turn up.

Aubrey Morris arrived in full flood wearing a fedora and a long scarf wrapped around his neck.....the movie star had landed....He came in with all eyes upon him. With that he swept over to my table and planted a huge kiss right on my mouth and then sat down waving a waiter over to take his order......This entire scene was unlike anything I had encountered with him before and as his coffee arrived he began to do our interview all over again by reminding me we never completed it and now here we go....Aubrey started to sing a song from a show he did in the West end called *Expresso Bongo*... at the Saville Theater in 1958...this was an entirely different show from the one Val Guest made into a film a couple of years later with Laurence Harvey. This *Expresso Bongo* was very transgressive for it's time as it was immoral dark and sardonic while the film version was cleaned up as a Cliff Richard showcase. Paul Scofield originated the role Harvey played in the film and was by all accounts stunning. Aubrey sang from memory a song called "Nausea" and then informed me that Charles Gray {whom I expressed an interest in earlier when we discussed Hammer films} and he became lovers during the run confiding that he was buggering good old Charles until doomsday, it seems Gray had the role Aubrey would have liked to play, the chic owner of the Diplomatique Club... Charles even had a song "The Dip Is Dipping." However it did not make it onto the soundtrack later on.

Aubrey was spellbinding in recalling the lost era of theater in London and a production that has since become legend as the film never came close from what he described as a landmark moment in theater history. The production is said to have inspired the classic Alexzander Mackendrick film *The Sweet Smell of Success*.

Looking back I wish the situation had been otherwise and I could have really been friends with this man since there is greatness in him and long after all the petty remarks and crazy behavior is forgotten there will always be *A Clockwork Orange* and dozens of cameos that dazzle the imagination with the talent and humor that will always be Aubrey Morris.

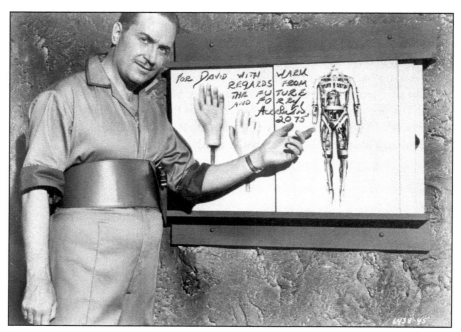

Forrest J. Ackerman – cameo for friend Ib Melchior.

22

The Forry Identity

Forrest J. Ackerman

"WHEN THIS YOU SEE, REMEMBER ME: 4E—4E—4E"

AS I WRITE THESE WORDS, 91 year-old Forrest J. Ackerman is on his deathbed in Los Angeles surrounded by die-hard monster fans and his caregiver. It was just a day or so since he was brought home from the hospital at his own request. This is a bittersweet reflection on a childhood relationship that went sour around 1988, and until this week I have kept my feelings private regarding the circumstances that ended such a powerful tie that bound FJA and me in the magical world of fantasy and imagination.

Who is Forrest J. Ackerman? He may be a well-kept secret to most of the civilized world, but if you are connected in any way to Science Fiction or classic horror films, this man is a legend whose lifetime on Planet Earth has been utterly devoted to becoming just that: a legend in his chosen field of Science Fiction. For those of us who write about film, his legacy is even more profound. From the early 1930s, Forry has taken the task of preserving, at least in memory if not material, all the genre films that would have fallen through the cracks regarded as worthless by critics of the day, if not for his magazine and his lifelong interest in them. If you look at film history in 2008, his influence is widely apparent, as we now respect the importance of cult films whether they are Ed Wood-directed fever dreams like *Plan Nine from Outer Space* with Bela Lugosi in his final bow, or a Z-grade Science Fiction film like *Robot Monster* with a gorilla wearing a space helmet.

Forrest Ackerman made himself known to me at an early age through the magazine that will always be his legacy, Famous Monsters of Filmland. This magazine united for the first time children around the age of 12 like me, who found themselves attracted to horror films thanks to the shock packages of Classic Monster Movies that were sold to television stations all over America during the 1950s and 1960s. This was the way baby-boomers were first introduced to Bela Lugosi as *Dracula* and Boris Karloff as *Frankenstein*. Nearly five decades cannot diminish the memory of the first issue of Famous Monsters of Filmland I ever laid eyes on. My mother and I were in Portland, Oregon on a shopping trip from Seattle where we were living at the time. We were staying in a large hotel downtown that had a newsstand, and from across the lobby I saw this bright yellow cover with blood-red letters that spelled Curse of the Werewolf. Above that was the masthead that cried out Famous Monsters of Filmland.

I must have read that magazine from cover to cover a dozen times before I could put it down and try and comprehend just why I was so excited. Looking back, the magazine justified my obsession with horror films, and for the first time I realized that I was not alone in my rapture for graves and ghouls. Because a guy named Forrest J. Ackerman cared about what I did, all at once as if by magic, I felt endorsed–not to mention part of a coven of like-minded kids that loved what I loved. We would all live then and there for the next issue, which turned out to be number 13.

Thus began my childhood as a fan of the horror genre in earnest, although by then, 1960, I had already seen most of the Universal classics and never missed a horror film in the theater. My poor mother had to sit through some pretty damaging cinema as I was never "of age" to see a film. When I first saw *House of Wax* in 3-D or, as she always reminds me, *Abbott And Costello Meet Dr. Jekyll and Mr. Hyde*, being just four years-old, I cried during the credits and had to be taken home.

This experience was not unlike what happened to all of us baby-boomers during those days, and Ackerman's monster parade was always a part of this as his magazine was akin to what the trades are for a Hollywood agent, keeping up with new releases as well as seeing for the first time movie stills from all the horror films that came before.

It was in following the development Famous Monsters of Filmland throughout this period (1958-1983) that Forrest J. Ackerman became more than just the name of its editor. "Uncle" Forry, as he advised all his admirers to address him, lived and breathed what seemed then like an enviable fan-ish lifestyle devotedly to be wished by every reader in each and every issue. He published pictures of himself with notables in the field of horror films and soon we would learn that he had been a fan of science fiction even longer than most of us were on the planet. By the late sixties he had even published an article in Famous Monsters of Filmland about a day in the life of Forrest J. Ackerman. When I read this article, which depicted an adult male, by then in his mid—forties, living by himself in the outskirts of Beverly Hills surrounded by nothing but books, Magazines, movie posters and file cabinet after file cabinet of photos from every horror film since *Caligari*, I realized that should be me. He even had his mail box rigged for sound to alert him to what goodies the postman would bring to his house every day. You see, Forrest J. Ackerman was the first of his kind – a FAN, and not just any fan, but a horror and science fiction fan who lived for that purpose only.

What most of us could not have realized at that time, being so young, was a not-so-subtle variation on the Peter Pan syndrome of never growing up. Forry was Peter and Captain Hook rolled together and we were the lost boys. By the mid sixties Ackerman was allowing the faithful to visit his home if any of us happened to be in Los Angeles and wanted to attend one of his "open houses," which took place on Saturdays. We all knew what his place looked like, having seen pictures of every room in the pages of Famous Monsters of Filmland which, by this time, was simply referred to as "FM".

This was the best of times for monster fans, remembered in the pages of Famous Monsters as "the Ghoul-don years," and Forry more than lived up to the image we all had of him as the "Pied Piper Of Horrordom" with a magic monster magazine that endorsed all of us who worshipped at the altar of Karloff and Lugosi and read EC comics instead of doing our homework. He even published an article entitled "Monsters are good for my children" just in case anybody should miss the point. All of this was perfect for that era where drive-ins were the teenage alternative to staying at home ignoring their hormones. At this point, up and coming studios like American International were grinding out Beach Party flicks as well as juvenile adaptations of Edgar Allan Poe, all of which premiered at the drive-in.

Throughout the late 1950s and 1960s, Ackerman maintained the hugely popular magazine without any reference to the reality of growing up in these turbulent times, yet the readership remained loyal as these monster kids would be among the last to tune in and trip out when the summer of love loomed over the horizon. By this time other monster magazines were beginning to show up on the newsstands, with one in particular standing out as superior in style and content, *Castle of Frankenstein*; yet even as adult an approach as *Castle of Frankenstein* was, it still owed its existence to the source of it all Famous Monsters of Filmland.

By 1962 I was traveling with some regularity from Sacramento to Los Angeles in time to catch Forry at the original home he had during the magazine's heyday. This address was located in the outskirts of Beverly Hills on Sherborne Drive. The Forrest Ackerman of those days is the way I will always remember him best. Forry dressed in business suits with silk ties as if he had a nine-to-five, and he was never without something under his arm, usually press materials from some new horror film, and dozens of genre magazines. He loved what he was doing, and why not? His work was his passion, the never-ending pursuit of all things fantastic in the visual medium.

He idolized Playboy and the lifestyle of its editor, the legendary Hugh Hefner who, like Ackerman, started a magazine from nothing and created a publishing empire beyond anyone's wildest dreams. At this time I think both Jim Warren, FM's publisher, and Forry still had hopes of creating a little empire of their own with spin-off magazines like Spacemen and Wildest Westerns. However, as influential as Famous Monsters of Filmland was for the baby-boomers of 1958, the kind of success and fame Hefner would enjoy with Playboy was always well out of reach for Warren and his editor. Ironically, years later, Warren would strike it rich with horror comics like Creepy, Eerie and Vampirella.

The first afternoon I spent at the old address was something a 12-year-old would never forget, walking into a house filled with paintings and posters of fantasy and science fiction, the walls lined with bookcases filled with first editions of rare science fiction, weird fiction and pulp magazines with covers of great beauty and imagination. Forry kept a section of his living room for displaying material that was placed there especially for trading to fans like me. Advance copies of Famous Monsters of Filmland, foreign horror magazines filled with rare stills of films I was yet to discover. It was Ali Baba's cave in the eyes of even a seasoned collector of such material. I still have the hard cover French film book he gave me that afternoon, which is now in shrink-wrap to keep the pages from falling out. He also collected people like Tor Johnson, who appeared in Ed Wood's essential *Plan Nine from Outer Space*, and my favorite, *Bride of the Monster*. To Tor and other exotic types, whose only claim to fame were their appearances in grade-Z horror films, Forry must have seemed like an oasis in the desert after being ignored by mainstream show business. Thanks to him, they all became part of our collective consciousness.

This youthful Forrest J. Ackerman was a wonder to behold, as he gave of his time to make sure others would follow in his example–that is, to always find a place for fantasy and imagination in your life. He loved to play music for his guests, and I remember hearing Marlene Dietrich for the first time singing "Falling in Love Again" in Ackerman's living room while he sang along; absolutely unforgettable.

I began to collect in earnest after that, adding movie posters and stills whenever I could, and of course having every issue of Famous Monsters was a given. Forry encouraged me to collect ALL monster magazines as they popped up, and in those days imitation was the highest form of flattery: Forry never felt threatened by any of them. What is amazing to remember is how nothing we collected was of any monetary value at that time. I hate to tell you what we would have in today's market if the twelve-year-olds of 1962 had kept everything they collected.

I saw Forry whenever I could get down to Los Angeles. As time wore on, high school began, and soon other interests would take hold, yet my devotion to the horror genre was now part of my imagination and would never leave me completely. After high school I moved to San Francisco and started college; it was during this period that I would see Forry at Science Fiction conventions in Oakland and San Jose.

Whenever I found something from *Metropolis* (which was, by the way, his favorite film), it never occurred to me to keep it; this was an item for Uncle Forry and I would make sure he got it if possible. Forry was forever buying books and movie material from dealers and fans alike. His collection was a work in progress.

Looking back at those conventions of the mid-1970s, Forry was not the Sci-Fi icon he is today, as we were still more or less a decade away from a major critical re-evaluation of these films, or from universities creating classes examining the films of the science fiction and horror genres. Forry had a reputation for being Sci-Fi's first fan during the early days of pulp fiction in the 1920s, when he corresponded with Robert Bloch and the master H.P. Lovecraft, who failed to appreciate Forry's enthusiasm and told him so in a famous letter to the young Ackerman. Robert Bloch, on the other hand, became a lifelong friend.

During the brightest period in the magazine's run, Forry was a welcomed guest on film sets and had the opportunity to interview actors no one else would have thought to question. This habit also gave Forry another career, that of the cameo player in such films as Curtis Harrington's *Queen of Blood* and *The Time Travelers* with Preston Foster. Forry enjoyed himself hugely on these projects and has since appeared in dozens of films including a moment in Michael Jackson's Thriller music video. You can spot Forry seated behind Jackson in the theater as they watch–what else?–a horror film.

When I finally relocated to Los Angeles in 1976 and subsequently opened a talent Agency, this would be the period when our paths would intertwine the most. By this time Forry Ackerman was living above Griffith Park near the Frank Lloyd Wright house that appeared in William Castle's *House on Haunted Hill* in 1959. This home on Glendower was nicknamed the "Ackermansion," even though it was anything but a mansion; it was a large home that once belonged to Jon Hall, a Universal contract player known for starring opposite Maria Montez.

Forry lived at this address with his then wife Wendayne and a South American housekeeper named Suzy, who lived in the quarters downstairs, where Ackerman maintained his office and housed the majority of his collection. Wendayne, a lady of German heritage, met Forry in 1950 and they stayed connected. She translated a science fiction series Forry edited called Perry Rhodan into German and this series is still running today.

At this point I was part of Forry's inner circle as I passed muster with then "assistant to the Ackermonster" Dennis Billows, who took care of Forry like a mother hen, and lived to regret it as did all those who followed who tried to bring order and keep the thieves away from his collection of increasingly valuable movie stills, props and posters. The reason these assistants never lasted too long was the tension that developed when outsiders would try and trade things away from Forry or make demands Dennis felt were unfair. Sometimes Forry would place Dennis in the middle and then side with the other person against him. Dennis left after a fashion, and this would go on until the magazine was no more.

As I write this I keep checking on Forry's condition which is still grave, and I can't help but read with amusement the evaluations of others who have only known him for the last ten years or so as a fragile elder with a legendary past, a Santa Clause from an alternative universe who gave of himself freely so fandom could flourish in his wake. Death is without a doubt the ultimate equalizer and I now fully acknowledge and appreciate that his intense devotion to the genre of Science fiction and fantasy far outweighs his shameless self-promotion and ego-mania that alienated many in his lifetime.

Let it be noted that Forry is and was a fascinating character, even by Hollywood standards, not without his faults mind you, but a decent man who did much for the genre he in many ways helped create. He could have been so much more, as I discovered the day George Pal died. Let me explain: for years as a reader of FM, I was accustomed to Forry's writing being juvenile and filled with puns, and it never bothered me because the photos were more than enough to make me happy at the time; in other words I never thought of Ackerman as much of a "writer" in the sense of, say, Ray Bradbury, although I knew Forry had once long ago tried his hand at fiction. The weekend of George Pal's passing both Chris Deitrich – my life partner, and I were on duty at the Ackermansion to give Forry an open window to draw up what he was going to say at the funeral as the widow had asked for Forry to deliver the eulogy. Forry put it together in one evening and no one saw it until he delivered the eulogy at the service. The day of the funeral arrived and as we all took our seats I was next to actor Ron Ely who had played the title role in Pal's last film, *Doc Savage*. Forry went to the podium and knocked the text right out of the park; it was fantastic. At the reception later in the day I went up to him and said, "You know, I just don't believe you, Ackerman. You can WRITE! Why in the hell don't you do this more often?" His reply was typical Ackerman: "Well for one thing we don't lose a George Pal every day, now do we?"

Chris had replaced Dennis Billows as Forry's assistant and because of that I was at the Ackermansion on Glendower almost every day for over a year. This gave me an unprecedented view into Forry and Wendy's daily routine, which revealed for starters a marriage that was all but in name only. When I say this I should explain that when a man is so in touch with his inner child as Ackerman was, there could never be children in such a marriage. He was always to play that role himself. Wendy had a son already from her first marriage named Michael, and Forry grew to hate this man, and with good reason. Michael was a spoiled and willful guy who tormented Forry. The relationship was like Dwight Frye and the Frankenstein monster for real. I recall seeing Michael come down the stairs with lit books of matches hellbent on setting fire to Forry's collection of a lifetime. He finally moved to Hawaii leaving the Ackermans somewhat alone, although Wendy would dote on her son throughout her lifetime.

Wendy was, in spite of her temperament, good for Forry because she prevented certain people from taking advantage of him, as she was more practical and refused to let his collecting excesses' climb the stairs into the main house. None of it was allowed to be displayed upstairs except for some very rare and valuable fantasy art and one bookcase with his first editions and rare Arkham house books. All of Forry's books and movie material was housed downstairs and out in a make shift garage he dubbed the "Garage-Mahal," which was filled to the rafters with posters and billboards and the original paintings for some of the covers of Famous Monsters. When Mayor Bradley came to the house and gave Forry an award in the form of a beautifully designed document complete with a seal from the mayor's office from the City of Los Angeles, this was to cement an agreement allowing Forry to donate his collection, especially his books, to the city. This of course never happened because Forry wanted them to build something to house the collection and then allow him to curate the result. I had the award beautifully framed, and Wendy reluctantly allowed it to be hung in the hall.

If only Mayor Bradley had pulled it off and Forry had not made so many demands we would have an amazing library today to honor his name and accomplishments. These failures were not lost on Forry and he became sad as the realization that the powers that be both in fandom as well as the city of Los Angeles were willing to bestow titles and nicknames on him without any real respect in a solid way he could take to the bank. What is tragic to think about is that all of it was finally lost in lawsuits and attorney's fees in a situation beyond repeating here, which led Forry to attempt to resurrect the magazine, and he spent the next ten years in courtrooms, casting a shadow over a lifetime of service. My friend Alan White, a longtime fan and supporter of both Forry and the Academy of Science Fiction, interviewed Forry on the subject of the frustration of being the first to carry the flag of fandom and the lack of appreciation for what for him was always a labor of love. Let Ackerman speak for himself on the subject:

"I've no hope whatsoever in fandom, none whatsoever. I'm a member of the Los Angeles Science Fiction Society. I was at the first meeting; I have been the director, the secretary, the treasurer, the publisher, the editor, the garbage man, everything you can think of. I've poured thousands of dollars into that club. I've been to over 1500 meetings of it. I have never once heard any suggestion that they pay a dime to help me out. I understand that over a hundred fans a week go to the club and I've put on the bulletin board that I have open house here. I'd be hoping for members of Los Angeles Science Fiction Society to come and see the place, but you know I just don't seem to exist and the unkindest cut of all...finally 50 years rolled around and I went to the 50th anniversary meeting—there I was the sole survivor of the very first meeting and I thought they'd like me to get up and tell how it began, the highlights the lowlights and so on. Well, the speaker of the evening was Harlan Ellison who continually claims he doesn't write Science Fiction and he began by saying something like, 'I don't know why you invited me because in 26 years I've only been to three meetings.' I sat there through the entire meeting as though I was the Invisible Man, nobody ever said, 'Oh Forry Ackerman...he was our first member.' So I drove back with my wife and I said, 'You know, have I lived too long or what?' She says, 'Well, young people, they don't care about history, the world began when they were born and that is all they are interested in – themselves.'"

I think this was a difficult time for him as he wanted too much to see a museum or a library come forth or the funds to build one. For a time he had interest from Japanese fans to raise money to create just that but something always got in the way, Ultimately Forrest Ackerman would become a victim of his own bad judgment.

During this period I would bring genre celebrities I thought Forry would enjoy meeting up to the Ackermasion and it was always an experience to see how each one would react to the situation. Beverly Garland drove me up there one afternoon and proved herself to be not only a great lady but a good sport as well. Once she got a load of Forry's collection she took us aside and told him this: "Are you nuts? ...You mean to tell me you have people come in this office space and do whatever without a watcher? You are going to be robbed blind!" Forry changed the subject and gave her two posters from her cult films and the conversation went south after that. Of course she was right but Forry would just disregard such advice and was robbed blind right up until he moved out of the home altogether. However, not all were so candid as Beverly; most of the guests I brought up to see him were always amazed at his childlike sense of joy at having this collection and being able to share it with anyone who cared to make the journey.

Forry at the "Ackermansion" with Reggie Nalder and David Del Valle.

There are so many memories I could relate regarding life with Forry, having experienced the best of times and the worst of times. However, as we baby boomers approach 60, looking back can be enlightening yet we can do nothing to change the past, and the future is what we make it. Forry has had a great run and for a man who lived on his own terms I can't think of a more glorious final curtain than to be surrounded by caring fans and know that somehow you made a difference.

I will always keep this image of Forrest Ackerman in my heart: When I was going to Europe back in the 70's Forry asked me to drop by on my way to the airport. I came up to the door and he walked outside wearing his favorite Hawaiian shirt loaded with buttons. He was smiling ear to ear and he handed me an envelope with a letter inside. He told me to read it on the plane and make as much use of it as I saw fit. I thanked him in advance for whatever it was and went on my merry way. At the bar at LAX I ordered a preflight Bloody Mary and decided to see what the Ackermonster had to say; the letter read as follows:

"For whom it may concern: this is my pal David Del Valle who has proven to me over time that he knows and loves all the same films and books that I do...Please treat him as you would my own son if I had one and let him purchase or trade for material that will ultimately serve us both." (This note was followed by Forry's unmistakable red ink signature on his one-of-a-kind stationary)

Forry and I often talked of time machines and how wonderful it would be to have one...Tonight I wish they really did exist because I would climb in one and go back to the day before we had our falling out and make it right. Having him out of my life all these years has truly been my loss. Goodbye, Forry.

How can you ever thank a man for giving you the key to unlock a world of Gods and monsters?

23

The Rocking Host Winner

Bob Wilkins

AS A BABY BOOMER PUSHING SIXTY it is difficult to wrap my mind around the fact that nearly four decades have passed since I did my first on camera interview as a "film expert". The first person to ever refer to me in those terms just passed away on January 7th.

Bob Wilkins was a slightly built man with sandy blond hair sporting high school teacher glasses and on occasion smokes a cigar, domestic of course. Bob was the premier horror host at KCRA channel 3 in Sacramento from 1966 to 1970. Bob then moved his Creature Feature show over to KTVU in the Oakland San Francisco area until the early 1980s.

Bob had come to Sacramento directly from the mid-west, Indiana to be exact, soon finding a place at the NBC affiliate Channel 3, where he worked behind the scenes until one day at a company dinner his toastmaster antics caught the eye of one of the executives who recognized Wilkins talent to amuse.

It was a common practice in those days at Television stations to have one of their own staff to introduce movies from their film library. Most of the time it would be grade Z horror films that the station would sign off with late at night. Bob was given a group of AIP films that included a lot of Japanese fare like *Attack of the Mushroom People*, which incidentally was the first film Bob Wilkins introduced as Sacramento's Creature feature host.

By the time I arrived in Sacramento to begin high school, I had already been exposed to the shock theater packages that debuted in Los Angeles in the mid—to—late 1950s missing Vampira by about five years. The lady I re-

Bob Wilkins with David Del Valle.

call was a character actress named Ottola Nessmith who dressed in Victorian purples and lace. She lived in a haunted house and would say things like "well it's midnight, the stores are closed, time to go shopping." Ottola kept a pet bat and introduced the films by playing an old Victrola record player. As she placed the needle on the record, the film would begin.

Bob Wilkins was unique as he would have none of that camp stuff as a host. Bob wore a suit and tie sitting in a yellow rocking chair on a small modest set. He would simply rock back and forth smoking his cigar and lament whatever he was asked to introduce as the evenings feature. He did this every Saturday night on his own most of the time but he would try and have guests to interview if he thought they could add something to the witch's brew he was serving up on Creature features.

I remember watching *Curse of the Demon* one Saturday night early in 1967 with Bob in top form asking his audience to write in if they had any encounters with witchcraft or black magic. Now can you imagine what he would have gotten himself into in today's mindset? Goth girls and Devil worshippers on the internet alone would be mind-boggling.

I decided to send Bob a letter explaining that I had just become a member of the Los Angeles based Count Dracula Society and really enjoyed his show. Within a week I got an answer back asking me if I would like to appear on the show as a representative of the society and maybe even recruit some new members. I was just a sophomore at Encina High school and had never been on TV so of course I said definitely to that!

I had at that time no knowledge of Donald A. Reed except in name and even less about the society itself save from their newsletter, The Count Dracula Quarterly, which seemed pretty cool in 1967 with members like Forry Ackerman and Robert Bloch among the faithful. It would be a few years later that Bob Bloch and I would sit in a bar laughing at the idea of Don Reed in a cape way to big for him trying to knight people like he was our king....well in his mind at any rate.

I taped my first Bob Wilkins show wearing a black cape extolling the glories of Count Dracula and his order with disciples mainly in the greater Los Angeles area. Bob showed *Son of Dracula* with Lon Chaney, Jr. I am grateful no tape of that show exists to come back and haunt me today.

We taped the show on a Thursday and I will never forget seeing myself for the first time on TV wearing that dammed cape while promoting Don Reed's cash cow in LA. The sins of youth and all that, however something clicked with Wilkins and myself and I was asked back to just talk about the films. The result of these appearances were immediate for me as everyone at school watched the show including the principal of Encina Jack Bassitt. As a direct result of my appearances on Creature features I was given my own film series at Encina beginning with *House of Usher* and then *The Fly*....some three decades later I would be sitting in a sound booth with star David Hedison recording an audio commentary for *The Fly*.

In 1968 Bob went down to LA with fellow KCRA anchor Harry Martin to tape interviews for the station. The highlight of this visit would be meeting Boris Karloff who was in town to do a cameo for the series The Name Of The Game...Bob got Karloff to say lines like "Who is Bob Wilkins?" and "I have never watched the Bob Wilkins show"...wonderful stuff all of it... it was during this moment that Bob Wilkins became my hero for life. Bob knew that Karloff was my idol and made a point during his time with him to inform the great Karloff that he had a number one fan in Sacramento that would appreciate an audience with the eighty year old icon if time would permit. Karloff was of course very modest that a young man like myself would know so much about his films and would be glad to meet me if I was ever in Hollywood when he was working. Karloff lived in England in those days, only coming into Hollywood for filming.

Within a month of Bob's return from LA I received a telegram from Karloff {which I still have to this day} asking me to come down and watch him guest star on *The Jonathan Winters Show.* I immediately phoned Bob to thank him and he knew by my voice I was on cloud nine. Now as luck would have it this experience of a lifetime was just beyond my grasp as one day before I was to fly down I got in a car accident that prevented the trip. I did get to speak with Karloff on the telephone which was filming what was to be his last appearance on television period. Karloff thanked me for being his fan and wished me god's speed in recovering from my accident. I will never know if Karloff could tell I was crying over the phone but it remains the greatest phone call of my life and I owe it all to Bob Wilkins.

By the time Bob took his show to the Bay area I was already going to San Francisco State yet I still appeared on his program no longer wearing capes or extolling the virtues of the Count Dracula society thank god. During these tapings I was beginning to become a film historian with interests extending beyond just the genre and Bob was as always supportive of whatever I was going to do.

Bob Wilkins, TV Host.

It was at this point that we discussed the possibility of me taking over from him if and when he left the show and I will always wonder what if…but I was determined to go to Hollywood and he understood that perhaps from the first time we met that nothing else would do but to make the journey for myself.

Bob Wilkins had made the show not only an institution in the Bay area creating a fan base that is still in evidence today. Bob made himself a much loved figure in the hearts and minds of film fans all over Northern California. He never put the fans down nor made the films look worthless; his comments were always fun with a genuine sense of wonder that would have made Forry Ackerman proud.

I was sorry to learn of Bob's battles with Alzheimer's disease which took its toll over the last years of his life, yet he never let it stop him from making personal appearances until just a couple of years ago.

I never did get to tell him personally how much he meant to me and what an influence his support was during my high school and college days. They were of course the best of times and Bob Wilkins will always be a part of that.

I can still hear Karloff's voice over the phone with that unmistakable voice saying to me "Your friend Bob Wilkins told me you like my work…well bless you for that."

Bless you Bob Wilkins you will be missed not just by me but the thousands of fans whose appreciation of fantasy and imagination were made all the better for you being a part of our lives.

BOB WILKINS 1932-2009

Les Baxter.

24

Les Is More!

Les Baxter

IT WAS THE MID 1980S, and I was sitting in a screening room in Hollywood, trying to watch a preview of John Boorman's chapter
The Emerald Forest. Sitting next to me was composer-conductor Les Baxter. The reason I say "trying" is that Les was well into giving me a non-stop audio commentary of how this film would have been if he were scoring it. As I was beginning to learn, Les Baxter had zero tolerance for rival composers in this field; however, there was a good reason for this, as I would discover much later on.

I was a close personal friend to Les for the better part of the 1980s. At that time he lived on a large, ranch-style estate in Chatsworth, California, surrounded by mountains. Les loved living large and had done so most of his adult life. The royalties from his film-scoring and album sales allowed for this lifestyle, and Les made no apologies for doing whatever came his way to keep himself in the manner he felt he deserved. In order to be his friend, one had to make allowances for his bitterness towards the music industry, particularly the Music Academy, which he felt (sometimes rightly so) had gone out of their way to malign his work and character to the point of spreading rumors that he employed ghost writers to do some of his composing, which was indeed a lie. This situation cost him dearly as he lost important friendships with colleagues like Nelson Riddle and John Williams, whom he sued during the time I knew him.

The tragedy of Les Baxter is that he really was a genius whose musical talents were towering and in a perfect world he would have been in the Hall of Fame with Grammys, as well as, be revered by his peers. One of the things he felt held him back was having scored so many grade-Z potboilers. The industry simply would not take him seriously. When Les had been considered for the big-budget film *Green Mansions*, he was shot down by those within the M-G-M music department who said film required class and style and Les possessed neither. M-G-M finally gave him their B-titles, such as *The Invisible Boy*, instead.

When I met him, the fact I was so enamored with the American International Pictures films that he had scored pleased him greatly, because it meant I sort of got who he was and wasn't just another young guy being taken to lavish meals by a wealthy musician. Les had audio cassettes of both his scores for *House of Usher* and *Pit and the Pendulum* in his car, complete with dialogue from the soundtrack, so we could travel about listening to them. He felt his score for *Master of the World* was his best and was very proud that it was one of the few ever released on vinyl during his lifetime. *The Dunwich Horror* was another, which was my personal favorite and the one he autographed when we first met.

I think one needs to know just exactly how important a figure Les Baxter was during the 1950s and early 1960s to fully understand his fall from popularity; the advent of Elvis, along with the British invasion, rocked his world to its very core, and he never recovered from it for the rest of his life. Les was an important part of the lounge music era; and especially for swingers with a taste for Exotica, Baxter was the man. His albums for Capital records were best-sellers (the best of this material collected onto a 2-CD set titled, appropriately, *The Exotic Moods* of Les Baxter), and he was on radio and television constantly, finally having his own show as well. When this suddenly disappeared, he was left feeling no self-worth for his abilities and he began to drift, turning down nothing, as he needed money to sustain his lavish lifestyle. Les had owned homes in Hawaii and had he held onto his assets he would have been set for life.

Les was a very sensitive and complex man with impeccable taste in art and music. His idols were Igor Stravinsky and Ravel; he also adored Rio, with special emphasis on Carnival. Les had gone to Carnival over and over, soaking up the beats and the rhythm in the streets of Rio. He was planning to do an album about Carnival with an eye for Broadway later on.

Vincent Price in *Pit and the Pendulum*. I think he realized the importance of the horror films he scored as he would never tire of playing the tracks if asked. He loved *Pit and the Pendulum* the most because this score was atonal score and ultra-modern for its time. He told me that when AIP chief James H. Nicholson first heard the opening cues for the film, he called Les into his office and with tongue firmly in cheek began in mock angry tones, "Les, this is not what I asked for on the picture." After a pause he then smiled at Les, adding, "It is so much more!" From that moment on Les had a patron in one of the two powers-that-be at AIP. Les recalled, "Jim was a colleague and a fel-

Les Baxter.

low Scotsman. We had many conversations together over the years. He was bright and progressive in his thinking. I admired him as he did me."

Les remembers Roger Corman, who produced and directed many of the Poe-inspired horror films that Les scored, in a totally different manner; he told me they never had any kind of relationship to speak of, in spite of several films in common. "Roger never paid any attention to the music for any of the films I scored. I felt Corman had no interest in music to begin with, so he didn't really pay attention. He never sat in on the recording and never asked anything of me as the composer. We simply did one after another as quickly as possible. As soon as Roger wrapped one he started up another."

Les was a lifelong admirer of Edgar Allan Poe and delighted in creating scores like the Poe Suite for Vincent Price's *An Evening of Edgar Allen Poe*, a television special that AIP asked Price to do while awaiting yet another film to fill up his contract. Les loved to play cues from *Cry of The Banshee* as he felt there were the moments in that score that were new and fresh for a period film (although the director felt otherwise).

Les was always interested in doing new things with music and was so knowledgeable regarding music from all over the world. As far as horror scores were concerned, he said, "The subject matter for horror projects always takes control dictating what I compose. I conducted each and every one of my scores for the Poe films and my commitment was 100%."

Les loved his film scores and was never really satisfied unless you did as well. One evening he invited the veteran Hollywood photographer Ted Allan and his wife Jean and their adult daughter Holly up to the Chatsworth house during a weekend stay-over for me. Ted had introduced me to Les in the first place, so it was like a gathering of extended family. After one of his more dramatic dinners, Les placed us all in his den, where he proceeded to darken the room until it was pitch black, and then he played the entire score for *The Beast Within*, one of his last genre efforts. Towards the end he threw a huge pile of rubber bands up in the air and as they landed on us we all began to scream like teenage girls. It was great! He told us he learned that little trick from "Screaming" Jay Hawkins.

Les was a riot when he felt like it. These were the times I will cherish when I think of Les now. I was pleased to show Les early pressings of the Poe films when they came out on laser discs, as I had provided the liner notes and artwork. I made sure he was given his due on those releases, and he seemed to bask a bit in their preservation. The interest in the music of Les Baxter is growing with each passing year; there are now websites devoted to him with more and more young musicians discovering and admiring his legacy. I just wish Les could have lived to see it for himself. He was some kind of a man…

25

Baroque Mirrors

Eric Portman

MY INTRODUCTION TO THE FILMS of Eric Portman was not an easy one by any means. He was brought to my attention by an alcoholic Hindu princess by the name of Rukhmani Singh Devi. She was odd even by my standards of eccentricity; Rukhmani was a bit like the willful princess that tormented James Mason with their past lives in James Ivory's sinister *Autobiography of a Princess*.

She behaved like a member of the British Royal family if they'd been brought up on Hammer films, and who am I to say they weren't? She was supremely intelligent, world weary and drunk, in that order. Rukmani worshipped at the altar of British Cinema, with actors Eric Portman and Peter Cushing as the jewels in the crown.

They say every actor has a special follower and I mean much more than just a fan since these people tend to personally morph into the object of their affection in act and deed. In Rukhmani's case she was to be referred to in these circumstances as "Patty" or "PC two"…her devotion to all things Peter Cushing was something to behold. For example she could tell you how many wardrobe changes Cushing had in say *The Creeping Flesh*…which, in case you were wondering, happens to be an amazing 12 changes in one film. I never really thought about what an Edwardian clothes horse Peter Cushing was until I met the princess, and afterwards I never ever regarded him as just a film star. Saint Peter was now an experience never to be taken lightly.

During this period she and I were meeting regularly, every weekend, in Berkeley to see films at the fabled "Telegraph Rep" cinema which at the

Eric Portman in Terrence Young's *Corridor of Mirrors*.

time (1973) was more like seeing a film at somebody's apt while sitting uncomfortably in rickety wooden chairs – inhaling pot smoke until you had a contact high. It was there that I first saw Eric Portman in Powell and Pressburger's World War II epic *The 49th Parallel* (1941). In it Portman played a Nazi U-boat commander to perfection. I was hooked. Who was this suave, slightly psychotic gentleman and where had he been all my life.

Rukhmani quickly filled me in on all things Eric by telling me she had a girlfriend, also from India, who was to Portman what she was to Cushing. This woman was to be known to me as simply Eurika Portman, a name she created to be on a more personal footing with the object of her adoration. So here I was living in San Francisco in the early 1970s, leading a very exhaustive night life, to now be further complicated by knowing these two wacky divas, both completely outré personalities of the twilight fringe of celebrity mania. The one saving grace of it all was the fact that these ladies approached it all with style, wit and class, all courtesy of the on screen personas of Messrs Cushing and Portman.

Eventually I began to seek out the films of Eric Portman on my own without the distractions of having to count their costume changes or how many cigarettes they lit during their various running times. One of the first things Eurika ever imparted to me regarding Portman was this comment he gave regarding acting, which is of course priceless: "Acting is like masturbation, one either does it or one does not, but one never talks about it." Lord Olivier could not have said it better.

American teaser one sheet advertised *The Naked Edge* trying to follow the example left by Hitchcock's "Psycho"…even written by the same screenwriter. However that is all the two films had in common.

Even in today's world of entertainment, men like Eric Portman remain sadly forgotten. I am ever hopeful that he will be rediscovered as his films turn up on you tube and Netflix with fairly contemporary titles like *The Bedford Incident* with Sidney Poitier and Richard Widmark. Eric Portman became a star on the British stage in 1929 with a breakthrough performance as Romeo at the refurbished Old Vic and this in turn led to many roles in Shakespeare there. He quickly created more modern roles as well.

By 1935 he was well known as an actor with great presence and range. By 1942 he began making films for directors like Michael Powell. Yet he always returned to the stage. In the early 1950s he created the role later played on film by David Niven in Terrance Rattigan's *Separate Tables*…in the play as well as the film the character was disgraced by being caught in a local cinema making unwelcome advances to a young girl, years later the playwright revealed the original script in which the character was gay and the offence was with a boy. Almost all of Eric Portman's characterizations had this coded sexuality, both on stage and screen.

In the early 1970's Norman Hudis (a well known screenwriter of the "Carry On" films), wrote a play about Eric Portman entitled *Dinner with Ribbentrop* which was a bit like the recent play about Tallulah Bankhead doing sound bites for *Die, Die My Darling*…only in Hudis's play we discover Eric Portman's Nazi leanings as well as his homosexuality, and how he managed to avoid ever discussing it with the press even as late as 1960. The truth of the matter is Eric Portman was a unique personality and the more we learn about him the more fascinating he becomes.

Among the many films Eric Portman would make during and after the war, the two I remember the best are the ones he made towards the end of his life. *The Naked Edge* is always remembered for being Gary Cooper's last film; he literally died before it could be released. And *Deadfall*, made just before Portman would pass away as well. In *The Naked Edge* Eric plays Jeremy Clay, a seedy opportunist who has a line towards the end, after much suspense has been made of a straight razor. Eric prepares a scalding hot bath for Deborah Kerr to cut her wrists in, and before he can put her in the hot water he looks up into the camera and says "Tell me, do you think women really like to get naked before they kill themselves?"

Deadfall was made at the time of Michael Caine's emergence as a star, and much is made of his sex appeal. The film was advertised as a heist caper, however the real plot was given to Eric Portman as the homosexual jewel thief whose daughter is used as bait to lure Caine into their web. The fact that Portman is supposed to fancy Caine is supposed to shock the audience, as is the revelation of incest later on, but through it all Eric Portman remains a legendary performer who commands the screen, making audiences wish to know far more about his character than Michael Caine's. It was a bittersweet way to say goodbye to such a remarkable career.

The stage work of Eric Portman is lost to us now but I was told that during his reign upon the British stage his performances were the stuff of legends. He apparently ran up against the equally legendary Tallulah Bankhead on more than one occasion causing the press at the time to speculate on which one of them was going to kill the other after screaming matches during and after performances, both actors fueled by alcohol. Tallulah never referred to Eric Portman in her memoirs as the scars were just too deep. She also managed to keep her encounter with Stephanie Powers all to herself after making her final film, *Die, Die My Darling*.

Perhaps the most flamboyantly artificial of Eric Portman's film appearances would have to be his star turn in Terence Young's *Corridor of Mirrors* which, if remembered at all today, is because the future "Bond" director introduced both Christopher Lee and Miss Moneypenny (Lois Maxwell) in the opening scenes of the film, giving each a line or two.

Corridor of Mirrors is a marvel of genre homage's all in one beautiful package. It references Cocteau's *La Belle et La Bête* even down to having Georges Auric compose the music, which is quite beautiful. The exquisite photography recalls *Rebecca* and *Jane Eyre*, with shadowy staircases and billowing curtains with a large white cat roaming the castle to invoke Lewis Carroll for good measure.

Eric Portman plays a wealthy Londoner who is traumatized on a visit to Venice where he catches sight of a portrait of a vixen named Venetia, and spends the rest of the film trying to find a reincarnation of her, which of course he does in the character of Myfanwy Conway played by new comer Edana Romney whose presence in this film is no accident since she is one of the producers along with Rudolph Cartier, who also wrote the screenplay to favor her as well. But no matter, the film belongs to Portman whenever he chooses to enter the frame. His performance is romantic, dashing and of course slightly psychotic, as this was how the British film industry coded gay actors since the days of Ivor Novello.

Yes, it is true, Erich Portman, like Michael Redgrave, Alec Guinness and Dennis Price were all gay actors working in the British film industry and doing their utmost to play straight. Fortunately for the viewing audience

Eric Portman in his last role; *Deadfall.*

this still did not prevent screenwriters from coding most of their parts with tell tale signs of Wilden allure. In *Corridor of Mirrors* for example, Portman plays Paul, an artist and from the looks of it an interior decorator who furnishes not only his mansion with antiques and all manner of Object Art. No, he does not stop there, he also installs a lavish wardrobe of ball gowns that would put Cher on fashion alert and place Elton John under house arrest until he got his game on.

How Edana Romney could not suspect her phantom-like lover was gay is just a device of cinema we must refer to as fantasy. For her role in the film,

Edana comes across much too mature to really be taken in romantically by his posturings of love. By the time she does sleep over at his gothic abode, our poor Eric is so worn out with all the costume changes that he finally hands her a set of velvet pajamas and toddles off to parts unknown for the evening. They never kiss or make love on camera. He might as well have worn one of those Jean Marais beast make-ups to justify his reluctance to go further than a waltz or an embrace.

The plot of *Corridor of Mirrors* is really divided into two distinct halves, the first being the fairy tale world represented by Paul's Regent Park estate, a re-creation of a palace in fourteenth century Venice. This part includes his gothic quest for the ideal woman, the Borgia-like Venetia who was wanton in the past and then again in Edana's recreation of her later on. The films greatest moment arrives with Paul's staging of a renaissance Venetian ball with masked party goers all behaving like the guests in Corman's *Masque of the Red Death*.

The second half of the film darkens and changes mood as we observe Paul descend into what we mistake for madness, leading to his death and then retribution through the faithful manservant that was looking out for his master all along. We also have a madwoman living in the villa not unlike the first Mrs. Rochester in *Jane Eyre*.

What really holds all this together is of course the performance of Eric Portman who has the style to carry off the costumes much like his colleague Peter Cushing. He lacks the necessary glamour of a matinee idol and knowing that, instinctively invests all his characters with breeding and intelligence, which makes him appear more attractive than he actually is. When it is apparent his character is going to his doom after the trial for a murder he may have committed, Eric is given another classic moment that even Dirk Bogarde (perhaps the most closeted of all British actors) could not have improved on. Portman tells his lost love the following:

"There is a time to be born and a time to die, so please don't spoil the exit I've chosen for myself. You ought to know I've always had a liking for dramatic effect."

What an exit for a remarkable performer. Eric Portman would make a number of other films before his demise in 1969, all of them graced with his impeccable sense of timing and a desire to entertain.

26

The Deathmaster Knocks at the Madhouse of Dr. Phibes

Robert Quarry

DURING THE PAST YEAR, I have been following the online trials and tribulations of actor Robert Quarry, from being victimized by a con artist posing as a fan to being rescued by caring admirers into the safety of the Motion picture home. Thanks to the personal generosity of men like producer Fred Olen Ray (whose heart is as big as the sky), when Quarry died last Friday, it was with the knowledge he was loved and respected by literally thousands of his fans and peers both in and out of the movie industry.

Bob had been on my mind a number of times during the four years I have remained out of the loop since leaving LA. There was a time as the 1970s ended and the 1980s took full swing that Bob Quarry was more like Uncle Bob to his friends – if by "uncle" you meant Keith Moon's outrageously antic performance as Uncle Ernie in *Tommy*, that is! I have already penned a memoir about those times entitled "The Bitter Tears of Count Yorga" in the July 2007 installment of my monthly column Camp David over at Films in Review, but I would like to take this opportunity to bring to light my impression of what Robert Quarry was like before the personal disasters took their toll. As I was reading the dozens of threads on the Internet from fans who met Bob over the last ten years, I began to realize that the Robert Quarry being discussed bore little resemblance to the man I knew and partied with in the mid-1980s in West Hollywood.

The Robert Quarry in those days was a savvy, worldly actor at the top of his game enjoying a night on the town. As I have already written in the Camp David piece, I was introduced to Bob by fellow actor Richard Deacon during

Robert Quarry as Count Yorga in *Return of Count Yorga*.

his birthday party at a dinner club on the strip. We hit it off and phone numbers were exchanged. From that came a lasting friendship that was based on having the same lifestyle with active interests in all things show biz.

Occasionally, Bob would enjoy watching one of his old films if it happened to show up on the tube. My favorite memory of watching a film with him was night they ran *A Kiss before Dying* on the nine o'clock movie. Bob set this one up by saying, "I was younger than springtime and stupider than shit if memory serves. Joanne (Woodward) was and is a close personal friend from that picture, and RJ (Wagner) was such a pretty boy that it was hard to take him seriously in those days." At one point the actress Virginia Leith appeared on screen, and Bob looked over at me and said, "Would you believe that girl is now remembered by the fans as *The Brain That Would Not Die* while I am now and ever shall be *Count Yorga Vampire*!! What kind of a crazy fucking business is this?"

I called him once when they ran *House of Bamboo* as I was taping it for Cameron Mitchell, and he said, "Well don't bother making me a copy. If you cough you'll miss me – I am in it that much". I do believe he liked watching some of his work, although from what I am told that changed in later years.

Robert Quarry was in those days jaded but optimistic about his career, since he was represented by a good agent and was doing his share of episodic television like *The Rockford Files* and *Battlestar Gallatica*. I remember Bob telling me that after he had done the James Garner detective show, he was made up as a half man half robot for the Sci-Fi show and felt completely disguised. He was walking through Universal in full regalia, and as he went by Garner, the Rockford star looked up and said, "Hi Bob," as if noticing nothing unusual – which just cracked Bob up. He also hit it off with co-star Elizabeth Allen, whose sense of camp matched Bob's. He told me it was such fun to get up and go to work with talent like that.

As many of his fans know, Bob was a gourmet cook who loved to give dinner parties at home, or he would pack up his pots and pans and do it at your place if that is what the party called for. This always fascinated me: Bob and Vincent Price had so many things in common and yet they never really connected after those two films (*Dr. Phibes Rises Again* and *Madhouse*) that they did together in London. Bob knew that I was in touch with Price, and so he explained that in spite of what I may have heard, Bob admired Price both as a movie star as well as a erudite, cultured man in private life. "We were put at odds by the bastard Sam Arkoff and his slimy errand boy Deke Hayward," Quarry explained.

When the AIP years were brought up at a dinner party or if he was in that kind of a nostalgic mood, these memories brought on a kind of angry vent from him. Bob did not possess the luck of the Irish when it came to his career. *Dr. Phibes Rises Again* should have brought him and Vincent Price together like Cushing and Lee; however, according to Bob, the atmosphere was decidedly Macbethian, with Price being told by Heyward that Quarry was being groomed to replace him. This coupled with Hayward's going behind Bob's back and talking trash to his London friends terminated any good will on the set for all concerned. Bob did bond with Peter Cushing whom he cooked for at his London flat on several occasions.

I had an opportunity speaking with Vincent Price personally about Robert when I was working as publicist on *The Offspring*. Price brought him up in conversation, asking, if I knew what had happened to him. After I explained that Bob was still around, Price shook his head and reflected, "This town can be a Paradise or a Hell, and I have seen it both ways in my career. He should have had a bigger career than he did. Robert was a good character man; he just couldn't carry a tune."*

These last two days have created a flood of memories with all the parties and dinners at my place or his in North Hollywood, where he lived with his mother Mabel, whom he sometimes referred to as "Mimi." She occupied her own quarters as his apartment was more like a duplex; this allowed him some privacy, yet he could keep an eye on her as well. Bob was a good son in every way. I remember how my heart went out to him when she was getting weaker. He called me one afternoon from the hospital, and I could tell he was worried.

"The doctor asked me if I would mind if they called a priest in to give Mimi the last rites, and I simply had to get out of that room – I couldn't take anymore." This is especially meaningful for me at this very moment in my own life, as I am caregiver to my mother, who will be 94 in June. Bob said to me that day, 'David, you will go through this someday, so try and remain strong when it comes your way." Now I think of that just about everyday of my life.

What stands out now more than anything else in my memory of Robert Quarry was the way he treated my domestic partner Chris Dietrich. From the time they were introduced he became Chris's Uncle Bob as well. After our first dinner with the three of us, Bob took me aside and said, "You know this kind of friendship comes around once in your life so cherish it. I wish to God I had someone as loyal and loving as Chris in my life." I lost Chris on December 4th 2004; he had suffered from both liver cancer and HIV. It would be later in the following year that I would see Bob at a Ray Court's show; he had put on quite a bit of weight but was still Uncle Bob. I went over during a break as I was doing Richard Stapley's table that day and knelt down by Bob's chair and told him we lost Chris. The look on his face said more than I could bear and we quickly hugged; then I went back to my table on the verge of breaking down for the umpteenth time.

I decided to go through my box of pictures from those days and could not stop looking at the ones with Bob and Martine Beswicke. I wish I could recall more of the night they met —all I can tell you is it was love at first sight. They decided they should play vampires together and soon. I did try to put a film together for Bob and some of my other friends like Reggie Nalder and Angus Scrimm, but the money could not be raised for something that did not have more explosions and sex, so another opportunity was lost and *The Boarding House* never got to open its doors to the public.

---

* Price was referring to an incident during the making of *Madhouse,* when Quarry was singing in the dressing room. Quarry told Price, "I bet you didn't know I could sing." Price jokingly replied, "Well, I knew you couldn't act."

Robert Quarry in a scene cut from *Madhouse*. Quarry is about to slap
Vincent Price with a newspaper as Peter Cushing looks on.

One thing that I am sure had never changed with Bob was his uncanny ability to remember nasty tales from his days of Broadway. "Oh my god, Richard Burton – let me tell you about Burton," he would say. "He had the worst body odor on the planet because he never *bathed*. I ought to know – I sat in his dressing room when he was on Broadway in *Camelot*." Robert was no stranger to theater, as he really shined on the stage. I remember he was doing *Butley* in the San Fernando Valley one year, and I thought his performance rivaled Alan Bates in the title role. I wish I could have seen his George in *Who's Afraid of Virginia Wolf*.

It is more than amazing for me to realize that I actually knew four men at the same time, all of whom had played master vampires in the 1960s and 1970s: Robert Quarry, Reggie Nalder, Ferdy Mayne, and William Marshall. Each and every one of them was a gentleman of the old school, classically trained, versatile and modest with their public. As of last Friday, the last of them—who played not only Count Yorga but also the vampire-guru in *The Deathmaster*—has passed into legend, leaving a void in the cinema that can never be filled.

I have wondered what it would have been like to have seen Bob out at the motion picture home during this last six months of his life and in a way perhaps it is better that I just keep my memories as they are now. In my mind's eye Bob is his old self, laughing that laugh with a devilish twinkle in those sparkling eyes. Somewhere in the scheme of things, if we wish to believe, the aforementioned gentlemen are having one hell of a reunion somewhere over the rainbow…way up high.

27

The Face That Launched a Thousand Trips

Reggie Nalder

INSTANTLY RECOGNIZABLE AFTER HIS ROLE in Hitchcock's 1956 version of *The Man Who Knew Too Much*, and a key figure in European horror cinema for over two decades, Reggie Nalder had a film career that truly stands alone.

One evening during the summer of 1969, I found myself on Hollywood Boulevard en route to the premiere of Fellini's *Satyricon*. As fate would have it, Reggie Nalder walked right past me dressed in a pale blue leather jumpsuit, a brown leather handbag over his shoulder. The assassin from Alfred Hitchcock's 1956 remake of *The Man Who Knew Too Much* was out for a stroll. I started walking behind him noticing how everyone that passed his way did a double take to make sure they hadn't seen a specter from some half-remembered cinema nightmare. "The face that launched a thousand trips." That was an appropriate counterculture expression in 1969 to describe the impact of Reggie Nalder's visage on the general public.

By 1977, I was a theatrical agent in Beverly Hills. One afternoon at a cocktail party for the Paul Kohner Agency on Sunset Boulevard, I ran into Reggie Nalder again. He was a client of Kohner's, but a dissatisfied one. Paul Kohner was a legend among agents in Hollywood. He represented such émigrés as Billy Wilder, Klaus Kinski and, early in his career, Erich von Stroheim.

By the end of the afternoon I convinced Reggie Nalder to become a client of Del Valle, Franklin & Levine. With that, I would see him on a regular basis for the rest of his life.

Reggie Nalder. Photo by Dan Golden.

In his later years Reggie withdrew from his social circle of artists and bohemians. In August of 1991, I returned from San Francisco to find a message from him on my answering machine saying "Auf Wiedersehen." I thought little of it at the time but later I was shocked to discover my mysterious and enigmatic friend had succumbed to bone cancer on 19 November 1991.

Reggie Nalder was a character actor whose aura of mystery and demonic physiognomy placed him in the forefront of Euro-horror personalities. His real-life drama was worthy of Sax Rohmer with a dash of Edgar Wallace. It is only appropriate that he be remembered in the same breath as Klaus Kinski, Anton Differing and Udo Kier. This interview was done with him in 1989 but never published in his lifetime.

Tell me about your early background as a performer.

Acting was a family tradition. Both my father and my uncle were actors. My mother was a celebrated courtesan who also acted in German films from 1919 to 1929. My uncle owned and operated a notorious cabaret in Vienna which was appropriately named "Hoelle" ("Hell" in German) in the basement of "das Theater an der Wien" throughout the 1920s. There are no filmed records of what went on in such a place. My early memories are filled with decadent, smoke-filled parlors where anything goes.

This environment must have been instrumental in your love of the theatrical.

When you are born into such an environment you know nothing else. I took dance, ballet and painting classes. This enabled me to help my uncle by painting backdrops and suggesting tableaux for the cabaret. It was a fantasy world and the only thing that changed it was the Nazis. I fled Vienna and arrived in Paris, where all my theatrical experience would be put to the test. I had no money and had to find work in very untheatrical venues. By the time the Nazis came to Paris I was established in cabaret, specializing in a dance called The Apache. It was considered shocking at the time as the woman, my partner, was made subservient during the dance. In fact, she was dominated and loved it.

This sounds intriguing...

It was. My partner became my lover and we performed in private for those that could afford it. At one point I employed a hunchback to procure customers for our more exotic shows. Believe me, sex has always been a best-seller. We were very successful. It disgusted me to perform for the Nazis but survival made me do things that seem impossible now.

Did you attempt a film career at this point?

Not really. I wanted to. But it didn't happen until the war was over. One of my first [pictures] was Le signal rouge with Erich von Stroheim that was filmed in Austria with French money in 1948. It allowed Mr. Von Stroheim the chance to go home to Vienna. He was a genius. The mayor gave him the key to the city. He was so highly regarded in France. I was honored to be in the same city with this man. So to make a film with him meant I was on my way.

What other films did you do at that time?

I also did *Echec au porteur* (aka *Not Delivered*, 1959) with Jeanne Moreau, a divine actress to work with. She was kind to the cast and crew alike. I loved her. Also *Demain Sera Un Autre Jour* (the working title of Rene Clement's *The Day and the Hour* [*Le jour et l'heure*, 1962]). It starred Simone Signoret who was what you Americans call an "earth mother." She was mad for her husband (Yves Montand) who was unfaithful. And she was always looking out for people like me who were starting out in films. Simone was all heart. I wish she could have been happier in her private life. I would not meet a woman like her again until Melina Mercuri years later, larger than life. But, unlike Simone, Melina was happy at all times.

Weren't you also in The Adventures of Captain Fabian *(1951)?*

Yes, with your great pal Vincent Price! *The Adventures of Captain Fabian* was shot in France in the summer of 1950. It was an amazing film for many reasons. Michelle Presle was the evil woman in the picture and a great friend. She had seen my cabaret act in Paris during the war. Errol Flynn was producing the film and the whole production was centered on him. Well, the cast and the crew spent weeks on salary without a frame of film being shot because Flynn was off being Errol Flynn and wasting a lot of money. Finally William Marshall [the director] walked off and Flynn directed the film from that point on. A disaster! Flynn was a great guy. He was well liked by the crew but he was no film director. It was a paid vacation for all of us. My part was small. I did get to work with a little monkey in that film. I love animals so much but I travel too often to own one. Vincent and I had one good scene together toward the end. I saw him again back in Hollywood. He came up to my apartment in Hollywood and we had cocktails. He seemed to be having some problems with his wife at the time. I lost touch with Vincent soon after.

Let's move on to the film that made you world-famous, The Man Who Knew Too Much.

Hitchcock was responsible for my coming to America, and I owe him a great deal. I didn't realize how much this film would change my life. I am recognized all over the world as "the man at the Albert Hall." Hitchcock never gave actors any real direction [and] I was a bit put off at first. You really didn't know where you stood with him. He told very crude and dirty stories like a schoolboy. He knew exactly what he wanted from you, and once you were there he felt it was up to you not to disappoint him.

What else do you recall about the filming?

Doris Day was such a pro and Hitchcock gave her little encouragement. She always felt unsure, which is exactly what he wanted. A writer named Donald Spoto asked me about this film and I told him that Hitchcock asked me to regard the man I was going to assassinate as if he were a beautiful woman gazing lovingly at the target before I shoot him. What I didn't tell Mr. Spoto was that Hitchcock stared right at my crotch whenever he talked to me, never once looking me in the eye. At the time I was convinced he must be perverted. I already knew he was a genius.

What was your favorite moment from that experience?

Oh, the touring. I went to all the major cities in America and some in Europe. Of course the Cannes Film Festival was unforgettable. I felt like a star. I posed for publicity pictures by the Carlton Hotel with Melina Mercouri and her husband, Jules Dassin. In fact, I was the centre of attention. One reporter remarked that the one scene at Albert Hall would be remembered as one of Hitchcock's greatest set-pieces.

Did you come to Hollywood after that?

Yes. After the Hitchcock film Paul Kohner got me a lot of television. I guest-starred in villainous roles of course, in *77 Sunset Strip* and *Surfside Six*. I did one feature with Rock Hudson called *The Spiral Road* (1962). I played a witch doctor that helps Hudson who is lost in the jungle. A very nice guy, Rock Hudson. Very polite and completely professional. He looked like a movie star.

You also did two episodes of Boris Karloff's Thriller.

My favorite was *Terror in Teakwood* that was directed by Paul Henried. The lead actor, Guy Rolfe, was very ill during the filming, very weak and pale at the time. I remember the scene in which I lead him to the tomb and describe the casket and the funeral service to him. When my speech was finished, Paul said, "Cut!" and the crew burst into applause. I felt like I'd just won an Oscar.

Did you meet Karloff at the time?

No. But I met him briefly during the second one, *The Return of Andrew Bentley*. John Newland, who also played the lead, directed it. There was also a talented actress named Antoinette Bower with whom I remain good friends today. I had no dialogue, just a black cape and a "familiar" who looked like a man in a furry costume. Newland did needlepoint between takes and loved Hollywood gossip. A sweet guy and a good director.

You also had a small role in The Manchurian Candidate *(1962) around this time.*

I remember working only one day on that film. Frank Sinatra remembered my face from the Hitchcock film and thought it would compliment the other spies. So John Frankenheimer asked for me. I had no dialogue in that one either. About the same time I remember working on a prison film where I had dialogue and it was later re-dubbed with another actor. I hated it.

That would be Convicts Four *(1962) with Ben Gazzara. Vincent Price played an art critic in that one.*

Yes of course. I played one of the prisoners and I suppose my voice wasn't hard or tough enough.

I understand that the Hitchcock film was also responsible for your casting in Argento's first feature, L'Uccello dalle piume di cristallo (The Bird with the Crystal Plumage, *1969).*

I went to Rome to see Argento who asked for me through my Paris agent. He worshipped at Hitchcock's shrine and insisted I be an assassin who gets killed immediately in his film. I enjoyed Argento very much, a strange guy fond of using his hands to direct. We worked well together. He wanted me to appear in *Suspiria* (1977). I was to have been a professor in it. I was about to do *Casanova* (1976) for Fellini and one scene was all he offered. I would love to work for him [Argento] now.

Fellini must be on your list of geniuses that have directed you.

Of course! Casanova was a dream for me as an actor but a nightmare for poor Fellini as he was always trying to get money. He is like a child, very sensitive. Aware of all that goes on around him. Fellini was wearing a big straw hat on the set and toward the end of my scenes pictures were taken of me wearing Fellini's hat. He put his arm around me and hugged me like a bear. I wanted to be around him always.

It was during this period of European activity that you made those two infamous German films, Hexen bis aufs Blut gequält *(Mark of the Devil, 1970) and* Hexen geschändet und zu Tode gequält *(Mark of the Devil Part II, 1972).*

The first film was the brainchild of my late friend Adrian Hoven, who produced both films and directed the second. In truth, Adrian directed them both. Poor Mike Armstrong, who wrote the script for Part I, arrived from England to Austria without any idea how to direct a movie. Michael and Adrian didn't like each other at all either. So after a couple of weeks Mike was removed as director and Adrian shot the rest of it. By this time Herbert Lom arrived and his presence made everyone work better. Little Udo Kier played his assistant. It gave me great pleasure to see my name on a Hollywood Boulevard marquee. I even took a photo of it: "*Mark of the Devil* STARRING REGGIE NALDER."

I know Michael [Armstrong], Reggie, and for the sake of film history, I should tell you his side of things. Mike wrote a script in which the Herbert Lom character is sexually impotent and becomes frustrated and begins to lust for Udo Kier, thus his motive for torturing beautiful women. Lom kills your character, Albino, because you know the truth. According to Mike, Hoven didn't like the gay subplot and rewrote it. So poor Mike was out on both levels.

The film made so much money for Hoven, it's too bad he and Mike didn't have a good rapport. He wasn't up to directing a feature and knew it. I remember the very well endowed actress Olivera Vuco, the one I try to rape at the inn, wanted to make love to Udo Kier. She was after him throughout the filming, even coming to his room at night. Since he was gay she became very frustrated. When it came time to shoot our scene I was supposed to overpower her. However this huge woman used her frustration on me and I was the one who was overpowered.

Reggie Nalder and David Del Valle at *Salem's Lot* wrap party at Warner Bros.

Wasn't Sybil Danning supposed to be in Mark of the Devil Part II?

Yes. She was cast. I like Sybil. Adrian Hoven was married at that time and had a roving eye for beautiful women. He began a relationship with Sybil that was so intense he had a heart attack trying to keep up with her. He gave her all of his antique furniture that she put in her apartment in Vienna. His wife discovered this and demanded the furniture back or she would get a divorce. That ended any possibility of filming with her.

The second one had Anton Differing instead of Herbert Lom. What do you recall of it?

The second *Mark of the Devil* went very smoothly. Tony Differing became a close friend of mine and I enjoyed working with him. It was our only film together. There was a scene of me having violent sex with a nun that was cut, as well as much more violence sexual and otherwise toward the nuns. A fan sent me a tape of *Mark of the Devil Part II* and I couldn't believe how much was cut from what we had shot originally, especially the scene where a nun is impaled on a giant wooden phallus until blood is everywhere.

Sounds like those vomit bags went to the wrong movie! You also did a Dracula film for Charles Band. How was that?

It was *called Zoltan: Hound of Dracula* (aka *Dracula's Dog*, 1978). It was okay, I guess. Albert Band was a nice guy to work for and Joe [Jose] Ferrer was a great actor. We felt embarrassed for a while. As usual I had no dialogue for most of the film. I only speak in the flashbacks. I also did an episode of McCloud and John Carradine played Dracula. I played his butler.

Speaking of TV movies, Curtis Harrington told me that he fought like a tiger with NBC to cast you in The Dead Don't Die *(1974).*

Curtis is a friend and I suppose he did. I remember Joan Blondell very well. She was very frail when we shot the scene where I am lying dead on the floor of the shop. After a take she whispered to me, "I can't get up." She had knelt by my side but could not get up. George Hamilton was a real pro on that too. The scene where I rise from the coffin even frightened him! Curtis is a real master of this type of film.

Salem's Lot *(1979) was also done for television with a shorter version released in Europe as a feature. Tell me something about making it.*

I had met James Mason before at the Cannes Film Festival. He is one of our best actors, highly regarded in Europe, a joy to work with. The director, Tobe Hooper, had asked for me from the start. The makeup and contact lenses were painful but I got used to them. I liked the money best of all. The scene where David Soul stakes me took many retakes because Tobe wanted me to die in a certain way. I never saw the other version but the cuts wouldn't have affected me anyway.

You played the title character in The Devil and Max Devlin *(1981) with Bill Cosby.*

Yes, I played the Devil. I went out to the Disney studio and read for that one. Once again I had few lines to say. I hated working with Bill Cosby. He is a pig. I first met him in Rome, where I did an episode of *I Spy*. Bill Cosby is rude, arrogant and very untalented. He walked right by me on the set as if I were a piece of furniture. I tried to be polite but he made it impossible. I have rarely ever worked with someone like him before or since.

Your Star Trek *episode ["Journey to Babel"] is memorable to me and made it possible to go to that amazing 20th Anniversary party on the Paramount back lot.*

It always shocks me that people remembered things so trivial. When we arrived I didn't even have to tell them my name. The boy at the door knew my episode and the character's name. There were so many stars assembled in one place and all because of *Star Trek*. Amazing.

You once wrote a treatment for a film you would like to see produced. What was it?

It is entitled *Forgotten Idols* and it is based somewhat on my mother. It takes place in the 1920s, and the lead character is a celebrated stage actress who retires at the height of her career. It is a mystery. No one makes this type of film nowadays. I will keep offering until someone is intrigued.

I know this is a little sensitive but didn't you do a porno Dracula?

You mean *Dracula Sucks* (1979), of course. It was a very nerve-wracking experience. The Marshak Brothers who wrote the script in pencil on large sheets of paper, handing it to us seconds before we did a take, did it. Nobody knew their lines because they were being changed all of the time. We were all staying in a small motel in Palmdale, California. And people were going in and out of people's rooms all night. It was an orgy. John Holmes was the star of the film but he stayed on the castle set. I finally saw what he was so famous for, and it looked like a huge snake in repose! If you know what I mean!

You weren't credited as Reggie Nalder on that one, were you?

No. I was called Detlef Von Berg. But everyone that saw it knew who it was. I don't care. Work is work. And the Marshaks were happy with it.

I also saw your last skin flick called Blue Ice *(1992). What's that about?*

What do you think? Sex, of course! I play a Nazi general who likes to watch sex acts. It was shot in San Francisco over two weekends. So it was like a vacation for me. But promise me you will never see it!

Blue Ice would be the final film appearance of Reggie Nalder in a career that spanned nearly five decades.

Michael Gough in Konga's Paw.

28

Konga, Put Me Down!

Michael Gough

DURING MY TIME as the Hollywood correspondent for *Films and Filming*, I enjoyed at least two trips a year to London to meet with my editor, John Russell Taylor, who at that time was always busy, being also the Art Editor for the London Times.

In the summer of 1984 I arrived in London only to discover that John had a conflict in his schedule and was out of the city for a few days, leaving me at loose ends while I waited for his return. His office suggested that I could interview some British actors that I might not see in America. Duly armed with a copy of SPOTLIGHT [the English equivalent of the Academy directory that casting directors use to find talent], I began to look for a subject in London. I soon discovered the very man I had always wanted to meet, the star of many a horror film seen in my misspent youth: Michael Gough. Now you may only be familiar with Michael as the butler Alfred in the mega successful franchise *Batman* of the 1980s and 1990s; however, our Mr. Gough has been a staple in British Cinema since 1947.

Michael Gough was doing a play in London at that very moment, an old chestnut entitled *Aren't We All*, at the Theater Royal Haymarket. The play had been revived as a vehicle for Rex Harrison and Claudette Colbert, yet from my research it appear that Gough had all but stolen the play right out from under the famous movie stars that headlined the performances.

I rang up Mr. Gough's agents and within an hour I was given an appointment to interview him backstage the next day. The Theater Royale Haymarket is one of if not the oldest and most beloved theaters in London. I was thrilled to be able to enter it, as if was about to go on myself.

The next morning I prepared for my encounter by arming myself with a tape recorder and a photo for Mr. Gough to sign as I was and still am a great admirer of his work. I arrived at the appointed time backstage, which was just as you would imagine it would be, complete with the stage manager, a sage old man standing guard inside the entrance in his private alcove, not impressed by stars or fame, just a bloke waiting for the actors to come and in and do their business.

I had just walked in and began to explain why I was there and the old man stopped me in mid-sentence "You're the American here to interview Mick Gough, aren't you? Well he already said for me to send you to his dressing room."

With that I was led by a stage hand to Michael Gough's dressing room which had his name plate attached to the door. Michael was almost right behind me as he had just arrived almost the same time as I did.

Now to try and explain just how surprised I was at how nice this man is in person, I must first explain that we had never met and Gough, while well known in his profession, is not a huge film star whom one sees on chat shows. I had only his film performances to judge what kind of a man he might be. As a result, I was fully expecting a bitchy prima donna or perhaps an aloof, cold man. Nothing could have prepared me for the Santa Claus that sat in his dressing table, offering me tea and begging forgiveness for not having any scones to go with it.

Michael Gough has a wonderful long face that radiates intelligence and wisdom; he resembles if anything an Oxford Don. He is gifted with a beautiful voice, which in private is mellow and soft much like the man himself. He looked at me a moment, as I sat there quite speechless, and asked if anything was wrong; I explained that I half expected him to behave a little like he did in his horror films.

Michael laughed and replied "Darling boy, it's called acting, don't you know?" Well of course, I felt embarrassed for being such a dope, especially because I had seen several of Michael non-horror films like *The Horse's Mouth* with Alec Guinness and *The Go-Between* for director Joseph Losey.

Michael explained that he did not have to go on until late in the play so we could chat in his dressing room, and if I liked he would find a little time when the play was over to continue the interview if I needed him to. As I set up the tape recorder and did a test, Michael began to look at his cards and messages that were piled upon his table. On his dressing mirror were postcards from Italy and photos of his children, including a charming snapshot of a beautiful little girl.

When I asked if she was his daughter, Michael turned around and put his hand on mine and in whisper like tones said "Yes... she was my daughter Polly, and we lost her in an automobile accident a few months ago: she was struck down by a car and killed. She was soon to be married."

The grace in his tone of voice with which he offered up his personal tragedy struck me to the quick. My first thought was: "How could he perform under such grief?" Yet somehow I knew he was working because that is what he did, and it was also his way of coping with his loss. This touching moment – which allowed me to care about this charming man more than I ever thought I would in such a short amount of time – was interrupted by well-wishers knocking at his door, paying their respects before the curtain went up. As a middle-aged couple pushed their heads inside, Michael greeted them by saying "Hello, my darlings. I am being interviewed at the moment, but do come back afterwards, promise?" As they made their exit he glanced over at me and confided, "He is a titled Lord and one of the biggest landowners in Britain; nevertheless, they are mad about Theater and quite adorable when you get to know them."

Finally, we were on our own, and I began asking him about his career with the essential question about how he decided upon acting in the first place. "It is very strange how things work out, isn't it? You see it was watching our dear old Rex Harrison many years ago, in a play called *Sailors Don't Care*, that gave me the courage to try and become an actor, I realized almost at once that a sensible job was just not for me anyway. I was fortunate to learn my craft at the Old Vic; I was mainly atmosphere in crowd scenes in those days, but it also made it possible to observe the likes of Michael Redgrave and Alec Guinness years before I would actually share scenes with them."

Michael then asked me a question as to what I had seen of his films that made me a fan. Before I could answer, he said "Let me take a mad guess and say *Konga*." His grin at saying this was positively wicked.

"How on earth did you know that?" I replied.

Michael continued, "Don't take issue with this, but your being an American, it seems to be the only film I am known by in the States. When my children were in school right after I made it, they were teased to death by their classmates over *Konga*. The other boys would yell at them, 'Konga put me down.' It took several years for my brood to forgive me for that one. *Konga* was such a howler: no one that saw it could ever let me live down my dialogue, once Konga had me in its paw – simply unforgettable."

Since we arrived on the subject of films like *Konga*, I asked Michael about his working relationship with its producer, the infamous Herman Cohen.

"I made five films for Herman Cohen as he seemed to like the way I played his characters or perhaps I should say character because the first three were cut from the same cloth. Cohen was a showman first, last, and always; his manner was always overbearing and his opinions sacrosanct. During the filming of *Horrors of the Black Museum*, he would show up unannounced on-set and tell our director Arthur Crabtree how to direct a scene and the actors as well. I mean this just was not on, and as a result Arthur began to loath Cohen on sight. He demanded all the walls of the set be painted a violent shade of blue or green; Herman Cohen was the boss on all that he produced – and not in a positive way either.

"The best experience I had on a film produced by Herman Cohen," Gough continued, "was *Black Zoo*, which was made wonderful because of those animals that I worked with that made filming absolutely unforgettable. The trainer who owned them was a fearless soul with total understanding of just how to get these animals to work in front of a camera. Since I played the owner of a zoo, I had to connect with these cheetahs and lions as if I had a lifetime of knowledge, which of course I did not. This man also played the victim in our film: he would dress up like the character about to be killed and actually roll around with the lions as if they were attacking him. I had to step into cages with mountain lions and pat them on the head. At one point I put my hand in the cat's mouth to show my audience that I was master, and the cat would not open his mouth on cue, so the trainer gave him a sock on the side of his head, which caused me to protest. He took me aside and explained that the lions play rough with each other, and he was not abusing the lion in the least. The most amazing scene was the one where I summon all my creatures into the parlor where I play the organ, and they all came in one at a time and sat around me. Let me tell you, I was completely at the mercy of their owner, who as I said was truly a genius with God's creatures, great and small. He loved them and had no use for circuses and zoo's that exploited animals; he was well ahead of his time. I will always have a fondness for that film out of all of those thrillers I did for Herman."

I asked Michael at this point how different were the last two films for Cohen with Joan Crawford as the star. Michael rolled his eyes toward heaven as he explained, "I appeared in the last two films Miss Crawford would ever make on this earth. Herman was still Herman, yet he always deferred to Madame in all things that related to her performance or wardrobe, which incidentally came directly from her own closet. Joan Crawford was a small woman with enormous eyes topped by an elaborate series of hairpieces some of which gave her more height. By the time we worked together, she had to rely on huge cue cards that were placed just off camera enough for her to see them without having to move off her marks, as she could no longer remember dialogue. I remember doing countless retakes for what would sometimes only amount to one line. I believe she was under enormous stress at the time, and of course she drank quite a bit. It was interesting to watch how Herman handled Joan Crawford: it appeared that she was genuinely fond of him and for the most part would do whatever was required to make the film come together. Joan Crawford was professional regardless of whatever else one might say about her.

"My most vivid recollection of working with Miss Crawford has to be the last day on the set of our final film together *Trog*," Michael continued.

"After we had wrapped the last setup for day Miss Crawford came up to me and said 'Michael this is our last day working together and after two pictures I'd like to give you something as a token to remember me by, so please come to my dressing room before you leave today.' The rest of the day all I could think of was: what treasure was going to be mine when I finally arrived at Joan Crawford's trailer? I realized that Joan, having been a Major Hollywood Star for the better part of this century, it must be some fabulous gold watch, or I just couldn't imagine what to expect. My moment finally came, and I walked over to Miss Crawford's deluxe Winnebago and tapped on the door 'Enter,' she said. As I came through the door, Joan Crawford was seated at her dressing table, adjusting her make up after a long day of filming. 'Michael, this is my gift to you for two wonderful pictures together.' With that, she reached into one of her small cases and removed two plastic fountain pens that were inscribed 'from the desk of Joan Crawford' and with great aplomb she presented me with them. As I stood there holding these two fountain pens in my hand, I was quite speechless. I gathered my wits as quickly as possible, thanking her for them and then making a hasty departure before I burst out laughing."

Michael recalled dining out in London years afterwards with his wife and running into Herman Cohen. "He always thought we were such close friends. I mean, we never were at odds during those films, but his behavior towards the director and people on the floor was something else altogether, so I never knew quite what to make of him as a man. I think he recognized a soul mate in Joan Crawford; they could both behave like bullies towards people they worked with in films. I just would never call the old sod a mate."

I asked Gough to elaborate on the difference, and he used our mutual friend Ferdinand Mayne (the Count in Polanski's *Dance of the Vampires*, a.k.a. *The Fearless Vampire Killers*) as an example of just what he meant by the term "mate." Michael explained that he and Ferdy went back a long way in the theater and in films. "Ferdy is a mate. I could always confide in him in complete trust, whereas Herman Cohen was my producer and could be a real prat on a set. There was no sense of a social bond between us after five films together. Andre Morell is a mate, but not say Christopher Lee, whom I've worked with on a few films, yet we were never mates."

After that explanation, I simply could not resist asking about Andre Morell, another British character actor who appeared in his share of Hammer films. Michael smiled at the thought of his colleague. "Andre was a wonderful man and a very good actor. I will tell you something about him you might not know: Andre has been a frustrated conductor of classical music all his life. When he is on his own, Andre will put on a record of one of his favorite symphonies and conduct it complete with baton. The sight of him standing on a stool before his record player conducting is indeed a sight to behold, and

I am convinced that Andre could have been one of the great conductors if he had not chosen to be an actor."

I had made a mental note to ask about *The Crimson Cult*, with Barbara Steele and Boris Karloff (known in the UK as *Curse of the Crimson Altar*). But after Gough's comment about Christopher Lee, I almost avoided the question, since Lee was also in the film. Michael laughed at the mention of the film and then explained:

"That was an absolute disaster from day one, yet Boris Karloff was such a sweet man and was adored by the crew. It was almost worth the effort just to work alongside him. The director Vernon Sewell had been quite good in his day, but this project was just too muddled with orgy scenes brought in just for the sake of exploitation. Christopher was devoted to Boris, and that was quite moving to observe, since I had never seen Christopher defer to anyone as he did to Karloff."

At this point I explained that Barbara was a close personal friend and asked if he had any words to pass along when I saw her back in Beverly Hills. 'Well, give her my warmest regards when you see her, although I seriously doubt if she would remember our meeting after so much water under the bridge. Barbara worked only a couple of days on it, and I don't think I worked more than a week myself. I had a terrible part of a butler that was mute, and having read the script I was grateful…Barbara was very grand in those days and quite the star, and so she was treated like one as I recall—a very striking lady with amazing eyes."

I decided to ask what projects meant something to Gough personally, and he replied, "I am what they call a 'jobbing actor.' That is to say, I basically will do whatever is asked of me within my ability. I am not a starry kind of actor, nor am I expensive to hire. That is not to say that I can always afford to do this, as I have had too many wives and too many children, so I rarely can turn things down; hence all the horror films. However, on occasion I will do a project if I am attracted to the material or admire the director. Derek Jarman is one director I would work for anytime he needed me. I believe in his talent as an artist. It is a joy to be in his company; mind you, he never has enough money for any of his projects, but thank God there are enough people like me that will work for peanuts just to see him get on with it."

Since we were now on the subject of specific directors, I asked about two of the most talented and controversial filmmakers in world cinema, Ken Russell and Joseph Losey. Michael laughed at the thought of Russell: "Ken is quite simply a divine daredevil; he is always pushing to extremes, regarding the censor. I am never sure with Ken directing when I might have to drop my knickers for the sake of art," he laughed.

"Losey is a craftsman in a very different way from Ken Russell," Gough continued. "On *The Go-Between*, Joe and his cameraman knew exactly what they were going for, and every detail was planned to perfection. I watched as Joe pulled a brilliant performance from Maggie Leighton, who played my wife. He knows actors and understands the process and as a result allows them to do wonderful work. Every time there is a thunder storm I think of Maggie and how Joe choreographed her acting to show what an astonishing range she has as an artist."

With time running out, I moved on to the Hammer film version of *Dracula*, known in America as *Horror of Dracula*. Michael first remarked, "You know next to *Konga*, I get asked about *Dracula* more often than not. It is somewhat of a classic now, isn't it? I know it is, and getting more so with each passing year."

I went on to ask about something only a cast member would know: the rumor that Hammer Films had had director Terence Fisher shoot additional footage—that was much more gruesome—for the Japanese market. Michael replied, "That was absolutely the case; during one sequence in particular with Peter Cushing, I was a victim of its practice. In the film I was supposed to react as Peter Cushing stakes the girl—what was her name?"

"Carol Marsh..?" I offered.

"Yes... dear boy you are clever. Well, Terry Fisher had decided to shoot my reaction to all this by having me actually vomit on camera. This disgusting thing required that I fill my mouth with oatmeal and at the proper moment throw it up against the wall of the mausoleum. Terry put a cameraman on a ladder above me to catch the whole bloody thing in one go: each time Peter would bring down his hammer into the coffin, I would turn and hurl my oatmeal against the wall; by the third take I was feeling ill myself, but we managed to finally get a take Terry was satisfied with and that was that. I haven't seen the film in years, so I have no way of knowing if it ever made it into final film or not."

This was the first time I had ever heard this particular story, and I promised Michael that the shot was not in American or British prints of the film, though I had no way of knowing whether it had made it to Japan. Michael responded, "Well, if it was cut out, it was a ghastly experience to endure for nothing —although at the time we all took the film quite seriously, as Terry Fisher was a serious if somewhat tongue-in-cheek director well suited to Hammer as they were at that time."

I followed up by asking about Gough's other Hammer Horror, *The Phantom of the Opera*. I just happened to have a still from that film, in which Michael, having just ripped away the mask from the Phantom (Herbert Lom) reacts in true horror film tradition by screaming. Michael looked at the photo and smiled that wicked smile of his.

"You want me to sign this one?' As he signed it, he reflected a moment, "I suppose this was the film that brought it all down. Hammer spent a lot of money [for them] on it, and it was not a success —although Herbert was

Michael Gough and friend in *Black Zoo*.

splendid as the Phantom, I thought. I know he fretted about doing a part like this, that Lon Chaney had such a reputation with. Terry Fisher took a lot of blame at the time for its lack of thunder commercially. I thoroughly enjoyed playing the evil Lord Ambrose, who was the real monster of the piece. Heather Sears was a darling to work with as well. I am very fortunate not to have been typed in those things like Peter Cushing was, since he is one of our best actors and should be doing even greater work."

Michael was the perfect host for this interview, and when I finally turned the recorder off, he said, "David, you cannot make me believe you came all the way from the States just to interview me, so would you like to meet the real stars of this production?"

"If you mean Rex Harrison and/or Claudette Colbert, then the answer is yes, but I really did come to see you."

Michael smiled as he explained what we were going to attempt to do. "Rex should be delighted to meet you, if but for a moment, as we are getting to his break; however, Miss Colbert is quite another story, as she is wary of talking to anyone before or after the show unless she has known them awhile. This entire production has been staged to accommodate Miss Colbert's left side, so you can understand the problem.

I kept trying to reassure him that I was there to interview Michael Gough and anything else was a treat. We left Michael's dressing room and went down a flight of iron stairs to the level where Rex Harrison was in his dressing room relaxing, or so we hoped. I was getting very anxious as the moment arrived; we entered a huge space that was Rex Harrison's dressing room, and in the center of the room was a table complete with a white table cloth with a silver tray containing the largest prawn cocktail known to man. We stood by the door as Michael explained that I was from *Films and Filming* and wondered if an appointment could be made for me to do an interview. Rex Harrison remained at table with those cobra hooded eyes that made him appear to be asleep, yet he was not. He could not have been nicer and he gave Michael a number for me to call the next day. I could tell that they had a history together and this was a true favor that Michael was awarding me as Rex Harrison does not grant interviews to just anyone, not even for a well established magazine like *Films and Filming*. Having accomplished our goal Michael explained he needed to prepare for his entrance and we could meet later.

My favorite moment of this amazing encounter was what Gough suggested as he left me: he showed me which way to go on down to get inside the theater itself if I wanted to watch his part; then just as he was walking away, he looked back at me and said, "Claudette's dressing room is the first door down hall, if you want to see if she opens the door – only you didn't hear it from me."

Of all the actors I have ever met, Michael Gough has to be the most gracious and thoughtful, and by the way Claudette would not come to the door.

Yvette Vickers "Feeling French".

29

Yvette Vickers

YOU WOULD THINK MY TIME spent around Kenneth Anger over the years would have prepared me for the news I was about to find on Facebook on May 4th, 2011. I logged on as I always do, only this time there were more than a couple of emails regarding the passing of my friend Yvette Vickers. Now Yvette and I went back a number of years all the way to 1980 in fact, but I had not really been in touch with her since 2005 when our paths crossed in Burbank at Ray Courts' Hollywood Collector Show. Yvette was selling her autograph as usual along with a CD she self-produced, a jazz tribute to her parents.

My partner of 20 years had just died in December, and Yvette and I needed to catch up as Chris had been close to her as well. She did not look well and I expressed concern but as always with Yvette, she had a real talent for getting on with it regardless of the reality of any given situation depending on her sunshine personality to shake all the blues away.

The macabre revelation that the mummified body of Yvette Vickers was found in her neglected ramshackle home off West Wanda Drive, having been decomposing there for the better part of a year was definitely a chapter out of Hollywood Babylon. How could something like this have ever happened in Beverly Hills or West L.A. since her address was really in L.A. County? Yvette had friends, many like me, that had known her for years, as well as the monster kid/fanboy element that she accumulated from years of attending horror conventions across the USA, signing autographs from the two films that really kept her legacy alive, *Attack of the 50 Foot Woman* and *The Giant Leeches*.

241

These films were rarely, if ever, off television so everybody knew her face and sexy figure from those films, so by the time *Mystery Science Theater 3000* got hold of them and camped them up, Yvette was rediscovered once again.

The more I re-read these sordid accounts of her death, the more I began to think of another talented blonde actress I used to know who also ended her life alone in a neglected house in Hollywood, the late Joyce Jameson. Both of these ladies put aside their own careers to act as faux trophy wives for selfish men who took their love for granted, all the while, pursuing successful careers of their own. Joyce spent over 12 years with Robert Vaughn while Yvette lived with Jim Hutton from 1964 until his premature death in 1979.

My memories of Yvette are now welling up inside me like a dam ready to burst. The more I try and put that image of her lifeless body lying in that decaying house on West Wanda Drive out of my mind, the more I remember just how she might have gotten there in the first place. You see, from the very first time I met Yvette it was clear she was a Hollywood lady on a bum trip. Her film career was over, except for cameos in feeble films like Gary Graver's *Evil Spirits* or the masterful *What's the Matter with Helen?*, which might have mattered for Yvette had she a real role to play. Curtis Harrington placed her in his film for the camp value of having a cast member from *50 Foot Woman,* a film he would send up again in *Ruby* a few years later. Even in her glory days, Yvette was doing cameo's, as in Martin Ritt's classic *Hud*, which features Yvette in what could have been a break-through role except according to Yvette, "Paul's wife Joanne demanded my part be cut because of what she perceived to be "funny business" going on between Paul and me. Paul was a flirt, but guess what? So am I." In any case, Yvette's showy role as Paul Newman's married lover was reduced to a walk-on. None of this would bother Yvette at the time because her real life lovers continued to pick up the slack, blurring the reality of a film career in decline. Yvette really came forth as an actress in 1957 with her showy role in James Cagney's only directorial effort *Short Cut to Hell*, followed by a couple of Roger Corman flicks and then, of course, her beloved cult horror films that forever preserved her image as a scream queen thanks to a certain *50 Foot* Allison Hayes and a swamp filled with driving men dressed in rubber suits hung together with safety pins, those *Giant Leeches*.

The first time Yvette and I sat down together and really got to know one another, she brought over a VHS cassette of her first break-through commercial in New York as the "White Rain Girl", a riff on Gene Kelly's 'Singing in the Rain' number. Yvette was adorable as the pretty girl caught in the rain. I loved the humor Yvette displayed in those days. She still had the acting bug but thanks to investments in real estate, she did not really have to work unless the right part came along. As time went by, those parts never turned up. At that point she moved onward to what she hoped would be a new beginning in cabaret as a jazz singer.

My most vivid memory of Yvette may also explain why she became more reclusive as the years went by. At the time, I was preparing my cable talk show, "Sinister Image," in Santa Monica and I was very lucky in securing a number of well known cult figures for the first few shows, among them Russ Meyer. When I told Yvette I had Russ for my next show, she became very excited, telling me on the phone, "Oh David, I really have to be on that show too because you know Russ photographed my Playboy centerfold." When I heard this I could not have agreed more that this would be a classic reunion show if nothing else and I already booked the studio for two shows as I wanted to do an entire show on just *Beyond the Valley of the Dolls*. Now I just assumed that Yvette had seen Russ since that shoot which took place in 1959 and this was now 1987. As the taping got closer, I reconfirmed her appearance, as I did with Russ. On the day of the show, Russ arrived first and he immediately adapted to the scene, as we arranged the chairs for the cameras and so on. I told Russ that Yvette was on her way and he affirmed that they had indeed not seen one another since 1959. When Yvette arrived, I could tell Russ was taken aback with Yvette's appearance, which is understandable if your last memory was of a pin-up girl at the height of her career and now here was Yvette nearly three decades later and bit worse for it. Anyway, Russ concealed his feelings rather well and greeted her with a hug and then we sat down for the duration. Yvette really didn't enter into the conversation until we reached Russ's 'Playboy' days and then she sprang into action, recalling Russ asking her to say the name 'Paul' over and over again to make her mouth pucker in a certain way. We taped for a half hour and then she had to leave, giving Russ a hug and a kiss as she left the studio. After she left, Russ looked at me and said, "What the fuck happened to Yvette Vickers? She looks like a boozehound to me, David. I've seen this happen to these broads time and again. What a shame because she had real sex appeal once."

A few days later, I invited Yvette over to a friend of mine who lived in Silver Lake to watch the finished product as I had just gotten it back from the lab. She was happy to do this and she too had something to share with me. It seems she had been working on her cabaret act and wanted to show off one of her new numbers. Russ Meyer's words were still ringing in my ears when she arrived, wearing her party gear and more than ready to break in her new material. But first things first, as I put on the tape of our show with Russ and Yvette slowly began to really look at herself, perhaps for the first time in years and she did not like what she saw at all. I waited to see what, if anything, she was going to say about how she came off but instead in typically Yvette fashion she went on about how good an interviewer I was and so on without really addressing what I knew was bothering her, ever since I showed the damn thing to her. We had been serving champagne and kept on serving it until we had gone through at least four bottles and she did not seem to care about driving all the way back home to Benedict Canyon from Silver Lake which is a long haul when you are sober and Mt. Everest when you're drunk. In any case, Yvette decided it was the time to do her number and whatever she saw on that tape, this song was going to wash all the clouds away. She chose the Peggy Lee standard "Fever" to do that night, pushing away all the obstacles on the living room floor. She then placed a large pillow in the center and then turned on the record player, making her entrance from the front door into the center of the room, bumping to the beat: "I give you fever...when you kiss me." In retrospect, it was very much like Marilyn Monroe doing her cabaret act from *Bus Stop*, the only difference being Monroe was, well, Monroe. When Yvette was through, we reacted like everyone else in her life, like the number was fan-fucking-tastic. "Great stuff sweetie...you go girl!" She was pleased for about 10 minutes before she started to fade back into a more depressed state. By now, my friend and I knew she was not going anywhere near her car until morning and we pretty much told her so. Yvette remained sweet about it all but insisted she was leaving. "I always prefer to sleep in my own bed thank you very much, so gang way boys, I am out of here, mama's going home."

I told her, "At least let us make some coffee and then call you a cab." After all we could drive her car back in the morning as we were not in any shape to drive either. We were out of the living room for no less than five minutes only to return to find the front door wide open and of course Yvette and her car were gone. I was horrified and pissed in equal measure, feeling more than responsible for the whole mess. My friend was a bit more level headed and asked me who I could call to help intercept her before she harmed herself, or worse, a total stranger on the road. I remembered she was, at that time, dating a mutual friend Dave Stevens. Dave was, at the time, becoming a star in the world of comic art as the creator of *The Rocketeer*. Sadly, Dave passed away in 2008 and I am here to tell you a finer man you will not meet. Dave was a prince in every way and he loved Yvette. Once we got Dave on the phone, he decided to start driving towards where we were, hoping to find Yvette before she got into Beverly Hills. After nearly an hour, Dave Stevens called back saying, "It's over. I caught up with her just as she was being arrested." It seems Yvette got as far as Hollywood before her erratic driving got her pulled over. She could not pass a breathalyzer so she was booked on suspension of drunk driving and that was that. We were all relieved she was unharmed and pulled through this without having an accident or worse. I still fondly remember Dave Stevens (whose grace and good humor made him the very best friend to have in a town like Hollywood) laughing at one point when he described what he saw when he pulled up to the spot where they were about to place Yvette Vickers in the squad car. She was yelling, "YOU LET GO OF ME THIS INSTANT. DO YOU KNOW WHOM I AM?...I AM A MOVIE

Yvette Vickers and David Del Valle (1988).

STAR, GODDAMN IT." I will always be grateful that Russ Meyer never heard about this since it was his observations that made this incident all the more tragic. Remember every day is Halloween in Hollywood.

I do have a few more similar anecdotes regarding Yvette but they all have this dark side as a common denominator. Yvette was a beautiful woman in her youth and achieved success in both her public and private life. However, nothing lasts forever and as I have pointed out in chapter after chapter in my book, sometimes it is important to know when it's time to let go and just be happy with what life has given you, rather than dwell on how or why the glow has left the rose. The worst thing Yvette did to herself was to use alcohol as an alternative to facing her demons and casting them aside. Her real beauty was within and always was, if only she could have understood this sooner rather than later.

It took her passing for me to open up about my time with her and I do this with the objective that anyone reading this, who has a eye on a career in this business, will take heed to stay focused on what is real and never ever believe your own publicity, especially when YOU are the one doing the PR.

Index

Lightning Source UK Ltd.
Milton Keynes UK
UKHW020906140821
388823UK00009B/1780